Managing Innovation from the Land of Ideas and Talent

Clas Neumann • Jayaram Srinivasan

Managing Innovation from the Land of Ideas and Talent

The 10-Year Story of SAP Labs India

 Springer

Clas Neumann
SAP Labs India Pvt. Ltd.
138, Export Promotion Industrial Park
Whitefield
Bangalore 560066
India
clas.neumann@sap.com

Jayaram Srinivasan
SAP Labs India Pvt. Ltd.
138, Export Promotion Industrial Park
Whitefield
Bangalore 560066
India
jayaram.srinivasan@sap.com

ISBN 978-3-540-89282-3   e-ISBN 978-3-540-89283-0
DOI 10.1007/978-3-540-89283-0
Springer Dordrecht Heidelberg London New York

Library of Congress Control Number: 2009927283

© Springer-Verlag Berlin Heidelberg 2009
This work is subject to copyright. All rights are reserved, whether the whole or part of the material is concerned, specifically the rights of translation, reprinting, reuse of illustrations, recitation, broadcasting, reproduction on microfilm or in any other way, and storage in data banks. Duplication of this publication or parts thereof is permitted only under the provisions of the German Copyright Law of September 9, 1965, in its current version, and permission for use must always be obtained from Springer. Violations are liable to prosecution under the German Copyright Law.
The use of general descriptive names, registered names, trademarks, etc. in this publication does not imply, even in the absence of a specific statement, that such names are exempt from the relevant protective laws and regulations and therefore free for general use.

Cover design: WMXDesign GmbH, Heidelberg, Germany

Printed on acid-free paper

Springer is part of Springer Science+Business Media (www.springer.com)

Würde man mich fragen, unter welchem Himmel der menschliche Geist seine auserlesensten Eigenschaften entwickelt, am tiefgründigsten über die größten Probleme des Lebens nachgedacht und Lösungen für einige von ihnen gefunden hat, welche sehr wohl die Aufmerksamkeit derer verdienen, die Plato und Kant studiert haben, so würde ich auf Indien zeigen.

(If I were asked under what sky the human mind has most fully developed some of its choicest gifts, has most deeply pondered over the greatest problems of life, and has found solutions of some of them which well deserve the attention even of those who have studied Plato and Kant, I should point to India.)

Max Mueller, German indologist and Sanskrit scholar

Preface

India has always fascinated emperors, adventurers, missionaries, scholars, hippies and travelers alike. However, only over the last ten years, it has started to attract foreign investment and the interest of multinational companies as a destination for sourcing and sale for goods and services. Today, nobody disputes the potential the Indian subcontinent has in our global world and the international success of its largest companies like Tata Group or ONGC.

Unlike the other BRIC (Brazil, Russia, India, China) countries, which built their success either on abundance of natural resources or cheap labor, India built a large portion of its economic success on knowledge and technology. The best showcase was the rise of its IT giants, which employ hundreds of thousands of smart engineers and the Indian IT sector meanwhile is called the backbone of the global IT industry.

SAP AG, the largest software company in Europe, is the undisputed world market leader in business software solutions. It did not only pioneer the way how business applications help running companies successfully and efficiently; it challenged as well the traditional way on how to distribute engineering work around the globe. By not following the trend of just off-shoring IT work at the lower end of the value chain, but integrating its Indian development center as one of the four major development hubs it innovated distributed research and development (R&D) processes. Today, its capability to build complete products and generate a tremendous stream of innovation out of India, serves as a role model for many other multinational companies.

Since its foundation in 1998, SAP Labs India has expanded from a small development facility with 100 members to the biggest R&D hub of SAP AG, outside Germany, with about 4,000 employees in 2009. Its growth has become a phenomenon that still fascinates internal and external stakeholders. Today, SAP Labs India contributes to every conceivable area of product development, starting from research and breakthrough innovation right through to mission critical customer support. As a pioneer in distributed software development, SAP Labs India has attracted many visitors, ranging from government dignitaries and global customers to professors and students.

This book attempts to capture the key learning SAP has made in the first 10 years of development in India. It has its focus specifically on organizational considerations, the development processes applied and on the people management across intercultural borders. The book uncovers for the first time some of the secrets on how to turn a 'captive center' into an innovation hub that attracts the best talents from many countries. However, it also throws some light on the challenges that SAP faced on this way and on challenges that still lay ahead. This book is not a historical description of a journey. It is a summary of the knowledge that SAP has acquired in running its largest offshore lab, and it can be used for anyone who is interested in the way multinational companies build and run successful research and engineering in India. It is meant for interested scholars, professionals and managers alike; specifically in the turbulent times of 2009 and 2010, it will be of great benefit to understand how SAP leverages the innovation potential of India. Creating ideas and intellectual property in India is a sustainable model that weathers through all the storms that might still lay in front of us.

Acknowledgement

During the second quarter of 2008, when we were fondly recollecting the early days of SAP Labs India, we started thinking about writing a book about its 10-year story of success and about our experiences in those years. At that time, the market was really strong, and SAP posted excellent results for the first quarter of 2008. Grand plans were made for the anniversary of the Labs. We planned to invite several internal executives, academics and speakers for the anniversary event in November, and our book was supposed to be released as a great surprise for everybody.

Everything was set to engage the audience in an intense debate to dream about the next 10 years of the Lab, but fate had different ideas when the financial markets crashed in September 2008. They even deteriorated rapidly in October, and 150 years old companies like Lehmann Brothers vanished into thin air. This left us wondering, if our 10 successful years of business in India were suitable celebrating. Accordingly, in the second half of 2008, SAP pressed the brakes on all expenses, and the anniversary preparations were brought to a grinding halt. We still had our celebrations in November, but in a limited way and much smaller as planned before. Léo Apotheker, co-CEO of SAP AG, and Peter Zencke, at that time executive board member and board sponsor for the Labs, participated in a small celebration and rewarded those who had been with us since the opening of our first office in 1998. Instead of launching our book, we made the announcement of its publication at the beginning of 2009 because we had no sight on how things would unfold afterwards.

Since then, the market has been flooded with bad news, and the economic outlook became really gloomy. It was surprising for us to see how the business environment deteriorated from the time when we started our book project in July 2008 to the time when we finished it. When the book was nearly completed, we almost felt like playing the fiddle when Rome was on fire. We went ahead with our work, because we are sure that the SAP Labs' story of growth, passion and perseverance, still could help to motivate people during a big financial crisis and a bad market situation. This reminded us of the quote by Winston Churchill: "The farther back you can look, the farther forward you are likely to see."

Many people helped us complete this book, and we thank all of them for their outstanding help and support.

First, we would like to thank Springer and Dr. Martina Bihn, Editorial Director at Springer, for making the publication of this book possible and for constantly guiding us during our work. We thank Markus Richter, our copy editor, Mary Bhalla and Theodore Benno Schachter, our language copy editors, for their support.

A lot of people inside SAP AG and SAP Labs India helped us with the research for this book: we thank the senior development managers Ramakrishna Yarlapati, Avaneesh Dubey, Sudhir Krishna S., Venkat Srinivas Seshasai, Srivibhavan Balaram, Uma Rani TM, Alain Lesaffre, Anita Venugopal, our HR head, our SAP Labs marketing team, Padma Dhotrekar and our colleagues of the department 'SAP World'.

In various interviews, a lot of people helped us with our research and to enrich our storyline. Without their support, the book would have definitely looked less interesting. We would like to thank Les Haymen, former head of the Asia pacific region, Dr. Udo Urbanek, Werner Konik, Martin Prinz and Georg Kniese, former Labs India managing directors, Dr. Dietmar Saddei, Ronald Lorenz, Narasimha B.T., Suryanarayanan V., Franziska Ahl, Ramesh B.G., Bhuvaneswar Naik and Satish Venkatachaliah, former HR heads of Labs India.

Eva Bonnewitz, our assistant from Germany, joined us in India and supported us for the entire duration of the project. We thank her for the management of the overall project, her motivation and high level of enthusiasm. Without her, it would not have been possible to complete our work.

We would like to thank Kush Desai and Ferose V.R., the current Managing Directors of Labs India, for their constant support. Special thanks go to Prof. Dr. Henning Kagermann and Léo Apotheker, co-CEOs of SAP AG and Gerhard Oswald, SAP Executive Board Member for supporting our project. Last but not least, we thank our families, specifically our wives Bea and Sharmila for supporting us and allowing us to take so much time during the weekends.

We would like to place our sincerest thanks to Dr. Peter Zencke, former executive board member of SAP AG and longtime board sponsor of Labs India. Peter encouraged us to write this book right from the beginning and provided us with valuable insights into his time and experiences at SAP AG.

Bangalore, March 2009   Clas Neumann
                                                          Jayaram Srinivasan

Table of Contents

Preface VII

1   SAP AG Profile 1

   1.1   The History of SAP AG 1

         The Beginning of a Story of Success 1
         Initial Customers and Success 2
         Growth and Internationalization 4
         The Way Forward with SAP R/3 6
         A New Millennium and a New Product Range 9

   1.2   SAP Today 16

2   Location Strategy at SAP AG 19

   2.1   International Locations Strategy 19

         The Initial Years of Internationalization 19
         The Markets' Need for Really Local Products 19
         The Building of SAP's First Lab in the Silicon Valley 22
         The Foundation of the First Market-Oriented Lab in Tokyo 23
         The Next Wave – Labs in Bangalore and in Nice 26
         The Next Expansion Wave – China, Eastern Europe
         and Israel 30

   2.2   SAP's Journey from a Global Player to a Global Company 32

3   SAP in Asia-Pacific and India 39

   3.1   SAP's Asia-Pacific Strategy 39

   3.2   Restructuring of the Asian Region in 1997 40

   3.3   Launch of the SAP Labs Project in 1998 41

   3.4   Structure of the Indian Software Industry 45

   3.5   Birth of SAP India – SAP's First Subsidiary in India 48

3.6   Increasing the Commitment Further to the Indian Market 51

3.7   Acquisition of Kiefer & Veittinger – SAP's Push into
       Front-End Space 55

3.8   SAP Labs India and Its Milestones 58

4   Organizational Structure at SAP Labs 73

4.1   Operating Environment 74

4.2   Innovation and Availability of Talent 76

4.3   Bringing Development Closer to Key Markets 77

4.4   Cost Containment and Reduction 77

4.5   Set-up Structure 78

4.6   The Role of the Management Bodies of SAP for
       Labs India 80

       Executive Board 81

       The Role of Labs Management 84

       How SAP Labs India and Its Internal Services Are
       Managed 85

4.7   Key Challenges of the Operating Environment 93

4.8   How SAP Operates Product Development from Labs India 95

4.9   Product Development Organization at SAP Labs India 98

       Labs View of Development Organization 98

       Compliance Adherence 99

       Compensation 99

       The Role of the Line of Business and Services 99

       The Local Branch of the Line of Business
       Development Organization 101

       The Evolving Organizational Structure at Labs India 103

4.10 Factors Influencing the Organizational Structure 112

4.11 Challenges of SAP Labs India's Organizational Structure 114

5   Product Development and Innovation 119

5.1   Development Process in SAP 121

       PIL at a Glance – Challenges of Providing Complete
       Software Solutions 123

Invent and Define 123

Develop 125

Deploy and Optimize... 127

5.2 Development Tasks in Labs India 128

NetWeaver Development 129

Business Process Platform and ByDesign Development 131

Localization Development 133

Industry Solutions.. 134

ERP Development 136

Installed Base Maintenance and Support 137

Custom Development 139

Development with Partners 140

Certification of Partner Products 141

5.3 Innovation at Labs India.. 142

Innovation in India 142

Managed Innovation.. 143

Bottom-up Innovation 144

Co-innovation.. 148

Process Innovation 150

5.4 Summary of Development in Labs India.................... 151

6 **People Management across Boundaries and Cultures** **155**

6.1 The Market for Talent in India 155

Mobility 156

Shortage Situation: "Demand Is Larger than Supply".............. 158

Skill Discrimination: "Vastly Different Skill Levels (Employability) of Graduates" 159

Strong Preference for the IT Sector: "Run into Engineering Jobs"... 160

6.2 Guiding Principles of People Management at SAP.................. 161

6.3 Culture and People Management............................... 162

The Indian Perspective 165

6.4   Management of People – the Role of Leadership 170

The Talent Management Process 173

The Life Cycle of Employees.. 190

6.5   Conclusion... 201

7   Infrastructure Challenges 203

7.1   How SAP Copes with the Infrastructure Issues
      in Bangalore 205

K+V and the Early SAP India 205

7.2   The Move to International Tech Park Limited (ITPL)............ 207

7.3   The SAP Labs India Campus 209

The Construction Phase.. 214

8   Mergers and Acquisitions 225

8.1   The Acquisitions Process at SAP 226

8.2   Acquisitions at SAP Labs India.. 228

Acquisition of Virsa 228

Acquisition of Yasu.. 230

Acquisition of Business Objects... 232

8.3   Summary 234

9   Evolution and Way Forward 235

9.1   Development Locations... 239

9.2   Labs India 241

9.3   Conclusion... 243

About the Authors 245

References.. 249

1   SAP AG Profile

SAP AG, headquartered in Walldorf, Germany, has evolved from a small German start-up to the world's leading international provider of enterprise software over the course of the last three decades. Today more than 82,000 worldwide customers run SAP applications – from distinct solutions addressing the needs of small businesses and midsize companies to suite offerings designed for global organizations.

1.1   The History of SAP AG

The Beginning of a Story of Success

SAP co-founder, Hasso Plattner, often enjoys recounting the story of how SAP might not have come into being were it not for his efforts one rainy day in 1972. On the day in question, Hasso accidentally dropped a box of 2000 punch cards onto the wet parking lot floor while transporting them from his car. These cards contained essential data vital to the function of a newly developed standard business software – software on which the eventual creation of SAP depended. It took Hasso two days to dry the cards and rearrange them into their correct order. Had the cards been irreparably damaged, the development of the software, and by extension the birth of SAP, might not have been possible (Ramge 2006).

Hasso and his colleagues Dietmar Hopp, Hans-Werner Hector, Klaus Tschira, and Claus Wellenreuther, all employees of IBM at that time, made the decision to start their own company when IBM rejected their recommendation to develop software designed to be used by several users simultaneously. Hasso recalled: "We got the notion that within IBM we would never have the freedom necessary to make this idea a genuine success." They launched their private corporation in 1972. Called SAP (*Systemanalyse und **P**rogrammentwicklung* – **S**ystems **A**nalysis and **P**rogram Development), it was named after the project on which they had been working at IBM. The company had its headquarters in Weinheim, and its main office in Mannheim, Germany.

C. Neumann and J. Srinivasan, *Managing Innovation from the Land of Ideas and Talent: The 10-Year Story of SAP Labs India,*
DOI: 10.1007/978-3-540-89283-0_1, © Springer-Verlag Berlin Heidelberg 2009

Therefore, in the 1970s, while their competitors were still designing various products to tie different parts of a business together, these enterprising entrepreneurs were in the right place, at the right time, and with the right skills to develop a single software system that would unite all of a companies' business functions. Their primary business concept, to develop standard application software for enterprises controlled through a centralized mainframe, was a ground breaking innovation. Designed to eliminate the need for individualized end-user installation, and to make it possible to interactively process data in real-time with the computer screen the focal point, their system was a giant conceptual step forward in business software.

Initial Customers and Success

Within a year of being established, SAP had already completed its first software solution for financial accounting. This solution was developed for the company's first local customer, ICI (Imperial Chemical Industries), a British chemical giant, which owned a nylon fiber plant near Heidelberg, Germany. ICI was not only SAP's first customer; its production plant also became SAP's first development center. It was at this center that the founders of SAP spent their days, and worked on their software solution mostly in night shifts and during the weekends. The reason was that they could not afford to buy such a system on their own and during day time ICI needed the mainframe for their operations. This single management system, designed as a real-time accounting and transaction processing program, tied ICI's information databases together. It became known as 'R/1': the 'R' stood for real-time processing, meaning that the data was processed immediately after having been entered. At that time, batch processing completely dominated the computer world: business data had to be entered manually at the entry terminal and was then saved and stored. After that, it was subsequently processed by the computers, batch by batch, at a specified time. Accordingly, there was always a big time lag between entering and finally processing the data. Therefore, the advent of real-time processing was quite a sensation. After a while, real-time processing became a genuine milestone in the 1970s.

This also brought up problems: the computer's memory had to cope with a double workload: it had to execute software processes and control dialog with the terminal at the same time. "This is really hard to imagine today. We were working with computers that filled whole buildings – and had just a fraction of the processing power of an average PC today," recalls

Plattner. So it was a certainty that SAP's R/1 formed the basis for the continuous development of other software modules. Nonetheless, with the support of SAP's first customer ICI, R/1 was an immediate success, and SAP grew to nine employees in its first year of operations. According to Hasso Pattner, as reported in an interview with the magazine 'Euro Business', it was important that ICI was a multinational company, because it broadened SAP's international exposure and provided opportunities that would facilitate its emergence as an international business in its own right. ICI was already a global player, so from the beginning, English was the *lingua franca* between SAP and its first customer. Apart from that, SAP obtained valuable insights on the business management of international corporations. "We were extremely fortunate to have ICI as our first customer," says Plattner, "the fact that ICI was a multinational company expanded our horizons immediately. I believe that it was during the early days at ICI that the seeds of integration and international software were first planted in our minds" (Zipf 2002: p. 10–14).

Soon, other customers in the region followed and SAP sold its standard solutions several times to different companies. For example, Roth-Händle, a cigarette manufacturer in Lahr (Germany); Knoll, a pharmaceutical company in Ludwigshafen (Germany); and other well-known customers like Freudenberg, Jacobs Kaffee, and Grundig. John Deere, a German subsidiary of the American tractor producer, played a special role in SAP's development. They wanted to align the processes of their different subsidiaries with the help of software that was to run on one computer, but serve several countries, several different legal entities, legislations, and languages. As a result, in 1975 SAP became multilingual. Hasso Plattner recalls: "John Deere asked us to internationalize the software and we did. It was the beginning of our international version of SAP systems" (Lofthouse 2000: p. 69). Apart from all customizations to the system, the overall aim was to sell and develop innovative software that could easily be implemented and be installed as often as possible.

The fast growth of the company went on continuously, and, in its fifth year of operation, the private corporation was dissolved and SAP became a GmbH (*Gesellschaft mit beschränkter Haftung* – Limited Liability Corporation) and revised the meaning of its SAP acronym, (*Systeme, Anwendungen, Produkte in der Datenverarbeitung* – **S**ystems, **A**pplications, **P**roducts in Data Processing) to better fit its new broader scope and context. At that stage, revenues were roughly equivalent to EUR 2 million, and the number of employees had grown to 25. Furthermore, for the first time, SAP installed its systems at customer sites outside of Germany: the Nettingsdorf paper mill, and the energy provider OKA of Linz, both in Austria.

Growth and Internationalization

In the 1980s SAP experienced a rapid growth and benefited from major developments in the software sector: IBM presented its first ever personal computer, which was quickly shortened to the acronym 'PC'. Mainframes were more and more replaced by networks of medium-sized computers, workstations, and PCs. Computers with drastically improved price-to-performance ratios entered the market and helped SAP to expand its customer base. The basic shape of a client-server architecture was developed during this time. All these major inventions made the utilization of hardware easier through, for example, increased memory space providing temporary storage for dialog information.

During this boom time, due to its close relationships with customers, SAP continuously enhanced its already distributed program modules, and in 1982, released the SAP R/2 system. It was a major upgrade of the R/1 system and it was made compatible with IBM as well as with Siemens mainframes and operating systems. With its R/2 system, SAP claimed market leadership for large corporations, and was ready to conquer the international software market. At that time, fifty of Germany's one hundred largest industrial enterprises were already successfully using SAP R/2. Along with this success, SAP moved from its office in Mannheim to an industrial park in the town of Walldorf where it occupied the company's first building, and began to operate its own computer center. This move united all development teams under one roof. On its 10th anniversary, SAP celebrated sales soaring by 48 %, roughly equivalent to more than EUR 12 million. SAP planned for its major growth by designing country-focused versions of SAP R/2, which was developed to handle different languages and currencies. For example, with the development of a French version of the accounting module and with the foundation of subsidiaries in Denmark, Sweden, Italy, and the United States, SAP's international expansion took a big leap forward.

When SAP crossed the edge of revenue roughly equivalent EUR 50 million in revenue, it was converted from a closely held to a publicly held corporation. SAP AG was from then on listed on Germany's stock markets in Frankfurt and Stuttgart, with about 1.2 million shares. By changing its structure to a publicly held corporation, SAP significantly strengthened its capital base and laid the foundations for its employees to benefit and share in the company's success. Additional steps were undertaken in 1984 by founding SAP's Austrian subsidiary SAP Österreich Ges.m.b.H. in Vienna and SAP (International) AG in Switzerland. These two subsidiaries were tasked with increasing sales of the R/2 system in international markets. Hans Schlegl, responsible for foreign business at that time, recalls: "When I got into a taxi, whether in Philadelphia or Singapore, and asked for driving me to SAP, I wanted the taxi drivers to know where to go in the same way as their counterparts in Heidelberg." This vision, by the way, came true to a lesser extent, however, in Singapore and Philadelphia than in Bangalore and Shanghai. Already one year after the foundation of SAP (International) AG, it achieved great success gaining new customers all over Europe, as well as in Canada, Kuwait, South Africa, Trinidad, and the United States. Also, by establishing subsidiaries across Europe and the United States, SAP continued to develop its international network.

In addition to that, development teams began to work on two new applications for personnel management and plant maintenance, while the production planning and control systems were installed at the first pilot customers. Further expansions also took place at the Walldorf headquarters, which had grown to 10,000 square meters of space, while at the Swiss subsidiary a new headquarters was occupied. Branch offices were also opened in Munich and Hamburg. It was only a question of time until SAP would start planning a new version of the R/2 system. Dietmar Hopp, co-founder and SAP's CEO at that time, explained:

"Our decision in 1987/88 to develop the R/3 system was probably the most important and most appropriate one we have ever taken. It was the golden age of mainframes and R/2 was booming – we could easily have sat back and taken it easy. But we were fascinated by the idea of developing multi-platform software. The timing was very fortunate, since a fairly dramatic demise of the mainframe began soon afterwards" (Schepp 2002: p. 21).

SAP (International) soon grew to twelve subsidiaries, including Canada, Singapore, and Australia. SAP's growing profile in 1989 was evidenced by a number of events, the large number of participants attending the first annual stockholders' meeting in 1988, the strong growth of employees to more than 1,000, and the expansion of its customer base. Recognizing this success, *manager magazine* named SAP 'Company of the Year', a distinction SAP received twice more in the next few years.

The Way Forward with SAP R/3

An anecdote tells that SAP R/3 actually grew out of the necessity of having something new to present at the annual CeBIT, an IT and telecommunication fare in Hannover, Germany. Hasso Plattner once confessed in an interview that this is a true story. At the end of the 1980s, IBM had announced its new System Application Architecture (SAA) programming in 'C' language, containing rules and standards for interoperable programming on different platforms. IBM expected SAP to use and stick to their standard, nevertheless, at the beginning of the 1990s SAP could already assume that SAA was not going to become an industry standard. Therefore, SAP decided to develop SAP R/3, including the ABAP/4 programming language on UNIX. However, SAP developers had difficulties in connecting IBM's C programming, which was designed to run on mainframe computers, with its ABAP/4 based applications. The aim was to make SAP systems run on mainframe computers. Peter Zencke then made a suggestion, to migrate the application from the mainframe to a workstation. "I simply answered that this was not the system we actually wanted to sell, but that it would certainly give us the opportunity to demonstrate our new system at the CeBIT", Plattner explained. This was the birth of the SAP R/3 system; it ran on a UNIX workstation, the Hewlett-Packard 500. For a long time the story was told that SAP R/3 was originally a mainframe system and ironically it never ran on a mainframe.

With its highly portable system, SAP's future was predictable; it would become the winning software provider for client-server systems across the globe (Schepp 2002: p. 22 – 23). The improvement of SAP R/3 formed the combination of a uniform appearance of graphical interfaces, the consistent use of relational databases, and the ability to run on computers from different manufacturers. With its new product, SAP ushered in a new generation of enterprise software – from mainframe computing to the three-tier architecture of database, application, and client interface. Until today client-server architecture remains the standard in large enterprise software, although we now see new software architectures and consumption models like SaaS (software as a service) or SOA (service-oriented architecture) gaining ground. With SAP R/3, a whole new market potential was found among the branch offices and subsidiaries of large companies, as well as among small and medium-sized enterprises (SMEs). The release of SAP R/3 in 1992 marks the most significant development in SAP's history, and triggered record growth. SAP became a trendsetter in IT globalization and the dream of the five founders, to offer companies standard application software that would allow business processes to run more efficiently at lower costs around the globe, had finally become true!

On an international scale, SAP made a big step forward with the expansion of business in Asia and in America. After the fall of the Berlin Wall in 1989, and the end of the cold war in the early 1990's, SAP began establishing subsidiaries in Central and Eastern Europe. At the same time, around the years 1991 and 1992, a Russian version of SAP R/2 was completed and SAP began promoting its software in the former Soviet Union, the Commonwealth of Independent States (CIS). A subsidiary was opened in Japan, which became SAP's 18th subsidiary, and developers worked on the Japanese version of SAP R/3. Accordingly, in 1995 a subsidiary in Beijing, China, was opened to support sales of the software in Mandarin Chinese.

Fig. 1. Dietmar Hopp and Peter Zencke at the opening ceremony of SAP Asia in Singapore in 1996

However, the SAP board members knew that expansion in America was even more crucial to the company's success. "We had clearly planned that we had to go to America. If you're not successful in America, you can't be successful in the rest of the world, either," Hasso Plattner said, looking back. With the opening of a technology development center in 'Silicon Valley', California, and the start of a USD 2 million advertising campaign, SAP won a large number of American high tech firms to run SAP software. In the mid-1990s, SAP's sales in the U.S. increased from EUR 46 million to 116 million. Henning Kagermann, who became member of the SAP executive board at that time, claims: "A crucial factor in our breakthrough was our ability to acquire renowned customers in the key market of the U.S., at an early stage, which paved the way for the success of R/3 there." Consequently, within a short period of three years, the U.S. became SAP's largest market and also influenced the management style of the company. Hasso Plattner promoted an 'Americanized way' of managing the company by promoting open-door policies and a more family-like atmosphere. Plattner later called it an 'informal hothouse culture'. Although SAP's corporate culture was never very 'German' from that point of view, for German employees this was a new move forward, as at that time the management style of German companies usually still tended to be more formal and was arranged in a strictly hierarchical way (Lofthouse 2000: p. 69–70). Driven by the success of SAP R/3 in the U.S. market, the pace of SAP's worldwide business picked up considerably. New subsidiaries opened in the Czech Republic, Russia, Poland, China, Korea, Thailand, Argentina, Brazil, South Africa, Malaysia, and Mexico City, which further increased SAP's international activities. In the first half of 1994, almost 60 % of its sales came from outside Germany. In 1995 SAP, continued to expand its sales organization and strategic alliances; more than 6,000 companies of all sizes were SAP customers, some two-thirds of which solved their IT tasks using the R/3 system. Eventually R/3 became the largest source of the overall revenue. The company had acquired 1,089 new SAP R/3 customers and SAP R/3 had been installed on more than 9,000 systems worldwide. It became obvious that the success of R/3 had propelled SAP to the top league of the global software market. As a result, at the end of the 1990s, SAP was represented in over 40 countries by subsidiaries, branch offices or partner companies. The 15 international subsidiaries were managed directly from Walldorf.

A New Millennium and a New Product Range

Already in the mid-nineties, the IT sector was again undergoing a major revolution, namely, with the rise of the Internet. Plattner recalls: "We had an employee from California working with us in Walldorf for some time developing SAP R/3. When he left the company to travel around the world, he wrote me a long letter. One thing he kept repeating was: 'Don't overlook the Internet. Nobody has an idea what it will mean to us in the future.' He was right. I, for one, didn't see the Internet coming. And suddenly it was just there!"

SAP had to act fast to get on board the speeding train of the Internet. Hasso Plattner, co-founder, co-chairman, and CEO at that time, knew that the company had to move on by adding a new product range to its best-sellers. As a first movement in the right direction, and in order to keep SAP state-of-the-art, SAP aligned with Microsoft, Netscape, and SUN Microsystems to make SAP R/3 Internet-compatible. With the first system, Business Application Programming Interfaces (BAPIs), which can be seen as a precursor of today's popular Web services, customers anywhere in the world could work with SAP software over the Internet. As a result, the 3.0 version of R/3 in 1996 provided the first comprehensive, Internet-enabled business application package, which increased the attractiveness of the R/3 system by making it more user-friendly. For many of SAP's clients, however, this move was still too early, so the BAPIs were used in some business-to-business scenarios, but they found very limited application in business-to-consumer scenarios.

In the meantime, SAP's globalization proceeded fast; Labs Japan was opened in 1996 to help entering the Japanese market, followed by the foundation of Labs India in 1998, another milestone in the globalization of SAP.

In 1999 SAP announced a set of completely new software products as part of its mySAP.com strategy, which represented a complete restructuring of the product portfolio and the beginning of a new direction for the company. Using the latest Web technology, mySAP.com combined e-commerce solutions with the existing Enterprise Resource Planning (ERP) applications. It enabled SAP to offer an integrated business platform that combined front-end processes with back-office systems. Consequently, customers were enabled to organize business processes with suppliers and partners, and to automate their business workflow. A important part of the mySAP solutions were the so called 'New Dimension Products', which were cross-industry solutions (for example, mySAP Customer Relationship Management, mySAP Supply Chain Management, and mySAP Business Intelligence) based on previous modules of R/3, but targeting new business segments. In addition to that, industry-specific solutions (for example, mySAP Automotive or mySAP Public Sector) were promoted more intensively while infrastructure and services (for example, mySAP Technology and mySAP Services) were put under the same umbrella. Within one year, the image and go-to-market approach of the company were revamped into a big player in the new Internet-based economy. What started in the New Economy with 'mySAP.com' and continued with 'mySAP Technology', ended up in SAP NetWeaver technology. Based on the Enterprise Services Architecture and the underlying integration and application platform, SAP NetWeaver provides its customers with solutions for end-to-end business processes. With SAP NetWeaver, companies can integrate people, information, and processes within the company and beyond. In 2004, SAP launched the first version of SAP NetWeaver 2004, which marked the foundation of the Enterprise Service-Oriented Architecture (ESOA).

At the end of 2002, the company's 30th anniversary, SAP's employee base had grown to 29,000. The following year marked the end of an era: With Hasso Plattner leaving the executive board and becoming the new chairman of the supervisory board, there were no more founders left in the day-to-day management of SAP (co-founders Dietmar Hopp and Klaus Tschira had left the excutive board already in 1998). Henning Kagermann became the sole CEO and chairman. His first trip abroad after assuming the new role was to India, which marked the first ever visit of any SAP CEO to the subcontinent. At that time India was already on the radar in terms of high growth rates in both sales in the market and development capacity at the Labs. In 2003, SAP opened its ninth development location outside Walldorf in Shanghai (China), adding another development center to its worldwide network. The 120 developers at SAP Labs China had an average of over four years of experience in the software industry. Most of the developers were Chinese, but some were from Germany, Australia, the U.S., and other Asian countries – this cultural diversity helped to drive innovation at the new SAP Labs, and it helped to integrate them into SAP's global structure.

In 2005, Dietmar Hopp, SAP's co-founder, former CEO and former chairman of the SAP Supervisory Board, retired from the supervisory board.

That same year, Henning Kagermann introduced six core values for SAP AG: customer focus, quality, product excellence, integrity, commitment and passion. He also added what is known as the 'new requirements': agility, high performance, simplicity, co-innovation, and talent development as an overall focus of the multinational company. With solutions based on the new business process platform (BPP), SAP aims today to significantly increase its customer base. It has the entire market on its radar screen, from large conglomerates to the smallest of companies.

In the year 2007, there are more than 12 million users working with SAP solutions every day. There are 121,000 installations worldwide, more than 1,500 SAP partners, over 25 industry-specific business solutions and more than 47,800 customers in 120 countries. SAP has become the world's third-largest independent software vendor.

Table 1. History of SAP AG

1972	— Foundation of SAP in Mannheim, Germany, and launch of the first SAP system R/1.
1976	— The private corporation is dissolved and transferred to SAP GmbH, a limited liability corporation named 'Systems, Applications and Products in Data Processing'.
1977	— SAP moves its headquarters from Mannheim to Walldorf and gains first international customers by partnering with two companies in Austria.
1978	— SAP has 50 employees and 100 customers. The SAP R/2 solution is born.
1980	— SAP moves into the company's first own building in an industrial park in Walldorf, near Heidelberg. — 50 of the 100 largest industrial companies in Germany are SAP clients. — SAP co-founder Claus Wellenreuther leaves the company for health reasons.
1982	— In its 10th year of operation, SAP numbers 100 employees. — SAP revenues increase to DM 24 million for the year. — More than 250 companies in Germany, Austria and Switzerland are using SAP-developed programs
1984	— SAP International AG is founded in Biel, Switzerland, to coordinate business abroad.
1985	— SAP systems are being used throughout Europe as well as in South Africa, Kuwait, Trinidad, Canada and the United States. — The first U.S. headquarters is established in Wayne, Pennsylvania.

Table 1 (continued)

1986 — SAP founds its first international subsidiary in Austria.
 — The first German branch office is opened in Ratingen, near Düsseldorf.
 — The company makes its first appearance at the CeBIT in Hanover.
 — The turnover reaches the DM 100 million mark earlier than expected.
 — SAP increases its capital stock from DM 500,000 to DM 5 million.
 — In Walldorf the company installs an IBM computer with a 64 megabyte memory – an investment of around DM 7 million.

1988 — SAP GmbH is converted from a closely-held corporation to the publicly-held corporation SAP AG and is from then on listed, with about 1.2 million shares, on the stock markets of Frankfurt and Stuttgart, Germany.
 — SAP gains its 1,000th customer, Dow Chemical, and subscribes capital stock increases from DM 5 Million to DM 60 Million.
 — SAP's international business is reinforced by the opening of subsidiaries in Denmark, Sweden, Italy and the U.S.
 — SAP opens the subsidiary SAP North America, Inc., in Philadelphia, Pennsylvania.
 — The SAP executive board inaugurates the international training center in Walldorf.

1989 — SAP presents its new user-friendly interface for the R/2 system. New tools, for example the programming environment ABAP/4, give rise to new developments. R/3 is also taking shape.
 — SAP stocks are traded on the Zurich stock exchange and SAP employs more than 1,000 people.
 — SAP now has 12 international subsidiaries, among them Canada, Singapore and Australia.
 — SAP holds its first general meeting of shareholders in Karlsruhe.
 — DM 83.3 million is spent on research and development.

1990 — The capital stock reaches DM 85 million following the issue of preference shares.
 — The economic and monetary union with East Germany and the subsequent unification of Germany opens up a new market for SAP.
 — SAP opens another branch office in Berlin.
 — SRS is formed in cooperation with Siemens Nixdorf and Robotron.
 — SAP invests more than DM 109 million in research and development.

1991 — 2,225 customers in 31 countries are now using SAP's standard software.
 — SAP software is installed in Japan for the first time.
 — The SAP Executive Board of the co-founders Dietmar Hopp, Hasso Plattner, Hans-Werner Hector and Klaus Tschira is extendend by including Prof. Dr. Henning Kagermann in early 1991 and Hans Schlegel between April 1992 and December 1993.

Table 1 (continued)

1992   — The SAP R/3 system is released to the general market.
　　　 — Revenues increase to DM 831 million, of which almost 50 % are
　　　　 derived from international operations.
　　　 — SAP enters the Hong Kong market.

1993   — SAP starts to cooperate with Microsoft, the world's largest software
　　　　 producer. One of the aims of this collaboration is to port the R/3 system
　　　　 to Windows NT.
　　　 — The construction of a development center in Foster City, California,
　　　　 U.S., initiates an SAP presence near Silicon Valley.
　　　 — SAP extends the executive board to include Peter Zencke on January 1.

1994   — The R/3 system for Windows NT is released for the general market.
　　　 — IBM, a long-standing partner of SAP, also uses the R/3 system globally
　　　　 to control its business processes. The IBM contract is the biggest at this
　　　　 stage in SAP's history.
　　　 — With more than 4,000 firms as customers and a turnover of DM 1.8 bil-
　　　　 lion, SAP is one of the leading vendors of standard application software
　　　　 worldwide.

1995   — Microsoft is yet another hi-tech company to invest into the R/3 system.
　　　　 With SAP shares listed in the DAX and the lowest par value set at DM 5
　　　　 SAP shares are proving very popular.
　　　 — German Telecom decides to install the R/3 system, with 30,000 R/3
　　　　 users, this is SAP's largest contract so far.
　　　 — For personal reasons, Hans-Werner Hector moves from the SAP execu-
　　　　 tive board to the supervisory board.
　　　 — The customer base grows to 6,000.

1996   — Three more members are admitted to the SAP executive board:
　　　　 Claus Heinrich, Gerhard Oswald and Paul Wahl.
　　　 — The European Business Press Federation (UPEFE) nominates SAP
　　　　 "company of the year".
　　　 — Bill Gates visits SAP.
　　　 — 1,089 new R/3 customers have been won. By the end of the year around
　　　　 9,000 R/3 systems have been installed worldwide.
　　　 — The system R/3 Release 3.1 is Internet-enabled.
　　　 — SAP Labs Japan was founded.

1997   — SAP begins developing industry-specific solutions.
　　　 — SAP celebrates its 25th birthday. The 1997 jubilee year is a particularly
　　　　 successful one. With approximately DM 1.6 billion, the profit breaks
　　　　 through the billion barrier for the first time.
　　　 — Hasso Plattner becomes co-chairman and CEO of SAP AG.

Table 1 (continued)

1998 — The company is listed on the New York Stock Exchange and launches new solutions for business information warehouse, business-to-business procurement and supply chain management.
— Establishment of SAP Labs India and SAP Labs France.
— Dietmar Hopp and Klaus Tschira move from the executive board to the supervisory board.
— Paul Wahl leaves SAP.
— Henning Kagermann becomes co-chairman and CEO of SAP AG.
— Henning Kagermann, Hasso Plattner, Peter Zencke, Gerhard Oswald, Claus E. Heinrich form the Board of SAP AG.

1999 — Co-chairman and CEO Hasso Plattner announces the new mySAP.com strategy, heralding the beginning of a completely new direction for the company and its product range.

2000 — More than 10 million users work with SAP solutions. There are 36,000 installations worldwide, 1,000 partners, 22 industry business solutions and 13,500 customers in 120 countries.
— SAP is the world's third-largest independent software vendor.

2001 — SAP's revenues top EUR 7.3 billion.
— Werner Brandt joins the SAP executive board on February 1, 2001, assuming responsibility for the company's financials.
— In early November at TechEd in Los Angeles, Hasso Plattner presents the new e-business architecture, mySAP Technology, the watchwords of which are openness and integration.

2002 — SAP celebrates its 30th Anniversary and has grown to 17,500 customers and 27,800 employees.
— SAP announces its new medium-sized business offensive.
— Two new management boards will help provide decision-making support: the Field Management Board and the Product Technology Board.
— As of January, a worldwide consultancy unit (Global Professional Services Organization) deals with all global and strategic projects.
— Léo Apotheker moves into the Executive Board and officially announced his replacement to head the North American subsidiary. William R. McDermott joins to head operations in the United States and Canada as CEO and President for SAP America, Inc., reporting directly to Léo Apotheker.

Table 1 (continued)

2003 — SAP launches SAP NetWeaver, its new integration and application platform.
— A change of leadership at SAP: CEO and co-chairman Hasso Plattner moves to the supervisory board and Henning Kagermann becomes sole CEO and chairman.
— SAP opens SAP Labs China in Shanghai, adding another development center to its worldwide network. The 120 developers at SAP Labs China have an average of over four years of experience in the software industry. Most of the developers are Chinese, while some are from Germany, Australia, America and Asia – this cultural diversity will help drive innovation at the new SAP Labs.
— Shai Agassi becomes board member

2004 — SAP announces a timeline for the service-enablement of its own solutions. By 2007 all SAP solutions will be Enterprise Services Architecture compliant.
— The new SAP Service Marketplace goes live with a new, harmonized layout and navigation structure, providing SAP customers, partners and prospects with a central point of access to SAP's entire portfolio via the Internet. The new SAP Support Portal also goes live.
— SAP's newest support center (GSC) in Dalian, China, officially opens on September 15, 2004.

2005 — SAP announces the development of its Business Process Platform.
— Dietmar Hopp, SAP co-founder, former CEO and former chairman of the SAP supervisory board, retires from the supervisory board.

2006 — SAP introduces SAP CRM on demand and an enhanced road map for SAP ERP, delivering innovation without disruption.

2007 — Acquisition of Business Objects S.A., SAP's largest acquisition in its history for USD 4.7 billion.
— Shai Agassi leaves the Executive Board.

2008 — Léo Apotheker becomes co-CEO.
— Ernie Gunst, Bill Mc Dermott and Jim Hagemann Snabe join the Executive Board.
— Peter Zencke, one of the father's of R/3 and 10 years sponsor of Labs India, leaves the Executive Board.

2009 — Claus E. Heinrich leaves the Executive Board.
— Henning Kagermann leaves the Executive Board.
— Léo Apotheker becomes the CEO of SAP AG (announced in summer 2008).

1.2 SAP Today

The SAP success story is easy to explain: The five former SAP founders invented the market in which they are now the market leader! SAP was the first company that offered standard business software for companies that wanted to organize their business processes with a computer system. Today, SAP has grown from a regional software company to the world's largest provider of business applications. At the beginning of 2009, SAP employed 51,536 people worldwide and listed more than 82,000 customers in more than 120 countries. SAP AG is listed on several exchanges, including the Frankfurt stock exchange and the New York stock exchange.

Based on the software revenue, SAP is the number one business software supplier in every industry and solution segment with a 32.8 % share among the core enterprise application vendors.

In 2008 SAP generated revenue in excess of EUR 11 billion. On a constant currency basis, its growth in 2007 was the strongest for seven years, with an operating margin at the high end of the market guidance. In 2007 SAP increased its market share by another four percentage points, respectively. In 2008 the company grew by 11 % despite a devastating fourth quarter.

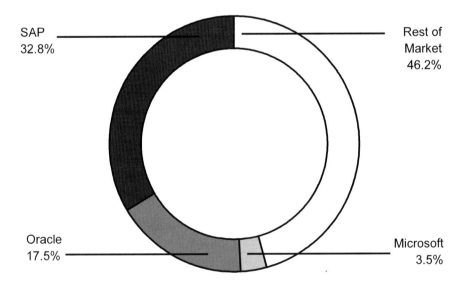

Fig. 2. Core enterprise application share as of January, 2009 rolling four quarters, based on software and software-related service revenues (Source: SAP Fact Sheet, http://www.sap.com/about/investor/pdf/SAP_FactSheet.pdf, February 2009)

Table 2. Sampling of SAP's 82,000 customers (Source: SAP Fact Sheet, http://www.sap.com/about/investor/pdf/SAP_FactSheet.pdf, February 2009)

Adobe Systems	Kellogg's
American Express	McDonald's
Apple	Nestle
BMW	Nike
BP	Nokia
Canon	PepsiCo
Chevron	Procter & Gamble
Chrysler	Samsung
Coca-Cola	Siemens
Colgate-Palmolive	Sony
Dept. of Defense	Starbucks Coffee
Disney	Target
Ford	The Body Shop
GE	Unilever
General Motors	U.S. Postal Service
Hershey Foods	Verizon
Home Depot	Wal-Mart

SAP continuously accelerates the pace of change through new technology platforms, new applications, and new best practices, to serve an ever-expanding universe of customers, industry categories, and business roles. Consequently, SAP's global development approach focuses on distributing development across the world in strategically important markets. Around 15,500 people are working in software development, at development centers in nine countries. These locations, known as SAP Labs, include major centers in Germany, the United States, India, China, and Israel, as well as smaller SAP Labs in Bulgaria, Canada, France and Hungary. By thinking globally and acting locally, the network of SAP Labs generates significant and lasting competitive advantages for SAP. The global distribution of the labs enables the company to secure the services of excellent employees from different cultures and with a wide range of market and specialist skills. It also allows SAP to make the most effective and efficient use of its resources. In 2008, SAP invested EUR 1.614 billion in research and development for business software solutions.

2 Location Strategy at SAP AG

2.1 International Locations Strategy

The Initial Years of Internationalization

SAP started its global journey during the 1980s, when it opened subsidiaries in neighbouring countries to Germany (Austria, Switzerland and France were among the first countries) and then started overseas with an office in the U.S. At that time, customers in many other countries, whether in Japan or China, were still served by central teams in Germany or by local SAP partners. In the mainframe world, it took some time to develop the idea of standardized software and to get customer traction. Big majors like IBM and DEC were dominating the hardware market, Nixdorf was strong in Europe and those companies were still selling big systems bundled with operating systems and the business applications to be run on them. The greatest technological revolution at the end of the 20th century was the appearance of the PC and the consequential evolution of client-server technology. Under the leadership of executives like Hasso Plattner, Peter Zencke, and Gerd Oswald, SAP was the first company to realize the potential of this new technology, and to make it available for its clients. R/3, which entered the market in 1992, was a real hit and created an unforeseeable global demand for SAP's products. SAP expanded quickly into new markets like Turkey and the Middle East (1992), Japan, Brazil (1993), India (1994), and China (1995), by opening subsidiaries and making the products locally available.

The Markets' Need for Really Local Products

This was also the time, when SAP for the first time had to strategically 'localize' its products. The first step of software localization is usually its translation, which includes the user interface and the help texts for the users. This may sound trivial, but in functionality-rich software like SAP's this task can easily span some million lines of text that need to be trans-

C. Neumann and J. Srinivasan, *Managing Innovation from the Land of Ideas and Talent: The 10-Year Story of SAP Labs India,*
DOI: 10.1007/978-3-540-89283-0_2, © Springer-Verlag Berlin Heidelberg 2009

lated, so that the user is able to use the product on a daily business. For SAP it was always clear that one can not expect the users to operate software only in one language like English.

Another need that emerged was the different legal requirements for software in different countries. Although different tax rates or the calculation of different social security payments can be customized in software, there are often much more complex requirements such as bonded warehouses or complex inter-state taxation schemes that need to be programmed. SAP was the first of the global Enterprise Resource Planning (ERP) vendors to understand this, and quickly responded by creating a department in 1994 whose sole responsibility was overseeing the legal localization of its products in different markets worldwide.

More interesting than purely legal requirements were the business needs of customers in different regions of the world. Best business practices were used in many countries around the globe, be it the payment by bill of exchange in Italy, or the 'Kanban' production principle in Japan. Kanban describes a pull principle that starts from customer demand, and runs through the whole company in order to match the product quality and quantity with the exact demand of the customer. At the beginning of the 1990s, German and U.S. companies still followed their traditional planning and budgeting cycles, so SAP's software usually reflected the Western way of doing business. Nevertheless, by enabling the software with tremendous effort to support the Kanban principle, SAP was one of the first software companies to support these typical Japanese production systems in its ERP modules. These efforts enabled its big Japanese clients like Toyota or Nissan to use their leading production methods not only on the shop floor, but also in their support systems. At the same time, the SAP software became much richer, as Kanban is one of the core principles of 'Lean Manufacturing', which became more and more a globally accepted practice during the mid 1990s. Following this, other enterprises around the world, specifically in the automotive industry, were keen to have lean manufacturing implemented in their production.

SAP was the first software company to persue the double approach of providing standard software that could be easily implemented and operated on the one hand, while at the same time watching for and integrating key global business trends into their software. This was not an easy task, though: the German developers needed to learn what those business principles were all about. This involved many communication problems. The result was that the new country specific functionalities sometimes did not meet the customer's expectations.

From then on, SAP started to fly in teams from its home base in Walldorf to locations like Seoul, Sao Paolo, Tokyo or Beijing to help them understand what was happening at these places. Dieter Schoen, one of the team members at that time recalls: "Every six weeks we used to fly to Seoul for about three to four weeks to work with Samsung, one of our initial key clients in Korea. We really got familiar with the country, but more important was that over there we learned how they run their business. It wasn't easy, though, as we needed interpreters all the time. We were not able to speak to users directly and at times we had difficulties in translating their needs into a software design, because the requirements seemed to be so far away from our usual way of thinking. When I think back, it was not only the client managers, but also our colleagues in the local subsidiaries who were putting a lot of pressure on us to solve things, as otherwise we would lose revenue."

Soon it became clear that this could not be the way for SAP to operate its global product business. Flying squads across the globe would not provide the needed input for the SAP's development hub in Walldorf, and neither would the consultants of the subsidiaries be able to do that job. A subsidiary at that time could only have two main goals: increase SAP's market share and be profitable beyond its industry's average. Consultants working on requirement analysis or on specifying the needs of a country for the developers, were seen as wasting their time because they were not at the customer site where their efforts were billable. SAP would need to get developers permanently into its key markets, to be closer to what was happening out there. As one manager from Waldorf expressed it: "Our board realized that it was either absurd or a sign of 'engineering overconfidence' to believe that we would be able to provide the world with suitable software out of a small village in Southern Germany. We were just too far away from it, so we needed to come closer – it was a matter of understanding the customer, but as well of economic realities, as we were blowing away a lot of money by traveling around the globe to visit our clients."

Supporting this was another trend, which had to do with the software itself. The R/3 system, designed to be one simple ERP solution which could be understood in its principles by one person, evolved to become richer and richer in functionality – which was it's key differentiating quality, setting it apart from the competitors in the years 1992–1999. One full-page advertisement in the New York Times was just a list of its functionalities – printed in 8 pt font across the whole page! And it worked. What may have been seen as a unique selling proposition by SAP sales and as a compelling offer by the customers, also had a downside. The complexity of the software was increasing constantly, so by the mid-1990s, there was hardly anyone who could understand all customer requirements across all modules of the software. Increasingly, developers and consultants were becoming highly specialized. At this point, the era of the flying mini-squads was over; there would have been the need of an "airbus" in the literary sense to bring everyone to his client and to cope with all the different development and requirement issues the customers might have.

The Building of SAP's First Lab in the Silicon Valley

By this time, it became obvious that SAP would need its own development hubs around the globe to get closer to the customers and to emerging technological trends. In 1993, SAP opened its first R&D center abroad, in Foster City, U.S.A. The U.S. was SAP's largest emerging market at that time. Although the U.S. still had not achieved the revenues of major European markets like the UK or Switzerland, it was the market with the highest growth potential for SAP at that point. Furthermore, the rules of business were different in the U.S., so a good amount of localization seemed to be needed for this market. However, regarding Silicon Valley, there was an even more striking argument: with the appearance of the client-server technology (and the disappearance of the last big European IT hardware players like Nixdorf), the dominance of the U.S. in the semiconductor and PC industry had become stronger than ever before. Intel and Microsoft were well on their way to conquering the computer market with the invention of the end-user PC, UNIX was the leading operation system in the market for business applications, and Informix and Oracle were the leading database vendors. In all areas in which SAP needed to cooperate closely with other companies to optimize its own system, their partners were based in the U.S. There was a compelling need to get closer to those companies, to understand and speak their language, and to establish direct people-to-people cooperation. German companies may be world market leaders, highly innovative in production machinery, the automotive industry, and specialized chemistry, but it was obvious that the trends of data and computer technology were set in Silicon Valley. That meant, 6,000 miles away, most of those trends would only reach Germany with a significant delay – a delay that would without any doubt be very decisive in the fast changing industry SAP was operating in.

It was co-founder Hasso Plattner, who was the man behind the opening and establishment of the Foster City lab, which later moved even more into the heart of the valley into a nice campus in Palo Alto, California. During those initial years, he convinced many senior SAP AG developers and architects to move to the valley. Some of them are still living there. Finally, he sent a very strong signal by moving himself to Palo Alto and living there for a good part of the year. Later, when Hasso Plattner was CEO of SAP, his presence in Palo Alto enabled SAP to hire key senior managers for the company like Shai Agassi, as these people felt that Palo Alto was not less a center of power than Walldorf. Many executives joined the Palo Alto lab – people whom SAP would never have been able to recruit if the pre-condition had been to settle down in a small town in Southern Germany. Some people in the valley seemed only able to survive there; but in the end, a company has to settle where it hopes to find the right talents.

Overall, it wasn't an easy start for Palo Alto during those initial years. Many colleagues back in Walldorf received the impression that their (ex-) colleagues were just having a good time in the bay area, preferring to surf at the beach, rather than surfing the latest technology wave. There were quite a number of voices saying that SAP was not getting enough tangible innovation from this expensive lab, compared with the resources put into it. One manager recalls: "The sweatshop work like solving customer messages and fixing bugs remained in Walldorf for us, whereas these guys got the fancy stuff like building the new graphical user interface of R/3 or the first Internet applications." Part of this was certainly perception, but specifically, at the time when the dollar was strong, the cost per employee in Palo Alto was about double the cost of an employee in the German headquarters. On the other hand, having large cash resources, SAP could afford the venture in Palo Alto despite pressure from global controlling and the undercurrent of perceived inequity emanating from Walldorf.

The Foundation of the First Market-Oriented Lab in Tokyo

It was in the years 1993/94 when SAP's board realized that Japan would become the number one market in Asia-Pacific, and that much more attention needed to be provided to this unique opportunity. Until then, SAP maintained only a small Asia-Pacific presence in Hong Kong, which mainly serviced scattered opportunities ranging from China to Indonesia. In addition to that, Australia was served by the U.S. subsidiary, so it was mainly handled like a 'province' of the U.S. in terms of support.

However, there was no clear marketing or product strategy for those markets. The customers had to use the SAP product in English; there was no translation available, neither for the product nor for the documentation. This worked for the early adaptors in those markets, specifically in more internationalized locations like Singapore and Hong Kong, where SAP quickly gained some market share. Nevertheless, the big opportunities in Japan and China were largely untapped. For Japan, it became clear that anything the company would do there would have to be strongly localized, starting from the management and ending with the product brochure. English is so uncommon even in places like Tokyo that one could neither sell service to customers through Hong Kong (at that time managed by a few Dutch employees) nor would it work to support Japan directly from Walldorf.

Dr. Peter Zencke, an executive board member of SAP, was the top manager in charge of the Asia-Pacific region during those years. He understood the message from the potential customers very well, and after having traveled to Japan twice, meeting customers and the first colleagues there, he made two strategic decisions that helped SAP to become, in an unprecedented move, the number one business software supplier in Japan. First, he installed a purely Japanese management team in Tokyo. The first president of SAP Japan, Sam Nakane, was hired from Pricewaterhouse-Coopers (PWC). He was the person with the contacts, the experience, and the local touch to win the first big Japanese clients for SAP. Peter's second important decision was to start the biggest localization effort for any country so far, by creating a big development hub right next to SAP's biggest clients: in Tokyo city. This was bold even by SAP standards, as the foundation of the Foster City Labs three years prior to that was certainly driven and accepted due to its technology spin. For Tokyo, there were many stakeholders within SAP who doubted that SAP would ever be able to recoup such an investment from one single Asian market.

Fifty smart developers were posted in Tokyo and another 10 in Walldorf to keep a link to the colleagues out there. The 10 colleagues in Walldorf, a few Japanese and a few German colleagues were organized in a structure called 'Japan Liaison Office' (JLO), which reported back to Tokyo. The development hub in Japan was managed by an American, Tom Shirk, who himself was a multicultural person, speaking English and German fluently, besides managing some Japanese. The newly formed Labs Japan not only incorporated Japanese business practices in the core SAP solution, it also helped their big clients add the custom developed solutions they demanded. Furthermore, they pioneered the technical challenge on the 'double-byte languages', which means making the software work well with Japanese characters, not only within the user interface, but also on the database level. That sounds trivial in today's world, but in 1994, the common codepage for the PC world was based on the assumption that all languages of the world would work sufficiently well with 256 characters – obviously not enough to cover the more than 30,000 characters needed in countries like China or Japan. This decision created a lot of creative work for key software architects in Tokyo and Walldorf, but it helped to make SAP's later entry in China and Thailand much easier.

In addition, Peter Zencke assigned himself a personal assistant to bridge the communication gap and provide management in the field as well as from the development hub (later re-named into SAP Labs Japan) direct access to him. The third important decision was to have Labs Japan report directly to him and not to the Asia-Pacific management. In this way, he underlined the strategic importance of the market and could get direct access to the key players.

The strategy paid off: the market share in Japan increased by 10 % every year, crossing the 50 % mark by 1997. A real success – by all measures: the local competition was virtually non-existent, and by the time the big U.S. competitors understood the game and got their acts together, it was too late. SAP had already gained such a high market share that it was seen as synonymous with 'business application software'. With its unique combination of German engineering and a completely local appearance in the market (many Japanese believed SAP to be a Japanese company), it was able to continuously gain market share and increase profitability. There was an important lesson for SAP: localization is needed initially to gain traction in a new market. The speed of localization is critical at the time of market entry and this need will slowly diminish when the product fulfills the market requirements. Sure, there are always continuous improvements and endeavors for perfection (especially in Japan), but after those crucial years the demand for localization usually reduces. That is true specifically for mature economies like Japan, where the rules and laws of business do not change as frequently as this might happen in places like India or Russia.

For example, in India the complete taxation is altered and at times significantly changed every single year in a process that is called 'annual budget' by the government. One can never predict whether today's rules will apply as well next year. Consequentially, the Japan lab was reduced in size after its fifth year of existence and disappeared as an independent research and development (R&D) location in 2005. Meanwhile SAP was able to build the necessary knowledge in more cost-efficient locations like India or China and could deliver the needed changes from there. Thus in Tokyo, only a small bridgehead remained, translating customer requests and changes of business needs into a language Japanese developers would understand.

The Next Wave – Labs in Bangalore and in Nice

By the end of 1997, SAP began wondering where to recruit all the people needed for its ambitious growth plans. The demand for SAP's products was still strong, the growth was double digit, but the products themselves were lagging a little behind the trends. Customer Relationship Management (CRM) had become much more than just a buzzword, as well as Product Lifecycle Management (PLM) and Supply Chain Management (SCM). There were previous niche players growing more quickly than SAP (like Siebel or I2) who represented a true challenge to SAP, not only in CRM or PLM, but also in its core application business. These new companies started building solutions around SAP's core functionalities and providing interfaces to integrate with core modules of SAP. SAP responded with the 'New Dimension Campaign' which gave its clients an outlook and a promise of future offerings in an effort to stall the competition's sales. At the same time, SAP was confronted by Internet hype, so it had to offer not only a compelling marketing story around Business to Business (B2B) and market places, but it also had to convince customers with its product story. Many customers were waiting to see how SAP would react to these challenges and many of SAP's global clients' 'purchase' decisions were put on hold to see whether SAP would be able to emerge victorious from those competitive battles.

In order to add the urgently needed product features and offerings, SAP had to expand its development base quickly. It went in two directions. First, SAP acquired other software companies in those new fields. It took over the sales-force automation software vendors and number two in its market 'Kiefer and Veittinger' to gain traction in the area of mobile solutions / CRM. It also acquired 'Commerce One', a company that was considered a leading vendor in the promising field of Internet marketplaces. Second, SAP took the decision to grow beyond its current R&D hubs in Germany, U.S. and Japan and open new labs at locations where talent would be easier to find.

As much as those acquisitions were successful insofar as the acquisition of new colleagues with specific mindsets and skills into SAP, the products of those companies had to be changed quickly, due to their incompatibility with SAP's core offerings. However, these acquisitions helped in the market in terms of mindshare, and it helped in the opinion of the analysts who recognized that SAP did understand the trends and was investing in those crucial areas to compensate.

Most of the new employees who came with those acquisitions were integrated into SAP, but a few left, as they could not find a suitable position in the new setup. Still, it took some time to make all of them productive, and the capacity added through those takeovers was still not enough to satisfy SAP's hunger for talent. It was obvious to the board, that SAP would also need to grow organically in engineering capacity if it wanted to keep the promises made to all those customers in the market with respect to future product offerings.

The 'Internet Hype' not only created thousands of start-ups globally, it also created a huge demand around the globe for software engineers and smart programmers. All those new companies, which sprang up specifically in the Western world at that time, were promising smart engineers quick bucks and work on really hot and exciting stuff. Whether it was in Germany, U.S. or in Japan – SAP faced severe difficulties in hiring intelligent young graduates, and it was close to impossible to hire from all those small and growing start-ups. In the job market and tech forums, SAP was often perceived using 'old technology', which was not really up to the trends. Some speculated that could even be in danger of disappearing from the marketplace, since all companies would soon drive their business via global market places and B2B scenarios, quickly making traditional software obsolete. As much as this view was of course too simplistic and proven to be completely wrong, SAP was having difficulty convincing investors in the stock market, and therefore could not offer compelling packages to potential employees. At the beginning of 1998 a full-page advertisement in one of Germany's leading newspaper (Frankfurter Allgemeine), launched to fill 10 positions in one specific engineering department, brought five applications. Only five! It was obvious – something needed to be done. The executive board of SAP put the need for talent on the very top of its agenda – it was identified as the main obstacle that impeded the company's growth.

At a ground breaking board meeting in 1997, the executive board decided that the company would need to reach out globally, beyond its current R&D centers (at that time in Germany, U.S. and Japan) and would either try to get talent from abroad into those centers, or open new R&D hubs around the world. A project sponsored by SAP's CEO Henning Kagermann and executive board member Peter Zencke was started in the beginning of 1998 to develop a proposal on where to establish the next labs of SAP. Two colleagues working as assistants at that time for Henning Kagermann and Peter Zencke, namely Thomas Vetter and Clas Neumann, were entrusted with the joint project lead. They were sent across Europe and Asia to scout for opportunities and to prepare the proposal. After two months, the team reported back with a proposal to open two new locations: one new lab in Sophia Antipolis (Nice, Southern France) and one in Bangalore (Southern India).

Sophia Antipolis looked compelling in terms of infrastructure, government support, and location attraction. The government of France wanted to promote this region very strongly as a kind of high-tech belt, offering subsidies and world class infrastructure for companies who wanted to invest. At the same time, this location just outside of Nice, overlooking the Mediterranean Sea, was absolutely suitable to attract talent from all over Europe, specifically Southern Europe, who might have found it hard to settle down in the more provincial area of Walldorf, but would find it compelling to be put up at one of the most beautiful spots in France.

Bangalore was chosen as the Asian hub. The predominant reason for this was the local availability of talent. Even Peter Zencke mentioned that during his trips to the United States and Singapore, he noticed that several Indians were working on important SAP projects and he asked himself: "Why can't these colleagues stay in their home country and still contribute to SAP?" This might also exemplify the supporting mindset for starting a lab in India. Although SAP can certainly not claim to be a 'first mover' to India, it has been one of the first to offer real product development for business applications to their employees there. Other early movers like Texas Instruments or Robert Bosch Software concentrated instead on system software, a highly specialized field that many people coming from those emerging new players of India's industry found it hard to identify with. Nevertheless, SAP now offered this unique combination of work, requiring a good knowledge of business processes combined with strong engineering skills. In an SAP board meeting in March 1998, both locations were approved by the executive board and were given a substantial budget to start-off and create the necessary infrastructure. Henning Kagermann became sponsor of SAP Labs France, whereas Peter Zencke was appointed sponsor of SAP Labs India. On November 13th, 1998, SAP Labs India was formally established in Bangalore. It started with about 100 engineers in the field of CRM, middleware technology and localization, and the first IBU developers were hired. At the same time, smaller teams comprising a handful of developers sited at locations like Thailand, Singapore or Australia were asked to either move to Bangalore or to different roles in their local subsidiary.

Strategically, SAP was now well positioned globally: it had significant development centers in some of its key markets like the U.S., Japan and, of course, Germany. At the same time, Palo Alto served as SAP's link to the Silicon Valley, providing the company with the necessary intelligence on

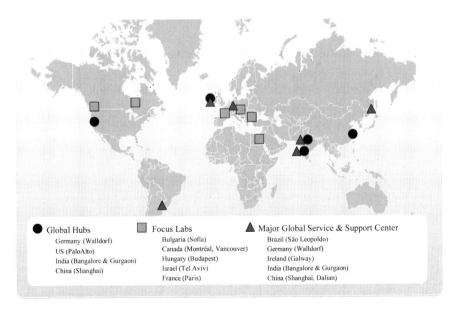

Fig. 3. SAP's global R&D and Service & Support network 2009. Globally 12,000+ developers and 7,000+ in Service & Support

the latest IT trends that were certainly, to a large extent, originating from there. For hiring new talent across the globe, two more locations were now available in Nice and Bangalore. This worked: within two years SAP was able to attract hundreds of new developers in both new locations, which enabled it to close product gaps in the 'New Dimension Offers' and in its e-commerce applications. At the same time, the global trend towards dedicated industry solutions demanded a significantly stronger product offer as well. The oil & gas industry and the high-tech industry were the main financially strong industries, for which the standard R/3 product did not completely meet the specific demands of their business. During this time, SAP initiated projects related to industries that were strongly present near the development facility. For example, in the Indian market there was a lot of requirements from big oil companies like ONGC, Reliance and BPCL and this led to the formation of the oil & gas development team in India. SAP firmly believed that this proximity was vital, as it would provide necessary business knowledge for the development teams.

Again it was Hasso Plattner and Peter Zencke, who headed some of those industry solutions and pushed the senior managers of SAP's global engineering to expand their development capacities to the new Bangalore location. Those were very crucial developments, since the distribution of work, specifically to a culturally diverse place like India, located in a different time zone, was something completely new to the company. While the managers accepted Palo Alto as a necessity to be close to the valley, and Tokyo to be close to Japanese business practices, it was a novelty for SAP to do work in Bangalore and France that had always been done in Walldorf. For the first time, development teams had to think of how to distribute work in a prudent and feasible way. Even more challenging was the cultural diversity which colleagues were asked to deal with. All of a sudden, there was an amazing number of new colleagues roaming around in Walldorf, looking different and also doing their work in a different way. So an extensive cultural adaption process was required, on which we will focus later.

The Next Expansion Wave – China, Eastern Europe and Israel

Labs France and India had proven that SAP is able to globally distribute its engineering and to meet the customer's expectation and needs, regardless of the location of its engineers. Peter Zencke became a frequent visitor in Bangalore and guided the management during the stormy growth phase. After the job market in Europe had cooled down following the Internet bubble burst, France lost a little relevance in terms of a hiring hub, as Germany now was again able to get a sufficient amount of talent. It became instead a focus lab that accumulated know-how for the telecommunication industry and the public sector and it built successful solutions in those areas. Recently, it got transformed into a service hub for South Europe.

Bangalore remained the only strong growth center of SAP's product development and gained further significance after September 11th, 2001, when SAP went beyond the usual cost cutting measures across the company and implemented, as well for the first time, a monetary budget for development instead of the usual headcount budget before. All of a sudden, the costs of the development locations became very important and Labs India could prove a significant cost advantage. Compared to the other locations, the factor was around 1:3 or 1:4. This further fuelled the growth of the India Lab in comparison to Japan, France or the U.S., especially from 2003 onwards.

It was within this context that SAP realized it could not put all its eggs into one basked (in terms of cost-efficient R&D locations) and thus started an initiative to look out for new locations. The search was based on two main criteria: the availability of talent and the impact on the market. China quickly emerged on top of the list, delivering on both factors: providing well-trained and technically very savvy engineers on the one hand, and representing one of the markets with the highest growth rates on the other. Nevertheless, the time zone difference, as well as the lack of a good command of English across all developers, posed a challenge to an otherwise good story. To overcome those problems, another location was needed, closer to Germany, but still cost-efficient. Sofia, the capital of Bulgaria, seemed to offer a good education system and to have engineers who speak either English or German. So another R&D hub was founded in Bulgaria. For those new R&D centers, SAP followed a strategy to avoid 'mushrooming' small engineering teams across the globe. Instead, it concentrated on a few locations with the aim to develop those significantly. Labs China was built up as a midsize market R&D location, focusing specifically on SAP's solutions for the midsize market A1, B1 and ByDesign, whereas Labs Sofia took responsibility for some of the projects around SAP's technology platform specifically the Java-based development.

The Israel Lab has a completely different background. It emerged from a couple of acquisitions which were made in Israel: first Ofek Tech, a specialized vendor of warehouse management software, and later Top Tier, a company with a strong portfolio in the area of portal-based applications, which later merged into the SAP offers 'SAP Portals' and 'B1'. As the locations in Israel had no strategic foundations, but basic acquisitions, their integration into SAP's main engineering hubs was a bit more challenging. Since the initial 'breeding and feeding' period was missing, people just did not know each other, and so they never developed the trust needed to develop software together. As a consequence, many of the initial managers have left SAP meanwhile and the new managers were then left with the task of building these relationships to make them stronger. Labs Israel has always worked more in the mode of having isolated teams adding complete products or separate tools to the SAP offerings, and discussing mainly requirements and Service Level Agreements (SLAs) with the rest of the engineering teams around the globe. Nevertheless, their contribution over the years has been significant and it focuses today more on the early lifecycle phase of product development and on research.

2.2 SAP's Journey from a Global Player to a Global Company

Over the years, SAP has opened subsidiaries and R&D hubs for its software development in all markets and countries of economic significance. This has always been accompanied by a parallel trend of change from a German company with global clients to a truly global company. The first international expansion efforts were still headed by managers who originated from the headquarters. Whether it were the first country heads of the U.S. (Klaus Besier, Paul Wahl) or Asia-Pacific (Eric van Houten, Lutz Kettner), all of them were expatriates who brought SAP knowledge and culture into those subsidiaries and markets. The same is true for the international labs in India, Palo Alto, France and Japan, which were all led by managers very much bound to the headquarters and predominantly assigned into those locations by SAP AG. It was felt that the initial trust between headquarters and those 'remote' locations was more important for their mutual success than the complete localization of their management team. Indeed, this may have been the appropriate approach. It is difficult to imagine that a manager in Germany would just pass a critical project to India without knowing anyone there and simply trusting the promises of someone who is foreign to him or whom he had just met for the first time.

Over the years, this situation has changed: in Europe and in the U.S., the field organization is now led by local people. The Labs in Israel, Hungary,

Bulgaria, India, and China are now led by managers who were born in those countries. However, even more importantly, SAP has also gained a lot of knowledge during this phase of becoming a globalized company. If you play globally, you have to adapt to the rules, which you may be able to teach your colleagues back at headquarters. So the awareness of different practices in all locations increases.

We mentioned the tremendous effort SAP made, selling its products globally and localizing its products. This has been the key to its success in the international markets. SAP already started learning the importance of localization, when the company expanded to France. At this point, it was already necessary to translate the software and to optimize it for usage under French laws and regulations. In this way, the development division prepared the software and its architecture to be most flexible for any adaptation and at the same time it provided tools for easy and consistent translation of text and help functions across all applications. When SAP's main competitors still believed the world would work like America did, SAP had already the leading edge in truly global product offers. Specifically in the early years of client-server architecture and the initial offerings by ERP vendors that used this technology, it was very crucial to be in the lead in those mostly new markets.

SAP combined a bold approach towards new markets with its capability to engineer diverse options and variations, thus making its products available to all kinds of regions and industries. What is valid for new geographical markets, is equally true for the early discovery of market trends across the globe. During the past years, many new industries have emerged (like semiconductors and renewable energies), new business trends (such as Lean Management, Six Sigma, TQM, and e-commerce), new technologies (RFID) or new global regulations (SOX compliance, anti-terror guidelines, and Basel II) – all those need to be reflected in a software product. More and more of these trends and rules appear somewhere on globe and then quickly become a standard – a software which a company builds all its business upon must be able to support those new processes or functionalities. Global presence helps to keep one's ears and eyes open for the emerging trends. It is impossible to sell software that does not support B2B, and in many countries, it is even illegal to run software that is not certified according to certain compliance regulations. This calls for trend scouts all over the world, to be on the spot when a trend is born, and to be ready with the solution when the customer needs it. And it requires a truly global development organization, which is able to transform all those regulations, trends, and technological advances into a well-engineered product at the end of the day. Software is never static, and the faster a company can react, the higher the customer satisfaction will be.

At the same time, while the significance of markets outside Germany were increasing, SAP also had to establish processes that would connect those locations. Be it the revenue split policy or customer message handling, all those things needed to be aligned and staff members around the globe had to be involved. The global labs structure played a very special role within this context: due to the fact that a significant number of projects and products were suddenly built outside Germany, a much higher effort had to be put into the inclusion of those international colleagues. The internal company language changed to English, and all the processes were redesigned to be applicable in any of the different locations. Many of SAP's policies and employee related programs like mobility or stock options were standardized across the globe. Of course, all these changes forced the colleagues in Walldorf to change as well. They quickly realized that it was important to learn English in order to be able to communicate with international clients. Since the developers in Walldorf were still the keepers of expertise in the core modules, they soon realized that it was impossible to understand the needs of the customers and to implement their requirements without a good command of English. They understood that their English skills would have a big impact on their career. Several senior managers took formal English classes to keep pace with the international expansion. Later, this became a vital success factor when SAP started distributing the development tasks around the globe.

Many of the supporting departments like HR, Purchasing, Controlling and others reached out to their equivalents in the other countries, and as a result they greatly improved alignment with their colleagues around the globe. This created a tighter bond and trust, even though in parallel, the local responsibilities were cut down to a certain extent. Nevertheless, in sum, the enablement of the new locations by providing them with fast and easy access to crucial knowledge was a determining factor and many of the global decisions could be made with significantly greater speed.

Communication itself became global as well. Now any staff meeting would not just be a gathering of the employees currently working at Walldorf, but it would be broadcasted via the Web to all the other locations, so that any single employee could follow the important announcements of the executive board either live or by watching the recorded version. Monthly mailers and quarterly board updates for all employees became a regular practice as well, as the top management understood that keeping the employees in the loop, would definitely not work any longer just by word of mouth. This helped a great deal to include colleagues on all levels in what was happening. Today, no matter whether one enters the SAP office in Bangalore, New York City or Walldorf – it will feel like SAP and the international colleagues would immediately be ready to work. Either with regards to the entry door (global access cards) or the network (harmonized wireless LAN everywhere) or the free lunch – the employees feel 'at home' and they can be productive anywhere without too much hassle.

In the field of external branding, a big step ahead in transforming into a global company was made as well, when SAP hired Marty Homlish, Sony America's marketing head, in 2000. Up to that point, SAP's marketing had been more of an advertising budget, and it did not involve consolidated global branding efforts. Actually, SAP's global brand image was rather shaped by its capabilities and its people rather than by its marketing (which is quite acceptable up to a certain point; however, there are also some battles that are decided on the marketing front, not only on the product front). Marty Homlish quickly realized that developing a global brand out of the rather provincial Walldorf would not work. In this place, he would neither find the right people for his team, nor could he talk to people from other agencies, market analysts, and so on. He therefore decided to move the headquarters of SAP Global Marketing to New York, into the center of global advertising, and into the center of global finance. This was the right move at the right time, since SAP's brand had to reshape quite a bit, from the rather fancy Internet mySAP.com brand to its origin as a serious partner of companies in doing business.

At the same time, he made sure additionally that globally a consistent Corporate Identity (CI) was applied and followed in all internal and external communications. This way he ensured that SAP's appearance was always the same, no matter whether one entered San Francisco Airport and saw an SAP advertising, or if one visited the SAP Event Hall in Singapore. These measures promoted global brand recognition quite a lot, and consequently SAP became ranked among the world's top 100 most valuable brands. Presently, it is among the top 50. In Germany, only the BMW brand has a higher value – which definitely is a great success. Given the increasing competition and the increasingly difficult differentiation between the many products available, the decision makers of SAP's potential customers do not want to go too deep into the product details, and mostly are not even engineers. To a certain extent, they want to believe in a brand promise – and in the time, SAP has developed the credibility of its promise that: 'The best-run companies run SAP'. Recently, its product portfolio has been up-dated for SMEs: 'Not only for large best-run companies, also for small ones'. One cannot overestimate the value of a strong global brand in the global competition. Large Chinese or Indian companies are cash-rich and they often have products that are successful in global markets, but they still have branding deficiencies. So when they go on an acquisition tour, they often do not go for a special addition to their product portfolio or for a cer-tain technology they need – they are simply trying to acquire a global brand to get on top of the competition. For example, when Tata bought Jaguar, or Lenovo bought the IBM Thinkpad brand.

The changes in SAP's top management were even more significant. Dur-ing the first 20 years, SAP was led by its founders, five (later four) German engineers. When they prepared for the next generation of company leaders in the beginning of the 1990s, they assigned four managers from product development to the board (Peter Zencke, Claus Heinrich, Gerd Oswald, and Henning Kagermann), to prepare for their succession. To tackle field issues, Paul Wahl was hired, and later Werner Brandt joined as CFO (to succeed Dieter Matheis). Paul Wahl did not stay very long, but left in 1999. But when Klaus Tschira and Dietmar Hopp left the executive board, the already established new management took over without any disruption. In 2003, Hasso Plattner resigned from the SAP executive board as well, but he designated Shai Agassi, the first non-German speaking board mem-ber. Léo Apotheker, who was heading Sales at that time, was also pro-moted to the executive board. He, being a German national, who grew up in Belgium and studied in Israel, was also an international addition to the board. SAP has kept following this 'approach of internationalization': with Ernie Gunst (Belgian), Jim Snabe (Danish), Bill McDermot (American) and John Schwarz (American), four other non-German board members were accepted into the top management. With Henning Kagermann, Peter Zencke, and Claus Heinrich leaving the board in 2008/09, there are only three Germans left (Léo Apotheker, Werner Brandt and Gerd Oswald), whereas the rest of the team comes from other countries and cultural back-grounds.

Maybe this is the most significant cultural shift in SAP's history, in becoming a truly global company in a true sense, not only with regard to the markets it serves or the locations where its products are built, but also with regard to its processes, its organizations, and the people who lead the company. Of course, this cultural shift is mostly felt by those who had to adjust from the previous world, so it is quite right to say that only the German employees feel a significant difference. These days, a lot of decision making power is positioned outside the traditional headquarters in Walldorf, and most meetings that include top managers are now made through global video conferences. Naturally, the ways people work, communicate and lead employees are mainly influenced by the culture in which they grew up and made their careers. It is going to be an interesting journey to find out where this melting pot of diversity will lead to.

Compared to all other German companies listed in the DAX, the main German stock exchange index, SAP is definitely the company with the most internationally represented executive board. Given the fact that SAP faces completely international competition, that the key growth markets are located outside Germany, and that more than a third of its engineering capacities is distributed across the globe, this company has managed its change to a global enterprise and it is well prepared to achieve its targets in this set-up.

3 SAP in Asia-Pacific and India

3.1 SAP's Asia-Pacific Strategy

Up until the beginning of the 1990s, Asia-Pacific was a largely untapped market for SAP. Though the first subsidiaries in Singapore (1989) and Hong Kong (1992) were already in operation, their presence was more a function of demand than a real strategic push into this region. Australia and New Zealand were at insignificant levels of revenue until 1993. Only when Les Hayman was hired by Klaus Besier in 1994 to run Australia/New Zealand, and Sam Nakane by Hasso Plattner to run Japan, was there a significant change: Both markets started to boom, with Australia becoming the third largest market for SAP after Germany and the U.S.

Les Hayman recalls: "At that time, a really professional sales team, which mainly worked commission-based, was only present in the U.S." In the European markets, SAP was still running sales with consultants, and sometimes developers. Australia was seen as a test case to prove that one could also run a professional sales organization outside of the U.S. It worked: Australian sales started from zero in 1994, grew to USD 30 million by 1995, and then tripled to USD 90 Million in 1996.

Japan saw a similar growth, coming very close to Australia, and from 1994/1995 onwards, SAP also intensified its business in India and China. Asia-Pacific had arrived on the map! As Hayman says: "The success we saw in the mid to late 1990s in Asia-Pacific was partly due to the unbelievable support and trust we received from the headquarters. Peter (Zencke) and Henning (Kagermann) were always there when I needed them and they always promoted substantial investment into our key markets. Dieter Matheis (SAP's head of finance until 2002) had a very positive outlook on Asia, and Gerd Oswald created support centers here in the region, which really made a difference in our commitment to Asia. So from all sides there was support!"

It's fair to say that SAP's success in Asia-Pacific was based on a set of really committed managers in the region, who had been working for SAP

C. Neumann and J. Srinivasan, *Managing Innovation from the Land of Ideas and Talent: The 10-Year Story of SAP Labs India,*
DOI: 10.1007/978-3-540-89283-0_3, © Springer-Verlag Berlin Heidelberg 2009

for a relatively long time. Les joined in 1994, was appointed to extended board in 1999, and stayed with SAP until his retirement in 2006. Klaus Zimmer in China joined in 1996, and stayed till 2007. Of course, there was also a lot of mutual trust and freedom given to the managers in Asia.

As Les comments: "At that time, we were running countries in a mode I would call 'creative anarchy'. We had a completely free hand, and as long as the top management felt that there was a strong commitment to SAP and we were bringing in the numbers, there was no interference whatsoever. In today's world, with a much bigger SAP, the listing in the U.S., SOX and all the related rules to follow – that would not be possible anymore."

3.2   Restructuring of the Asian Region in 1997

Les Hayman was promoted to president South-East-Asia-Pacific in 1996. At that time, three MDs / presidents were reporting to Peter Zencke, the board member responsible for Asia-Pacific: Klaus Zimmer (Greater China), Sam Nakane (Japan / Korea), and Les Hayman (all other Asian countries).

Peter Zencke designed it that way, in order to optimize SAP's sales and consulting activities in the Asian region and to reflect the cultural, political, and economic differences inherent to Asia. He also wanted to keep a power balance between South-East-Asia-Pacific and Japan on the one hand, and to nurture the 'new kid on the block', SAP China, on the other. The three regions were called:

- South Asia / Pacific (headquartered in Singapore);
- Northeast Asia (headquartered in Tokyo);
- Greater China (headquartered in Beijing).

The office in Singapore was in charge of all operations in Australia, India, Indonesia, Malaysia, New Zealand, the Philippines, Singapore, and Thailand. Tokyo was responsible for Japan, South Korea, and for the Asia Language Support Organization (ALSO). Accordingly, subsidiaries in China, Hong Kong, and Taiwan reported to the office in Beijing.

The Asia-Pacific region was one of SAP's fastest-growing markets, both in terms of sales and of the size of its workforce. About one third of SAP's international subsidiaries were located in this region, employing roughly 10 % of the SAP group's total workforce at that time.

Moreover, in 1997, the Asia-Pacific region registered sales of DM 785 million (1996: DM 465 million), an increase of 69 %. In all, the region accounted for 13.1 % of group sales. The countries with the largest sales were Japan with DM 380 million (up 67 %) and Australia with nearly DM 183 million (up 61 %). Based on these numbers, Japan took third place after the United States and Germany; Australia occupied the sixth place after the UK and Canada. The other, smaller countries of the South-Asia-Pacific region also experienced high growth rates – however some of them started out from very low levels. The leader was Singapore, which increased its sales by 121 %, followed by Indonesia with growth of 108 %. They were followed by India (up 90 %), Malaysia (up 74 %), the Philippines (up 33 %), and Thailand (up 5 %).

Out of the three Asian regions, SAP formed one Asia-Pacific region, and in 1999, Les Hayman became its president. From then onwards, China (Klaus Zimmer) and North East Asia reported to Les Hayman. The reason for this was that while International Sales and Consulting was restructured on the board level, with Henning Kagermann taking the lead of all regions worldwide, it was felt that China would not need direct 'spoon feeding' by Walldorf any longer.

3.3   Launch of the SAP Labs Project in 1998

During the first quarter of 1998, the executive board of SAP AG initiated a project to come up with a comprehensive document to answer some fundamental questions regarding decentralized software development: Why should SAP develop decentralized labs? What should be the development strategy for SAP Labs? What will be the type of development that will be done in SAP Labs? How will a global network of labs be managed? It was expected that the answers to those key questions should help SAP to highlight the main changes that would happen to core development with the formation of SAP Labs around the globe.

This project was supported by Gemini Consulting, and internally the project was headed jointly by Thomas Vetter, assistant to CEO Henning Kagermann, and Clas Neumann, assistant to executive board member Dr. Peter Zencke. The core team included team members from Corporate Human Resources, Kiefer & Veittinger, the SAP technology team and team members from the international development group, which was responsible for the localization of SAP products in different countries. Thomas Vetter and Clas Neumann toured Asia as a part of this project and conducted series of interviews with different internal stakeholders like Service and Support, Industry Business units, Technology Group, Quality Management and System Build Group. This project team tapped the wealth of globalization experience within the SAP organization. However, more importantly, were visits to companies like Texas Instruments, Deutsche Software (a software wing of Deutsche Bank Group, which was later divested to HCL technologies), Infosys Wipro, and Satyam. These visits helped to gain insights into the industry, its potential, and to learn about best practices that had already been established. Executive support was guaranteed as the co-CEOs Hasso Plattner and Henning Kagermann, as well as executive board member Peter Zencke, participated directly in the discussions and reviews. Inventories of the development teams in different geographical locations were taken, and the topics addressed by the different groups were also analyzed. In the end, SAP decided to expand and organize decentralized development activities under the SAP Labs concept. The global development strategy was to focus on key markets by ensuring national development presence, to attract the best people from different parts of the globe, and to reinvigorate the innovative and entrepreneurial spirit within SAP. In this context, 'SAP Labs' was also defined as an organizational unit in which SAP would perform parts of the software development process outside of Germany. As a consequence of this major project, SAP identified four different types of labs:

- Research lab;
- Development center;
- ABAP factory;
- Test center.

It was also agreed that each lab could have satellite locations within its geographic region and different content focuses, for example on specific industry solutions or particular technologies. Within this structure, SAP Labs in Palo Alto was planned as a center with a strong focus on research and development. SAP Tokyo was defined as a test center with focus on the Japanese market. Sophia Antipolis and Moscow started as smaller labs and were planned as development centers. The lab in Bangalore was planned to be initially established as an so called ABAP factory, and to develop in step two into a full-fledged development center. Overall, it was envisioned that SAP Walldorf would remain the main development hub and would delegate responsibilities to other labs around the globe. SAP also planned one test center in a time zone at least six hours different from Germany in order to reduce the overall development cycle time and to react faster to the market needs. The strategy at that time was clearly aiming towards a hub and spoke system in development, recognizing as well the dominant workforce in R&D at SAP to be in Germany (90 %).

The project paper proposed that each location should have a significant piece of the ongoing software projects, (because Labs had no prior knowledge) in order to reach minimum economies of scale and to support engineers in Walldorf with their high workload. A minimum number of 100 developers was set as base line for an SAP development location. It was also felt that breaking the software into too tiny pieces would only lead to low quality as a result of communication overload across different locations. Development of dependent pieces at one single site was identified as a critical success factor since it would allow resolving most of the issues in face-to-face meetings within the same time zone and location. The initial funding for the development center in India was from the corporate budget for R&D tasks, but it was also agreed that in the second step the global lines of business would fund their teams and the administration overhead in each location.

The project members further came to the conclusion that two major criteria for decentralized development are the complexity of the task and the degree of coordination needed. The option of encapsulating tasks in discrete modules was considered as the basis for identifying the work packages. Seeing that, the project team came up with the first set of projects and tasks in the areas of industry solutions, technology prototype development, localization of industry functions and also the development of standard tasks like reports, workflow, SAP Scripts and BAPI's (Business Application Programming Interfaces). Customer Specific Development Projects (CDP's) were also identified as a possible candidate for decentralized development.

The central part of this initial study was the proposal of the future locations of the different SAP labs. Many factors were taken into consideration, like human resources, availability of management systems, and closeness to growing markets. For the initial setup of the global labs network, the locations were approved and executive board sponsors were assigned as presented in Table 3.

Table 3. The SAP Labs locations concept

Location	Focus	Board Sponsor
Bangalore	ABAP factory	Peter Zencke
Moscow	Test center	Gerd Oswald
Palo Alto	Reseach & Development	Hasso Plattner
Sophia Antipolis (Nice)	Development center	Henning Kagermann
Tokyo	Development center	Peter Zencke

SAP also decided that a lab should be headed by a local lab director with administrative leadership knowledge. For the initial set-up of new teams in the labs, 10 engineers per manager was seen as ideal. The manager should be local, but another experienced development manager with a clear objective to coach the local manager could be brought in for some months. In addition to that, SAP Labs should not be part of the local field organization in the target country, but become an independent entity. However, mutual synergies should be nevertheless exploited in areas like Human Resources, administration, and legal considerations. For each development location, the actual situation and target situation was analyzed, and the project team clearly highlighted the changes that would be triggered as a result of the SAP Labs concept within the overall SAP development organization. The main success factors were identified as:

- Clear definition of tasks and mission statement to motivate the local workforce;
- Quality and availability of skilled people;
- Strong local leadership to create early success stories.

Major risks were identified as:

- Redundancy of work;
- Uncoordinated activities in the projects;
- Hiding of knowledge between development centers;
- Insufficient protection of intellectual property;
- Lack of acceptance of new location by senior developers in Walldorf;
- Loss of control within the development organization.

This proposal was first discussed in separate and repeated sessions with Hasso Plattner, Henning Kagermann, and Peter Zencke, and in April 1998, it was finally approved by the executive board. The project entered the implementation phase, and SAP Labs project teams started incorporating the concept as a part of their on-going activities.

Given the strong need for concentrating all India localization efforts in the country itself, and given the parallel acquisition of Kiefer & Veittinger in Germany and India in 1997/1998, Bangalore quickly made it to the top of the list of labs locations in Asia-Pacific. Considering the availability of talent, initial experience, and the fact that SAP already had 100 developers in Bangalore, everything pointed to Bangalore. To begin with, SAP Labs in Bangalore appeared to be practically a 'no-brainer', but it was nevertheless a milestone in SAP's history, and needed to be formally sanctioned by the executive board.

3.4 Structure of the Indian Software Industry

The history of Indian software industry can be traced back to the 1970s when American companies started searching software talent in India, Israel, and Ireland. India was selected because of the abundance of English, the understanding of technology, and its favorable cost structure.

During the 1970s, the industry and taxation policy in India was quite hostile, and it favored indigenous development of technology with the support of state owned corporations. The government discouraged multinational companies and smaller private firms from setting up operations in India. The import tariffs were high (135 % on hardware and 100 % on software), software was not considered as an important industry, and private firms had no access to financing. The regulatory measures did not help to get India on a growth rate beyond the 'Hindu rate of Growth', which was always in the lower single digit numbers. State owned companies were inefficient, over-staffed, and did not create output of world market quality. The labor force lacked basic skills, the motivation in state owned companies and government offices was very low, and the corruption was high.

Because of protective policies like the Foreign Exchange Act in 1973 (FERA 1973), the only way for foreign firms to operate in India was with minority interest (maximum 40 %). Due to those regulations and the lack of intellectual property rights protection, many foreign companies decided to leave India (e.g. IBM and Coca Cola). It is fair to say that FERA 1973 made production in India very difficult for multinational companies. A few Indian IT companies, however, found early on innovative ways to overcome the restrictions. For example, by exporting software developers to other locations and to customers outside of India. By 1980, 20 IT service firms in India counted annual exports of USD 4 million. IT expertise in India was restricted to the thin workforce returning from overseas assignments and very few scientists from the Indian Institute of Science. Those became the main source of knowledge for advanced technical and project management skills.

In the 1980s, the PC was invented and 'Wintel' became the worldwide standard for computing, which resulted in a decline of hardware prices and in an increased demand for business applications. The adoption of 'Unix' and 'C' as the standard operating system and programming language provided the first opportunities for Indian firms to develop device independent software components. By the 1990s, the success of database software like Oracle, Informix, Sybase and Power Builder further simplified the creation of application software.

In 1984, the now late Prime Minister Rajiv Gandhi introduced a new computer policy, which included reduced import tariffs (60%) on both hardware and software. Foreign firms were now permitted to establish fully owned subsidiaries in India. In addition to that, a chain of software technology parks that offered infrastructure at below-market costs were set up. The first company to make use of this policy was Texas Instruments; they started an Indian offshore center for software development in 1985. In the following year, export revenues, including software exports, were exempted from income tax. After the new policies had been established, the first software technology park in collaboration with elite institutions like the Indian Institute of Science, and large public sector enterprises like Hindustan Aeronautics and the Indian Space Research Organization was created in Bangalore. It was an ideal environment for the growing Indian software industry. Before that, most of the Indian business was headquartered in Bombay, but as the costs were getting higher in Bombay, the industry started looking for alternative destinations. Bangalore became the location of choice for foreign investments, because it is located in the center of the four southern states, Karnataka, Tamil Nadu, Andhra Pradesh and Kerala, and at that time, more than 50% of India's engineering students graduated in these states. Additionally, many of the leading state owned aeronautic research and production facilities were located here, as India moved all those defense-relevant establishments far away from the border regions with Pakistan, China, and Bangladesh. Multinational companies also liked the moderate climate in Bangalore. In spite of the fact that Bangalore had no international air connectivity at that time and the fact that the power supply was erratic, it became the most preferred location for establishing IT operations. The largest software exporters at that time, like Wipro Technologies and Infosys, were headquartered in Bangalore. Also several multinational companies like Texas Instruments, HP, IBM, GE, and Bosch settled their development centers in Bangalore. They all stood at the forefront of a new ecosystem for distributed software development in the new 'flat' world.

During 1991, the Indian government, headed by Prime Minister Narasimha Rao, faced an unprecedented situation due to an acute balance-of-payment crisis, and the government was left without reserves to meet its obligations. Dr. Manmohan Singh, the minister of finance, prepared to mortgage its gold reserves to the Bank of England in order to obtain cash reserves that were needed to run the country. During this time, the government initiated reforms to liberalize the legal framework in the economy: Foreign direct investment was promoted in most sectors, the capital markets were reformed, many rules for domestic business were simplified, import tariffs were reduced and the Indian market was exposed incrementally to international competition. This was a pivotal point in the economic history of modern India.

In parallel to these governmental efforts in India, there were significant technological advances taking place, mainly triggered by companies from Silicon Valley in the U.S.: object-oriented programming, client-server technology, and the broader usage and availability of Internet facilitated encapsulation of software development projects into manageable parts as well as their distribution around the world. Combined with a sharp decline of communication cost, it became a viable business model for companies to distribute software development across different geographic locations in order to reduce costs and to speed up their projects. Governmental institutes struggled to keep pace with the changing technological environment, and this encouraged domestic players like CMC, NIIT, and Aptech in getting into the lucrative business of teaching technology and software development. Most of the engineers spent many months in these institutes to learn the basic concepts of client-server, database, and programming languages before venturing into the software industry.

By 1998, the government recognized the important role of the software industry as it demonstrated phenomenal growth in the preceding years. The export earnings rose spectacularly. The growth was 40 % for the software industry as a whole and 50 – 60 % for the major enterprises. The new estimate of software exports per year was USD 5 billion by 2002. The top five Indian IT enterprises TCS, Infosys, Pentafour, Tata Infotech, and Wipro increased their turnover by 72.17 %.

The income tax act was extended in its definition of 'software' to 'transmission of data pertaining to information technology'. From then onwards, any kind of software export, IT service export (typically smaller projects for one specific customer) and even IT enabled services export (typically business process outsourcing like payroll processing or accounting of companies done from India), was completely excluded from direct taxes for a duration of 10 years. This tax exemption for interest on external commercial borrowings applicable to other sectors was extended to the IT industry. There were also additional tax exemptions for royalties to be paid on transmission of IT data. The depreciation of IT products was allowed at a rate of 60 % per year in order to accommodate the fast obsolescence of hardware products. With regards to indirect taxes, special concessions were announced. This included a full exemption of customs and excise duty for computer software, and a reduction of duty on several computer parts and peripherals.

These concessions granted by the government in 1998, created an ideal environment for multinational firms. Several companies like SAP, Intel, Microsoft, and Daimler started their research and development centers in India (Dossani 2005: p. 1 – 27).

3.5   Birth of SAP India – SAP's First Subsidiary in India

Before 1996, SAP did not have a sales office in India, and all sales activities were coordinated from Singapore. Siemens Information Systems Limited (SISL) which had been a logo partner for the SAP R/3 solution product, later became the first value added reseller and partner of SAP in India.

Incorporated as a Siemens subsidiary, SISL had already been in India since 1992. It started its SAP focus as a country logo partner for SAP in India in

1994 and continued in this capacity until 1996. A year later it went on to become a national business partner for SAP from 1997 to 1998. With the growth of SAP in India, SISL further strengthened its position to become a consulting partner and pioneer of SAP implementations in India.

One of the first management tasks of the new management team (Les Hayman and Rokiah Ahamed) was to negotiate the terms under which SAP would take over Indian business from SISL and 'downgrade' SISL to a consulting partner. According to Les Hayman, there were no alternatives: "We had to convince them not to be SAP's exclusive representative in India any more. At the end of the day, we would have only been one of many business streams for them – doing it on our own, I believed we could get much more heart and soul on the job."

SAP India was set up in March 1996, with its headquarters in Bangalore, and offices in Bombay and New Delhi as a hundred percent subsidiary of SAP AG, Germany. The company's objective was to sell and implement SAP's software. In the beginning, SAP Indian customers belonged to three main segments: First, there were the subsidiaries of global accounts like Dow Chemicals, ABB, and Colgate Palmolive; Second, were state owned enterprises in India like ONGC and BPCL; Third, a segment formed of large private enterprises like Mahindra and Mahindra, Tata Group, Reliance, Arvind Mills, and Essar Steel.

It was not all that easy in those early years. SAP had always taken the approach not to 'localize' the sales price of its products along with the purchase power parity, "SAP looked terribly expensive to Indian customers", Les recalls, "We had to explain to the customers the reason for being expensive and how they would benefit from our products. However, on the other hand, Indian companies always had and still have this global view. One day, Anand Mahindra hit the nail on the head saying that their reason for buying SAP was that they were a global company which happened to have their headquarters in India. By the way, this is as well how I saw the difference from the big Chinese companies. Indian companies always aimed to be become global players offering globally valued products and services, whereas Chinese companies always wanted to be global suppliers. And this is a major difference between those two countries."

As a result, sales picked up and India was soon seen as one of SAP's strongest growing markets around the globe, even though the pricing was absolutely on par with the prices SAP would charge in Europe or the U.S.

Another difficulty came from the fact that there was very little knowledge about SAP's products and capabilities in India. Traditionally, SAP requested partners to implement SAP software at the customer sites; SAP consulting only provided expert support to those partners, whenever required. However, as there were hardly any partners in India, and as the knowledge about SAP was virtually zero, SAP India took a novel approach to build up SAP's publicity in India. All the customer projects during those early days were taken up directly by SAP's consulting organization.

SAP consultants help customers to derive maximum advantage from the implementations. Good consultants often possess deep product knowledge combined with knowledge about business processes. During the early days of SAP Labs India, it was hard to find even good business consultants and knowledge about SAP's product was virtually non-existent. Therefore the consulting organization hired a mix of professionals with good line experience in areas like operations, finance, human resources, and information technology. Consultants were then sent to SAP software development locations in Singapore, Australia, Germany and the United Kingdom for training in SAP software. In addition to that, SAP hired ABAP (Advanced Business Application Programming) consultants from remote locations in South Africa to come to India and train the initial group of software developers.

Senior consultants from Germany and America were given long-term contracts in India to implement SAP solutions for the first customers like Mahindra. The newly trained SAP consultants joined those senior consultants in the implementation projects and helped SAP to create its first successful SAP R/3 installations in India. This initial group of consultants later became the core group of SAP India, and they went on to coach and train the next generation of consultants. When these consultants matured, SAP India started passing the knowledge to partners and began offering services in more sophisticated business areas like industry specific solutions. After few years, SAP India consultants had reached a point at which they would only provide expert support, since most of the implementations were done by the big consulting firms. Even later, SAP India copied this approach for complex implementations: when the first oil & gas solution was adopted by ONGC and Reliance, SAP India consultants closely cooperated with the experienced developers in Walldorf to first understand the solution before sharing their knowledge with partners.

In a famous interview in 1998 entitled 'SAP's Worldview', Plattner explained the thoughts behind the company's incremental global strategy: "Technology companies that wish to expand internationally have to think like missionaries and to first establish small advance groups to learn the language, business climate and culture. You cannot just arrive and preach your product. You have to give each subsidiary the freedom to establish its local identity." These words in many ways explain the initial approach of SAP in the Asian region.

3.6 Increasing the Commitment Further to the Indian Market

SAP's sales organization in Asia soon encountered a new challenge. On the one hand, it seemed to be easy to win the customers as they were already aware about SAP's phenomenal success in Europe and America. On the other hand, each country brought new challenge in terms of language, legal requirements, and business practices.

At this point, SAP's experience in Europe came in handy. In most cases, a team comprised of an experienced user from the customer's side, a consultant from the business consulting house, and an experienced SAP consultant, were brought together to analyze the requirements. The team's mission was to examine what was unique to that country and what could potentially be addressed by using the customization features of the software. Whatever could not be customized, resulted in a unique set of enhancement requests for the software. These requirements were forwarded to the developers in Germany, and they provided their feedback and recommendations. This became the basis for setting up the localization project.

In 1994, SAP founded the International Development Group' under the leadership of Georg Hage-Huelsmann. It was formed by developers from all over the globe, mostly with a background entailing several years of consulting in their respective countries or regions. The small localization team for Asia-Pacific consisted of Germans who had previously worked and lived in Australia, Singapore, Japan, Korea, and China. As a first step, in countries where the business language was not English, a translation project was started to transfer the software into the new language. After this, additional requirements for a specific country were mostly resolved by changing the configuration settings in the software. The new country specific settings were later bundled as a country specific template. This template approach helped countries to jumpstart implementation on the customer side. Apart from customizing, reports were submitted to meet legal requirements and also, in some extreme cases, changes were made in the software itself to satisfy the needs of the customers.

SAP started its localization efforts in India at the end of 1995 when Siemens Business Services, a unit of Siemens Information Systems Limited, was selected to hire the first set of software developers in Bangalore. Their task was to develop a country specific localization of the ERP (Enterprise Resource Planning) system's Human Resource module. The country specific legal requirements in the Human Resources module were mainly in the area of taxation, payroll processing, and the generation of related reports. Developers worked in the Siemens development center in Bangalore for the first few months before moving to Singapore to become part of the more comprehensive HR and payroll localization project for Asia-Pacific. In addition to modifications in the human resource module, customers in India started asking SAP to address local legislation and business in the area of logistics. The customers demanded this as it would be impossible for any manufacturing unit to receive and send goods from its facilities without this functionality. Most of these country specific features for India were related to 'SAP finance and logistics modules'. Projects were initiated to address the excise duty (also known as an 'excise' or 'excise tax'), the 'Central Value-Added Tax System' (CENVAT), withholding tax (also known as 'tax deducted at source'), 'Sales Tax Maintenance', and the printing of 'Statutory Excise Registers'. A small team of five developers from Siemens Business Services had already developed the first version of the 'Country Version India' (CIN) which addressed tax requirements on goods movement even before SAP had started its operations in India. Each functional module of SAP was managed by a different internal department inside SAP. While both departments approached Siemens due to the local presence in India, they followed different execution models. The Human Resource development department decided to locate all the developers in Singapore to address the requirements of the countries in Asia. The logistics related gaps were far more complex and hence logistics department decided to create a small development team within the Siemens Organization in India.

In early 1997, SAP India decided to establish a dedicated development team to enhance the 'Country Version India'. This team took over the solution developed by SISL under the leadership of Dr. Thomas Vetter. During this time, SAP India also hired additional developers to focus on industry solutions for Banking and Health Care. Unlike the Indian engineers doing payroll localization in Singapore, these developers were sent on a long-term assignment to Germany. Werner Konik, who was the head of the Asia localization project at that time, roped in Martin Prinz, who was a consultant at SAP America, to take over the development of the Country Version India.

Martin recalls his start at SAP Labs India as follows: "I was looking at the internal job postings in 1997/98 in the U.S., and I came across this position, a 'country representative' for India, which was based in Germany as part of the 'International Development Group', but including travel to India. That got my attention. I thought it could be interesting to get more exposure to India and its culture (my wife is an Indian national). Everything went on really fast: I had a few calls with Georg Hage-Huelsmann, Werner Konik and Thomas Vetter, and before I knew it, I had the job and moved back to Germany. After that, only within a few days after having started in my new position, I was already on my way to India. A customer meeting together with Thomas Vetter in Mumbai with around 100 Indian users followed and that was pretty much my first exposure to the localization endeavor and the 'Country Version India'. Henceforward, I was in charge of the India localization project, which was of course quite a big challenge, because it was totally different from what I had done before. I had not done development before, at least not within SAP, but I had a strong affinity to software development and had gained some knowledge earlier at university. Even being a consultant, I was among the minority of consultants who could actually do some debugging in the code and could understand software code. I was quite keen to move closer to development, but of course there was a lot for me to learn in software development at SAP. However, it was part of the challenge I accepted at that time. I was lucky and fortunate to settle a small team of good people, who worked with me and who built the country version for India."

According to Martin Prinz, there was no real distributed development at SAP at that time. It had to be proven that development could also work in a remote location, because a lot of people had concerns. "In India, we proved that there was a different way (than the traditional one of centralized development) and that it was feasible to cooperate with co-developers in other locations. In our case it worked because we were so closely connected with the core development team in Germany and we did have a lot of support from there." Prinz further admits: "We had a bit more liberty in development since our project was not part of the core product: 'Country Version India' was an add-on solution. We could have done it differently and we could have developed the solution in a more integrated way from the start, but at the end of the day speed was also an issue. We had to quickly deliver the products to the Indian market. There was a high demand of SAP solutions at that time, and we didn't have the luxury of working on the India solution for a couple of more years just to make sure we'd done it at hundred percent as part of the standard package within our standard release cycles."

Ramkrishna Yarlapati, Senior Vice President and one of the earliest developers in the 'payroll development', recalls: "The working style of the engineers at that time was like in a start-up: a small team comprising of four developers did everything, starting from pre-sales consulting, post-sales consulting, development, training and customer support. Accordingly, team members were actively involved in discussions with the customer interest groups in India. While this was a heavy burden on the development team, it provided a unique opportunity for the developers to get a 360 degree view of the customer's challenges … There was a lot of pressure on us, but not in an unfair or in an unexpected way. I think customers were right to demand those things from us and it was never done in a way that would cause us sleepless nights. Everything happened with a good human spirit." Prinz states: "It all helped the developers to get a deeper insight into the customer needs, which in turn translated into mature solutions."

In addition to that, frequent releases were made to meet the growing needs of the customer base in India. Prinz recalls: "One of our main struggles was to get whatever we had built as an 'add-on package', back into the standard SAP product. That was the 'retrofit discussion' and it went on for years and it also consumed a lot of energy and time to make the case. We went through many add-on releases, which was quite a challenge because we had to manage so many different versions of the software, and we were out there with so many customers. With every version, we had double maintenance and different requirements; therefore, it was a big challenge for the young team to manage that complexity."

In 1997, SAP became the ERP software market leader in India in the large enterprise segment. Thus, a local support team was established to help the growing customer base quickly, whenever they experienced problems with the software. Partners came up with complimentary solutions, particularly in the area of printing statutory registers and for addressing export and import related compliance requirements. Thus, a healthy SAP Labs Ecosystem was developed to support the growing needs of the Indian customers.

In December 1997, SAP made clear its intention to expand the development center in Bangalore beyond the local requirements.

SAP decided to shift the 30 developers working on the country specific 'payroll localization' for Asia, from Singapore to Bangalore to support the development. Along with the developers focusing on India specific localization, they were brought under one roof in order to gain synergies. SAP also decided to take over the responsibility for the Country Version India from SISL to further enhance the capabilities of the solution.

3.7   Acquisition of Kiefer & Veittinger – SAP's Push into Front-End Space

At the end of 1997, SAP sent out a clear message to its customers about its commitment to extend the leadership of the front-end space by acquiring a 50 % share of Kiefer & Veittinger (K&V), a privately held Sales Force Automation (SFA) software specialist. Dietmar Saddei, head of SAP CRM development at that time, recalls: "K&V worked on Sales Force Automation, which is a type of mobile application solution designed for sales people. Both engineers and their customers had a look at the solution, as all the applications had to be mobile to meet the day-to-day business demands of sales people who are constantly traveling. SAP came from a completely different field; it had learned how to develop software on the big mainframe computers in the headquarters in Germany. The Sales Force Automation was a 'strange new beast' to SAP, and it was Hasso Plattner who decided that this was not in the typical 'DNA' of traditional SAP development, and hence the decision was made to acquire K&V."

Founded in 1986, Kiefer & Veittinger GmbH was headquartered in Mannheim, Germany. It was the European market leader in Sales Force Automation systems. With the SALESmanager family, K&V was the only software provider at that time to offer industry-focused sales process management features and seamless integration with R/3. "After the acquisition we went on with a broader picture of what we called CRM, and one of the major pieces was the Sales Force Automation of K&V. At that time, K&V

had a lot of customers, but there wasn't a standard software at all. Most of their customers worked with individual products, and it was a big decision to rewrite a whole lot of the K&V applications. We made efforts to link mobile client technology to ERP related solutions.", Dietmar Saddei adds.

Over 18,000 users at more than 250 global corporations used SALESmanager to effectively manage their entire sales and marketing process. K&V employed 300 people worldwide, but only ran development units in Germany and India. 90 software engineers were working in its Indian center in Bangalore.

Ronald Lorenz, a former manager of K&V, once called Klaus Veittinger, the co-founder of K&V, an 'extreme visionary'. This is quite understandable since Klaus was instrumental in installing a software development center in Bangalore, way back in 1995, at a time when even tourists from Germany thought twice before travelling to India. Klaus' Indian friend Dr. Amardeep Kainth, a corporate lawyer in India, motivated and helped him with the set-up in Bangalore. The environment in India was quite different at that time, and the initial employees stayed in the lawyer's house and went through tremendous hardship before getting the center up and running. Dr. Udo Urbanek decided to move to India in order to lead the K&V initiative, and he worked closely together with Ronald Lorenz in Germany to turn vision of K&V in India into a reality. Klaus Veittinger, Ronald Lorenz, and Udo Urbanek hired the initial set of employees, supported by a corporate hiring firm called 'Search House'. They used a sophisticated test designed by a German psychological institute to test the aptitude of the interviewed candidates. This test was followed by technical interviews on C, C++, and Microsoft technologies. Then, finally the candidates were tested on their communication skills, since with regard to the cross-border interaction, those were identified as a critical success factor.

K&V provided a unique opportunity for the employees in India to work on product development, which was quite rare during that period. Very few firms like the Center for Development of Advanced Computing (CDAC) and HCL research offered opportunities for Indian engineers to develop products using C and C++ technologies. Apart from this, K&V offered comparably high salaries to lure intelligent employees to become part of their team. Taking into account the strong brand names of other potential employers like Infosys, IBM, and Texas Instruments, K&V aimed to be seen as the top paymaster in the market.

In Germany, K&V had a unique setup as well; its workforce was relatively young, the average was in the mid-30s. Many of them were consultants, and they were required to travel to customer sites in Germany, Scandinavia, France, and the UK. The employees were able to communicate in at least two languages. Their command of English was much better compared to employees of other German companies during that time. This was as well a key factor which helped to decentralize the development to the location in Bangalore in these early days.

Dietmar Saddei remembers: "Initially, K&V used to have a type of working model in which most of the architecture and design work was done in Germany, while the coding itself was done in India. One thing we learned even at those days, was that communication is a big challenge for distributed development. At this point, we had our developers in Wallorf, and we had a growing team in India, which worked not only on the traditional Sales Force Automation, but also took over more jobs on the CRM field. The strength of K&V was that the business language was English, whereas the SAP staff was still used to communicate in German. So for all German colleagues at SAP, especially for many of the senior developers, this was a big change. They had a lot of difficulties in learning English and communicating with their counterparts in India. For example, quite a few staff members in India had a strong accent, and you can assume how confusing those conversations with German colleagues might have been when those were not fluent in English. When we decided that English would be the company language, i.e. that all mails and specifications should be written in English, – and let's assume about 80 % of the staff was German – you can imagine how difficult it was to get people to switch over to the new working style. So we started sending people to training classes and tried helping them to improve their English skills."

K&V in India was characterized by a unique culture: 'work hard and party harder'. Work packages were given to the employees using a software called 'Job Biz', and the managers estimated the target time for those tasks. Employees were paid high incentives when the tasks were completed before the target time. This motivated the employees to work very hard to deliver the piece of code before the due date. The incentives were calculated based on the productivity figures determined by 'Job Biz', and this motivated the workforce to stay for overtime and even at times sleep in the office. Friday evenings were reserved for company parties, and this brought employees closer to each other. This combination of monetary incentives and an environment engendering closeness among colleagues seems to have had the desired effect as K&V started delivering quick results.

Looking back at K&V from today's perspective, their methods rather look simple, but several practices followed by the management and the employees deserve further analysis as they resulted in reducing the time needed for the overall development cycle and they also accelerated the 'go to market' efforts of K&V.

The office had an expert from Germany in India for three to six months and in return, it also sent its key people to Germany to understand the requirements. These experts served as consultants for the rest of the staff and the communication between the groups happened through these channels. In those days, the cost of communication was exorbitantly high, and even the electricity supply was erratic in Bangalore. The development centers in Germany and India devised certain practices and procedures to communicate requirements and to synchronize the software code on a daily basis. Primitive technologies like Telnet and FTP used with dial-up ISD connections for transferring data and home-grown systems, which anticipated the present-day e-mail systems, were used for communication. Dietmar Saddei admits: "One of our big learnings at that time was that we had to make all efforts that both teams in Germany and in India were working on the same page. The challenge was to put things on one blackboard to make technology and the application teams work together. So overall one can say that we underestimated the communication challenge of distributed development. But all the time, I never had any doubt that we could not develop software from Bangalore. It was not like an island where nobody knew what was going on; it was rather well connected to the rest of the SAP ecosystem."

3.8   SAP Labs India and Its Milestones

In 1997, SAP India, the sales and consulting organization of SAP in the country, had established a small team to localize SAP payroll, accounting, and logistics within the Indian legal framework. K&V, acquired by SAP in 1998, had 90 employees working on the Sales Force Automation (SFA).

The foundation of SAP Labs India was based in three pillars: First there were the teams to localize SAP payroll, accounting and logistics within the Indian legal framework. Second there were the 90 employees working on the SFA, who were part of the acquisition of K&V. And third there was the SAP Labs Project launched by the board, which was the binding glue to establish a full fledged Lab out of these pieces. It was clear, that as well some of SAP's core products would need to follow, if the Lab would really like to excel. Consequentially, based on the initial success, in 1998 SAP started setting up teams to work on three different industry solutions: high tech, aerospace & defense, and oil & gas.

As Dr. Udo Urbanek, SAP's first co-director for Labs India recalls: "Hasso (Hasso Plattner) asked two Senior Vice Presidents of development to establish teams in India, even before SAP Labs India was formally established. Those were Nils Herzberg, responsible for the IBU Aerospace & Defense, and Mayur Shah, responsible for the Industry Business Unit (IBU) High Tech. Both had the advantage of being relatively new to SAP, as they were hired from outside. In that sense, they were not completely pre-occupied with the usual 'Walldorf thinking' at that time, that the only place where software could be developed was this small village in Southwest Germany. They were open to the idea and grabbed the opportunity to gain new experience in India. Both teams started early in 1998 and were just put up along with the K&V developers. Only later, they formally became employees of SAP Labs India. In parallel, Peter Zencke convinced Dieter Rafalsky (SVP, IBU Oil & Gas), who had as well previous experience in working with teams distributed around the globe, to start a group for the oil & gas downstream development. At those times, such decisions were taken very fast and without bureaucracy – so we were able to execute them within a matter of weeks. And with having the right attitude on both sides, all three teams had a quite successful start."

On November 13th, 1998, employees of SAP Labs India moved into their new office facility in the posh International Technology Park Limited (ITPL) at Whitefield, Bangalore. The ITPL was the talk of the town, and it was a state-of-the-art technology park, jointly developed by the Singapore Development Board, Tata Group, and the Karnataka Industrial Development Board. This technology park had three towers, 'Innovator', 'Explorer' and 'Discover', and it housed many international and Indian IT companies. The basement of the technology park also offered food courts, banks and convenience stores. Dr. Peter Zencke, executive board member of SAP, and the German Consul General from Chennai were the guests of honor at the inauguration of the SAP office in the park. Zencke was the executive board sponsor for Labs India and during the inaugural address, he mentioned that the focus of the labs would be developing software in the fields of CRM, localization of R/3 for Asia-Pacific and the newly formed IBU's.

Peter Zencke once told the press that the move to expand the role of the Indian development center was aimed at creating a 'virtual development center' for SAP spread across three continents: Europe, America and Asia. He went on adding: "Using high-speed telecom links, software professionals at all three points of this triangle – Foster City, Walldorf and Bangalore – would collaborate seamlessly and on round-the-clock projects."

In March 1998, SAP started searching for the Managing Director of SAP Labs India. As mentioned above, the global SAP Labs concept suggested that every lab should be headed by a local lab director with executive administrative responsibility. However, for Labs India, a unique form of local leadership was chosen. Due to the fact that the employees were actually brought together from two different companies, SAP Asia / India and K&V India, it was felt that for an initial period of two to three years, it would make sense to run Labs India in a 'two-in-a-box concept', which

Fig. 4. Inauguration of SAP Labs India. From left to right: Werner Konik, Dr. Peter Zencke and Dr. Udo Urbanek, 1998

Fig. 5. Dr. Peter Zencke at the inauguration of SAP Labs India, November 1998

is to say, by assigning one senior manager from both companies each as joint lab directors.

In addition to the merged staff of both companies, positions were advertised in the corporate portal, and managers from all around the globe applied. Peter Zencke screened candidates and finally made decision for two senior managers who both had more than 15 years of IT experience, Werner Konik and Dr. Udo Urbanek. Konik, who was already responsible for the Asian International Development, had a vast experience in Asia, knew the specifics of India quite well and had spent many years of his career outside Germany. Dr. Urbanek, holding a PhD in Mathematics, was the head of K&V operations in India and had spent many years in Germany, the UK, and India. They split their responsibilities in terms of sponsoring different sections of the development organization. Urbanek, who was hundred percent on-site in Bangalore, ran the local day-to-day operations, whereas Konik, based in Germany, came in for regular visits and took care of corporate integration, transparency, and reporting to the SAP executive board.

The first month was a period of excitement and anticipation for the employees of SAP India and K&V. Naik Bhuvaneswar, Head of HR initiated a project to integrate the employees from both companies. Series of workshops with members from K&V, SAP India, and the newly formed IBU teams were conducted with the support of a professor from the Indian Institute of Management in Ahmadabad, and they were called 'Synergy Workshops'. These off-site workshops were conducted every month, and they involved employees of all levels of the organization. A separate workshop was also held for the two co-directors.

The cultural fit/misfit of those two companies was a major hurdle in the beginning months. Dr. Udo Urbanek explains this in the following words: "Actually we had to merge two completely different companies. K&V consisted of mainly young, very enthusiastic developers; they were used to work in a project environment under high pressure, and fifty percent of the compensation was variable. The colleagues joining from SAP India came from a product development background, which naturally had much longer planning cycles and less of the typical project pressure. They appeared to be much more settled, and their compensation was mainly based on a fixed salary. Joining these cultures was more difficult than I had thought initially. Being a mathematician and trying to get through things in a more rational way, I had to keep the communication channel open at all times. Often we thought we had a brilliant idea, which would make perfect sense, and then we were taken back, as we faced stiff resistance from some parts of our organization."

When the new company was formed, Naik Bhuvaneswar, Head of HR, formed a new framework for Human Resource (HR) policies and a new strategy regarding compensation and benefits. All employees got new contracts harmonizing the conditions between the ex-K&V and the ex-SAP India staff. All employees were evaluated and were assigned to appropriate career levels. This also created quite some initial disturbance among the workforce, which, however, subsided subsequently as the Labs was on a growth trajectory. Finally, the co-directors released an overall mission statement for SAP Labs India:

"SAP Labs India will deliver software solutions of the highest standard by ensuring quality, on-time delivery and extensive functionality enabling our customers to achieve their business goals."

Local HR policies and processes played a very crucial role in the merger. There was a lot of focus on trying to keep the best of both companies – and the situation was also quite unique: SAP was the acquiring company (from a global perspective), so the former staff of SAP India at times maintained an attitude suggesting, 'We bought you – so we can decide what is going to happen.' At the same time, 80 % of the initial 113 employees were former K&V employees, including all managers responsible for the service functions like HR, administration, or Finance. Werner Konik comments on that: "The situation was of course not the one of a typical take-over, with the vast majority of employees coming from K&V. Therefore, we wanted to avoid any impression of using sledgehammer tactics. We realized that there was as well a lot of good working practices coming from K&V. However, these guys appeared to be working all the time in a fire-fighting mode and had no real clue how standard development in a long-term product cycle would work, they had pioneered a lot of things in the way of how software development can be distributed and how to keep remote teams very engaged. And we had many brilliant people from K&V; one had to give a lot of respect to their management and HR for the selection of people."

SAP Labs trained all its new employees in the SAP development process and the highly motivated management team started working with co-directors to drive the company forward. SAP Labs India continued the K&V tradition of Friday evening get-togethers; even after the formation of Labs India, there were frequent and lavish parties for the employees.

On the other hand, the system of calculating incentives based on 'Job Biz' (inherited from K&V) came under heavy criticism by the former SAP India developers and managers. It was seen unsuitable for long-term product development, as it focused a lot on immediate rewards for project goals, sometimes just based on the number of lines of code produced. As Labs India was designed to have a focus on long-term product development (the original idea of an ABAP factory was dropped quite early due to the success of the initial software projects), the short-term focus 'Job Biz remuneration' was regarded as unsuitable, and the system was dropped. Instead, a new quarterly bonus calculation system was introduced, based on several productivity criteria since Dr. Urbanek believed in giving clear targets and in calculating the salary in an objective way.

Although the two co-directors Dr. Urbanek and Konik were quite different personalities, they had complimentary qualities. Werner Konik, being among the first 250 employees at SAP worldwide, had well wide-spread connections within the development organization at headquarters in Germany. He believed in people, networking, and teamwork. He also had a very good sense of humor, and the unique ability to quickly strike a chord with new people. Dr. Udo Urbanek, on the other hand, was a mathematician, and he believed in nothing other than facts. He always wanted a clear plan, and he always stressed on executing projects exactly within the predefined conditional framework. However, in all instances, they both directed the team with one voice, which was one of the crucial factors to make this arrangement, and finally SAP Labs, so successful. Werner Konik remembers these initial months: "Udo and I were on the one hand completely different managers and personalities, but on the other hand, we formed a perfect match. It took us some time to realize the qualities of each other and of the different approaches we would take to solve issues. Udo had a vast experience in India, whereas I had been on a business trip to India just once or twice before. On the other hand, I knew how SAP product development worked, and I did as well know all the relevant people in SAP development. We both learned a lot from each other during those days."

The efforts in merging the two companies went all through 1999. On paper, the merger was completed by November 13th, 1998, but in reality it took much longer, even longer than the two co-directors would have envisioned: "We had a long learning curve", says Werner, "And initially, we were carrying a lot of incorrect assumption. I always thought everybody should be completely happy about this merger, but I got to learn that we did not communicate enough. Besides, it was a tough job in those initial months to convince colleagues in Walldorf that Bangalore wasn't a temporary phenomenon. Simple things like setting up English as the standard language of communication had to be establish, we also had to deal with the belief that every development manager should come from Walldorf."

Dr. Udo Urbanek adds: "Initially, we were concentrating too much on the rational side of things. And too often, we were only talking to managers, ignoring the real influencers behind the scene. I learned that emotions had to be handled with the same due diligence as the policy framework or a development process. In the end, we had to build a new culture at SAP Labs India, a real 'fusion' of the two previous cultures. You can only do this by winning the hearts, not just by winning the minds. Looking back it's a good feeling to realize that I developed a very good relationship with colleagues even in the tough discussions during the merger."

It was in the year 1999 when all those initial grievances had to be sorted out, but by the end of the year, the headcount increased by 60%. With all the new people, the history became less important and a shared view of the future was what kept everyone engaged.

By the end of 1999, Werner Konik laid down the responsibility of a co-director of Labs India, and Clas Neumann, who was assistant to SAP executive board member Peter Zencke, took over together with Udo Urbanek. Under this healthy combination of highly motivated managers, the headcount increased from 200 in the first year, to 391 by end of 2000. Additional teams were started to handle the new mySAP.com development and a small team was established to handle the year 2000 (Y2K) problems. Nevertheless, the Y2K team had just 10 members since there were little or no problems expected for the users of SAP software due to the anticipatory design.

The development teams delivered quick results, and SAP Labs India created a positive impression within the internal SAP ecosystem. Visitors from Germany and other locations were fascinated with the new facility and with its young, energetic and enthusiastic employees. SAP Labs India gained popularity as most of the visitors carried many interesting and positive stories back with them.

The management of SAP Labs India also started some new practices which laid the foundation for the strong growth of the Labs. The directors

Table 4. Commitment at SAP Labs India

Commitment from the company	Commitment from the employees
• No. 1 software development company in India	• Dedication, responsibility and pro-activeness within projects
• Fully embedded into the SAP group	• Maximum quality approach: work according to quality processes
• Full-fledged software development – no coding factory	• Fulfillment of specifications by long-term design
• Using the latest technology	• Reusability and integration into existing SAP products
• Providing excellent career opportunities	• Focus on stability, performance and ease of use to provide superior customer support
• Excellent compensation and benefits	• Cooperation and team work
• Open and enjoyable (overall) working atmosphere	• Long-term association with the company

announced the yearly goals for the Labs, and these were shared with all levels of employees in a yearly kickoff meeting. The management team comprised of all development managers and the service department heads, would meet in a team managers' meeting every Thursday afternoon. During these meetings, the managers had intense discussions about the policies, practices, and the overall direction of the labs. The general inclusion of those who were responsible for the software development into the administrative and HR processes, made the difference in arriving at a system that really served the needs of the engineers.

Apart from project reviews with project directors in Germany, the development managers had periodic reviews with the lab directors. The performance of the local development managers was assessed jointly by the project directors in Germany and the co-directors in India on a quarterly basis. The co-directors of the labs had a monthly meeting with the program directors in Germany to collect feedback about the progress of the projects in India. During that phase, the lab directors still had the 'bandwidth' to run SAP Labs as a real matrix, monitoring the progress of each and every development team together with the line of business managers in Germany. Monthly staff meetings were conducted, and quarterly company parties were as well organized to create emotional bond with the employees.

By 2001, the headcount of Labs India increased to 522 with the addition of teams in the area of customer specific development, central quality and information management teams. The teams that were set up during the initial days also increased their coverage and headcount.

In 2002, Udo Urbanek moved back to Germany, and for the first time since inception, the growth of SAP Labs India slowed down due to the 'Dotcom bust', and the headcount dropped to 506. In 2003, Martin Prinz, the development manager from the international development team in India, took over responsibility as co-director of the lab along with Clas Neumann. At that time, Martin Prinz stated the direction of the lab: "We need to keep in mind that we will grow; SAP Labs India is a place for SAP to scale for the future, and we have to demonstrate that we can scale in Bangalore, that we can have a healthy growth here and that we can grow fast while remaining stable and reliable. Overall, we need to become better and better in what we are doing, and the key to that is that we hire the best people and develop a highly engaged workforce."

Neumann, who was responsible for finance, administration facilities, and IT in the lab (HR was always shared between the two MDs), was keen to develop an independent, campus style infrastructure for the Lab. However, it was clear that for 500 colleagues, such an investment would not make sense. Thus he initiated a project called 'Project 750' to provide additional push to increase the headcount of the location to 750. During this period, SAP Labs India conducted detailed discussions with several stakeholders in Germany. SAP Labs India deliberated on several ideas like creating product management and architecture teams in India to fuel the growth of the location. Clas Neumann recalls: "Within 'Project 750', for the first time we started to make a big sales pitch for the lab as a development location, even in Germany. It marked a fundamental change in mindset that we decided to do active marketing for Labs India on all different management levels inside the SAP ecosystem. We had done advertising before, but not with so much focus and commitment to growth."

During this period, SAP also embarked on a worldwide restructuring by sharpening the focus of the development organization. Prior to this, the development teams were responsible for both development and support of the solutions developed. With the new structure, all support activities were

Fig. 6. Inauguration of the campus in 2003, Dr. Peter Zencke, Heimo Richter, German Ambassador, and the Karnataka IT minister Inamdar

aggregated under the responsibility of the executive board member Gerhard Oswald. He became responsible for customer support and development support within SAP. Oswald was the first board member to count on the cost advantage in India, and he pushed his managers to make stronger use of it than in the past.

Gerd Oswald explains: "With the joint efforts of all managers, the headcount of the teams in India increased significantly, and Labs India grew to 748 employees by the end of 2003, hitting the 750 target planned under 'Project 750'." In November 2003, Labs India opened its 20 million, state-of-the-art campus in Whitefield. It was inaugurated by Peter Zencke, the German ambassador Heimo Richter, and the Karnataka IT minister Inandam. By early 2004, SAP AG embarked on the next organizational change code-named 'SCORE – Strategic Cross Organizational Realignment Process.' SAP intended to create dual roles in development, one for project management, another for people management. While the project management focused on delivery according to the master plan, the people manager ensured competency development for the employees working in the teams. The staffing was organized jointly to ensure both long-term competency development and short term project completion.

New mission, vision and strategy statements were published to provide a next level of direction to the staff. The new mission statement of SAP Labs India from then on was:

"SAP Labs support SAP's business units in developing competitive products for global markets and customers, from high-tech centers around the world. By discovering new technological trends and best business practices, SAP is able to diversify its technical and business expertise, and increase its innovation potential.

At Labs India, we want to be a community of talented and committed people, who are passionate about their work.

Our high standards of work and the ability to consistently deliver results above expectations will make us trusted solution providers within the SAP ecosystem.

We will be a role model for software development organizations worldwide."

The game plan itself was highlighted with the following strategy statements:

- Collaborate proactively with SAP's business units;

- Work jointly with SAP's field organization on selected customer projects;

- Network with local thought and innovation leaders in technology and business;

- Leverage synergies between development themes at each location;

- Develop, apply, and promote best-in-class internal processes and operations;

- Tap into the local talent pool for software development and invest in people.

To achieve the vision, Labs India created a three year roadmap, which stated:

"SAP Labs India will be a powerhouse and will be a leader of the industrialization of enterprise software development."

In January 2005, the new 'Research and Breakthrough Innovation' board area was formed and Clas Neumann took over the responsibility in India as Senior Vice President of this group. He was entrusted to develop the top-layer of SAP's new SME solution 'Business by Design', and he headed teams in China, Germany, and India from Bangalore. Georg Kniese, who was assistant to executive board member Peter Zencke, joined as the co-director of Labs India along with Martin Prinz.

In addition, the year 2005 saw many visitors from the SAP executive board, and SAP Labs India opened a second satellite lab in the North of India at Gurgaon. The fact that the Bangalore office outgrew the infra-structure, the lack of engineers and the idea of general risk diversion had pushed SAP to look for an alternate location within India.

By the end of 2004, the headcount had been 1,352, and at that point, every line of business was already present in India. In the year 2005, though, SAP Labs India launched a massive investment of 34,000 man-days of training, in order to further consolidate support and development units in India and to create a knowledge hub of a truly global scale. By end of 2005, the headcount reached 2,287.

In 2006, SAP acquired a compliance company named Virsa, which included employees at a new location, Chandigarh, in the North of India. Those employees were later consolidated in the Gurgoan location. By the end of 2006, the headcount stood at 3,230 as a result of intensive growth in the customer specific development as well as in the research and breakthrough innovation areas.

On September 17th, 2007, SAP inaugurated 'Phase III' of the campus to house additional 2,300 employees. By the end of 2007, the headcount of SAP Labs India reached 3,230, and it became the second largest lab right after Germany. SAP also acquired another company in India named Yasu, which had expertise in Business Rule Management, coming with a development center in Hyderabad.

In 2007, Georg Kniese returned to Germany, and for the first time nine years after its establishment, SAP Labs India got an Indian lab director. Kush Desai, who had been the CFO of SAP Labs India since 2002, became Managing Director of the labs. In addition to that, Ferose V.R. became lab director in Gurgoan, in order to have the Northern hub established as a unit on its own on SAP's global R&D map, and not only as a satellite of Bangalore.

In summer 2007, the executive board divided and restructured the global SAP Labs landscape, and formally established four global R&D hubs in Palo Alto, Ra'anan (Israel), Shanghai, and Bangalore. The other labs would either become satellites to those four hubs or be called 'Focus Labs'. Starting from that point, a 'President' was established in each global hub, which had to be a senior manager of SAP, being responsible for a significant part of development as well. Thus, the SAP board wanted to achieve better synergies within the lab structure. A defragmentation of the strong silos created meanwhile by the different lines of business, should bring back a certain closeness between the labs management and the actual people who did the software development. In India, Clas Neumann took over as the President of SAP Labs India in addition to his role as Senior Vice President for SAP Business By Design, which was the role he had in the global product development.

A very important milestone for Labs India was of course the 'Board Week' in New Delhi in August 2007. For the first time, the Senior Executive Team (SET), the Global Jour Fixe, the Product and Technology Council (PTC), and the Field Leadership Team Meeting took place within the Asia-

Pacific region, specifically in India. This was done to underline the strategic importance of India in two ways, as a R&D sourcing location, and as a sales market for SAP's products. The 200 top managers of SAP, including all of the eight executive board members, came to India – and most of them also came to SAP Labs as part of their visit. The international press coverage of that 'Board Week' was huge, and the board members took being in India as an opportunity to intensify their relationship with the big Indian service providers and with the local government.

India had finally arrived on the strategic map of SAP. At this point, Ranjan Das, MIT undergraduate and graduate of the MBA program at the Harvard Business School, took over from Alan Sedghi as head of the Indian subsidiary. This change of leadership at both SAP Labs India and SAP India sent the message that the company was very committed to local leadership in India.

The year 2008 saw the integration of the largest acquisition of SAP so far – Business Objects and 300 employees working at Business Objects India became part of the labs in India. This integration was the most comprehensive one SAP Labs India had to complete in its history, but the experience it had gained from the previous smaller acquisitions helped a lot. Without a significant 'brain drain', all Business Objects employees were integrated into the SAP Labs India campus in August 2008. In November 2008, the SAP Netweaver and Business Objects development teams were merged. More accurately, the two organizations were successfully merged, and the legal documentation got completed in December 2008.

4 Organizational Structure at SAP Labs

Transparency, integrity, trustworthiness, and a sense of responsibility are basic values on which SAP's solid global reputation is built. These principles of corporate governance, transparent for all stakeholders, set the standard for the work of SAP's executive and supervisory board. These values are reflected and substantiated by SAP's products and services; solutions that help both its public sector and its private sector clients improve the transparency and accountability of their operations. SAP's corporate governance structure follows Germany's legal framework of corporate governance, which separates management and supervisory functions into two distinct bodies: the executive board and the supervisory board. Due to the German Co-determination Act, half of the SAP supervisory board members

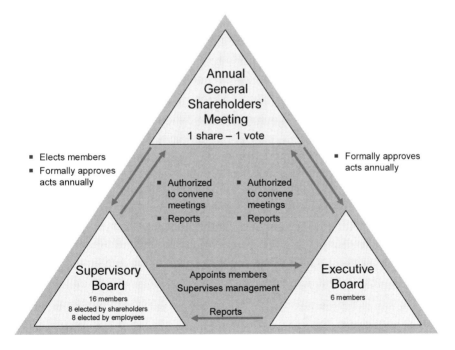

Fig. 7. Corporate Governance at SAP AG

C. Neumann and J. Srinivasan, *Managing Innovation from the Land of Ideas and Talent: The 10-Year Story of SAP Labs India,*
DOI: 10.1007/978-3-540-89283-0_4, © Springer-Verlag Berlin Heidelberg 2009

are employee representatives. Additionally, the German Stock Corporation Act provides for a third body – a shareholders' organization known as the General Shareholders' Meeting.

4.1   Operating Environment

Today, the operating environment of SAP Labs India is vastly different from the time of its inception.

Externally, India has established itself in the global IT landscape. NASS-COM (National Association of Software and Services Companies) estimates that in 2008 more than 65% of all IT outsourcing projects worldwide were given to Indian companies. The biggest three Indian IT majors TCS, Wipro, and Infosys have close to 100,000 engineers on their payroll, a massive increase from where they were some years ago. Bangalore holds more than 1,000 companies today providing IT services or that were established as captive centers by multinational companies. And those centers, which are basically exporting software or R&D services, are not only run by the usual suspects like Microsoft, Intel, IBM, SAP or Siemens – the list includes industrial firms as well, like GE, Volvo, Daimler, and Huawei, a Chinese semiconductor and telecommunication equipment firm.

All these movements on the market have created a big IT cluster in Bangalore; 45% of all Indian software engineers are working in the 'IT capital of India', which is unprecedented in the world. Many have tried to directly compare this environment with the Silicon Valley in the Bay Area, but these two phenomina are not comparable outside their own contexts. Even though one may find a similar number of companies here and there and as well a comparable number of engineers working in both locations, there cannot be any doubt that in terms of patent creation, start-up foundation or business idea generation, the Bay Area South of San Francisco is far ahead. The question is: Why is that the case? Indian engineers can be as proactive or innovative as any other engineers around the globe, they have proven themselves not only in the Indian aerospace, aeronautic, and defense industry, but also abroad as leading scientists, business leaders, and scholars.

Many explanations could be offered, but one of the most compelling seems to be offered by V. Raghunathan, who comes to the conclusion that his country men are very intelligent and at the same time very rational. He writes: "In India nearly every situation is encountered as a first-time situation, and people respond to them as such – so for the sheer survival, one has to be extremely intelligent" (V. Raghunathan, 2006).

Indian engineers, while intelligent, are a product of their environment. The Indian business environment, by virtue of its extreme competitiveness for good jobs, and what is still essentially India's old world hierarchical social structure, demands for the sake of personal survival a certain caution. Intelligent people in an ostensibly dangerous employment environment will naturally err towards the side of caution, and when every innovation carries with it the inherent possibility of failure, people are much more comfortable not drawing attention to themselves unless they are very certain of a positive outcome. Even when the company culture rewards innovation, it is unreasonable to expect individuals to easily cast aside inherited cultural survival strategies.

Having a rational mind also means making the best use of opportunities. Thus, most Indian entrepreneurs in IT do not waste any time or energy on far reaching inventions that may or may not have a fair chance to become a viable business. Instead, nearly all of them have opted to pursue established and tested opportunities, for example, simply hiring a few good coding guys and opening another offshore firm that offers IT services to Western companies. The comparative cost advantage and performance record of such ventures is just too compelling; the chance to generate profit is more or less 'guaranteed' when compared to research and development options. The business model – indeed a real innovation by its pioneers from Infosys, TCS, Wipro and others – has proven to be very successful with very healthy margins, and from this perspective a 'me-too strategy', while perhaps specializing in some niche, makes perfect sense.

Any manager who left SAP Labs India in the last 10 years to found his or her own company went into exactly the same business. And most of them (though not all) were moderately successful – at least employing today some dozen to some hundred engineers and offering – guess what – SAP services within the SAP's ecosystem. Nevertheless, most of the Indian entrepreneurs have applied themselves to innovative business models and new quality and project management approaches, rather than groundbreaking products. The same is true for all those engineers who are working in companies, where razor sharp project margins are a fact of daily life, where on-time project completion, careful adherence to specifications, and maybe a design given by the customer are their mantras, rather than sitting on a bean sack and discussing with fellows the future of software architecture for mobile devices. However, all this could lead one to the conclusion that Indian software engineers are only capable of working like bees in their cubicles, according to detailed orders given to them. One might think that only because of India's history of successful business service providers. However, the opposite is true; if the space, environment, and management recognition is provided, amazing results can be the reward.

4.2   Innovation and Availability of Talent

Meanwhile, many multinational companies have realized that the limited availability of bright talent represents a strong hurdle for developing their business globally and for spurring innovation. However, the demand for excellent IT engineers has undergone quite some ups and downs in the past 15 years (with peaks in 1998 – 2000 and 2006 – 2007). A consistent inflow of talent with a background that is broad, diverse, and technologically savvy is a crucial success factor for all global companies today. For the sake of talent sourcing, no global company can afford not to be in India, which is as crucial as being in China, Europe, or in the U.S.

For some of the multinational companies, beside their talent sourcing, innovation is also a major goal for their set-up in India. Specifically, SAP has always focused on fostering innovation. Different models of engagement were implemented in an event-based form like the 'Code Olympics', which is basically a weekend programming team competition, to 'SAPnovation', which is a multi-week competition of prototypes based on an underlying business case. Many of those events and initiatives only actually exist in India. It is not that other locations like Germany would not like to have such events, but the absence of a managing director (MD) at 'Labs Germany' might be one of the factors preventing such initiatives from being started in the first place. The success of these innovation programs at Labs India is ensured by motivated staff in combination with the right kind of management intervention. The rollout of the Patent Program into India was also a big success. It offers rewards for invention disclosure and successful patent applications, and many colleagues at SAP Labs India have their cubicle plastered with patent registrations from the European or the U.S. patent office.

4.3 Bringing Development Closer to Key Markets

These days, all multinational companies have understood that when looking at Asia, the question cannot be 'China *or* India', rather it must be 'China
and India'. India is still a developing key market, based on its strong Gross
Domestic Product (GDP) growth since 2001/2002 and its rising middle
class. Not only companies that sell to the end consumer see this opportunity; but also those that sell to businesses see their chance. The gigantic
necessary infrastructure investments, as well as the demand of Indian industry's rising corporate stars create demand for world class goods, be it
equipment, machinery, or software. Even in the middle of the Asian financial crisis in 1997, SAP has understood the future significance of the Asian
markets and their growth potential. The R&D hub in Bangalore was also
meant to underline its commitment to the Asia-Pacific region and to set a
specific focus on the strongly growing Indian market. In 2007, of all SAP's
global markets, India grew strongest; their revenues doubled.

SAP India, the sales wing of SAP in India, has profited from being local.
More often than not, sales deals were actually closed after some big meetings that took place in Bangalore. Their local presence clearly convinced
the customer of two key points: first, that SAP is here to stay, and second,
that there will always be core knowledge close by in case of any difficulties with the software or in the event that enhancements are needed. No
expensive consultant would need to fly in from Germany for that, because
the consultant is local.

4.4 Cost Containment and Reduction

The need for talent and the emphasis on the Asian markets were the reasons for the establishment of many R&D centers in Bangalore, as well for
SAP Labs. However, most companies are measured against certain objectives, which the CEO has set three months or a year back, on the guidance
of the company. These objectives are expectations that are to be fulfilled.
The operating margin and cost structure play an important role in this context. The analysts want to hear offshoring stories – so they would like to
see that the company takes measures to reduce the costs to a minimum,
without jeopardizing deliveries and innovative power. Thus, the obvious
cost advantage of the Bangalore location plays a major role. Even today,
despite annual salary increases of 15 % and above over the last three years,

Table 5. HC distribution in Labs India as per February 13th 2009

Board Area	Main Units	HC	in %
Jim Snabe	Business Solutions and Technology	2,331	53.70
Gerd Oswald	Global Services and Support	1,081	24.90
John Schwarz, Jim Snabe	Business Objects	437	10.07
Ernie Gunst	Internal Services (HR, IT, F&A)	250	5.76
Bill McDermott	Global Field Operations	166	3.82
Léo Apotheker	Field Services, Field Analytics	76	1.75
Total		**4,341**	**100.00**

Labs India enjoys a cost advantage (based on fully loaded costs including travel and side costs) of 75 % compared to Germany, SAP's headquarters.

Today, Labs India runs major operations in all areas of SAP's value chain. The exact headcount distribution can be viewed in Table 5.

4.5 Set-up Structure

With the strategic decision to offshore key parts of its value chain to India, SAP chose to set up a so-called 'captive center', meaning a 100 % owned subsidiary of SAP AG, Germany, completely managed and controlled by SAP. The advantages were very clear: complete control of the intellectual property (IP), project execution and the human resources management, and a much easier collaboration between the main development hub in Germany and the newly formed Lab. In most instances, the transfer of processes and knowledge was seamless. SAP pioneered the bold implementation of this model. According to a survey done by the Kelley School of Business in 2005, out of the Top 200 Fortune companies, only 65 were running a captive center in Asia-Pacific, and out of those, only 40 % (i.e. 30 companies) were actually doing substantial analytical or technical work there. Goldmann-Sachs, GE, HSBC, Siemens, and Microsoft are some examples of such companies.

The initial and continued success of SAP Labs India was based on two factors:

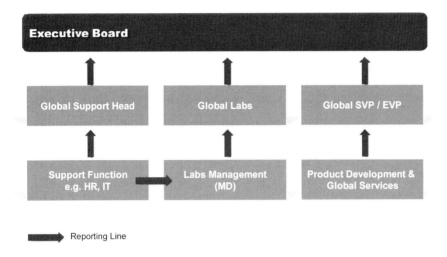

Fig. 8. Organizational structure of product development at SAP Labs

- The Labs India management, with full support from SAP's board, was able to overcome many challenges by initiating trust building measures.

- SAP's Global operations management benefited from early lessons on how global services should be delivered, and how collaborative software development, as well as skill and knowledge sharing should be organized across the globe. As a result, the organization developed and introduced new global processes and guidelines such as the change of SAP's official language to English. This helped SAP become a truly global company.

Today, the product development and global service teams at SAP Labs India do not have any direct or indirect reporting line to the Labs management (cf. Fig. 8). The reason behind this is a practical one: given the diversity of six different board areas, having colleagues working in Bangalore, and below this level at least 16–18 Lines of Business – it would be just too much for the Labs managing directors to go into all required details to understand what is going on within the Lines of Business. Therefore, these lines actually report to global stakeholders which in all cases are not based in India. And those report either directly or via another level to SAP's executive board.

During the initial years, the local service functions were built by the Labs management. However, today, as SAP works to increasingly globalize all these functions, reporting is done solely to either regional or global stake-holders, so that global capabilities could be accessed by the local teams.

Organizationally, this operating environment demands a lot of communication and networking skills from the Labs management, since basically all areas, development and local services have global reporting lines. And as the human brain works in such a corporate environment, we all align first of all to our boss who decides our bonus and our next salary increase. Therefore, Labs management has to drive its initiatives (like innovation and HR) across all Lines of Business. This often not only requires alignment with the local Line of Business Heads, but also with their global heads. The same is true on the other side for crucial functions like facilities, HR, or training. Local departments belong to global lines, so any decision that has budgetary impact would first need to be aligned with them.

Does this make things slower? Sure, it does. However, on the other hand, if these processes are managed well, they make sure that SAP moves in one direction globally and that every local subsidiary does not determine its own strategy and service levels for its employees. Accordingly, through discussions and constant communication, knowledge is also transferred to the local teams, knowledge that would previously have to be extracted – that is, if one even knew where to locate it.

The key to working within this structure is to find a way to minimize the time needed for decisions, decide which to accept locally and which to risk executing without aligning each and every person who might have something to contribute.

4.6 The Role of the Management Bodies of SAP for Labs India

It is quite clear that any captive center in the field of R&D needs to be connected tightly to management forums and to the global management structure. This can only be achieved if the basic structure is consistent across a country and is replicated at the different subsidiaries.

In the following section, we try to explain the role of different management bodies and specific management levels for Labs India at different points in time, since it is obvious that the management levels and their importance for a specific location change over the years. For example, whereas in the early days, a visiting Vice President of Development from headquarters was treated like a 'demigod' in India, that title has meanwhile become something much more common, with more than 40 VPs operating at SAP Labs India alone.

Executive Board

At SAP, the '**Executive Board**' is the topmost managing body, and it is responsible to develop and execute SAP's strategy. Its members duty bound to exercise their management power in the interest of the company and in pursuit of the sustained growth of corporate value. The board discusses and settles the company's strategy with the '**Supervisory Board**', ensures compliance with the requirements of the law throughout the group, and maintains appropriate risk management structures and risk controls. Overall, the executive board provides the supervisory board with regular, prompt, and comprehensive reports about all essential issues of business, corporate strategy, and potential risks. Under German stock corporation law, the executive board may comprise one or several members, regardless of the company's size. The supervisory board appoints executive board members

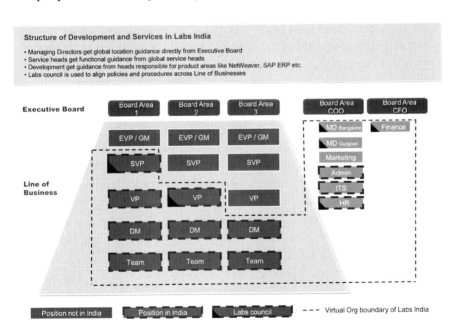

Fig. 9. Structure of SAP Labs location

for a maximum of five years, but members can be reappointed. The executive board usually tries to balance the interests of four major interest groups: customers, partners, employees and shareholders.

When the SAP Labs concept was established at the beginning of the 1990s, the main responsibility of the executive board was to make decisions with regard to SAP Labs global network function. When a new lab is established, the board defines the focus area for development and decides upon the initial resource allocation. Furthermore, the executive board approves its initial budget and investment plan. In addition, it reviews the development status of individual labs when presented by the board member in charge. Approvals for starting a new lab site, satellite sites, and the closure of a lab is also decided by the executive board, although new sites were only established through acquisitions during the last years.

Going forward, growth of a Lab is a function of the growth plans of its internal customers, the lines of business. A lab has to remain attractive to its customers with respect to scale, ramp-up times, cast, availability of talent and innovation spirit.

For many years, every lab has had one specific so-called **'Board Sponsor'**. This individual board member was responsible for a particular lab and acted as a representative of the lab in the SAP Executive Board. This was the typical start-up setup that supported the growth of the Labs through the initial years.

When SAP Labs India was formed, Dr. Peter Zencke took responsibility as its Board Sponsor. Starting from that time, he took special care of the Labs for a period of eight years. Except for two years in between when the Labs responsibility moved to Dr. Claus Heinrich, Dr. Peter Zencke has been the Board Sponsor for Labs India throughout its history. From its inception, Dr. Peter Zencke set its focus on localization, industry solutions, Customer Relationship Management, and base technology components. Since India was identified as the location with the strongest growth, the Labs added headcount in diverse areas including research, customer specific development, service, support, and field services activities.

During the last years, the service, support, and development organizations were located at Labs India. This helped to make it the biggest SAP hub outside Germany. A significant portion of new generation research activities in the areas of Business Process Platform and Business ByDesign are currently developed in Bangalore, which also increased the overall contribution of the location. Dr. Peter Zencke visited Labs India frequently to review its development status and guide the young development workforce in the intricacies of complex enterprise software development. He became a board member of the Indian School of Business, and when SAP's annual technology event, TechEd, took place in Bangalore in 2008, he delivered the key note address outlining the product and development strategy. All these activities, which Dr. Peter Zencke did as a Board Sponsor, greatly enhanced the reputation of the location and also created a unique name for SAP Labs India, within its ecosystem and throughout SAP AG.

Additionally, it was of great importance that Henning Kagermann, after having becoming CEO, made his first trip abroad to India in June of 2003. He brought his positive impressions back to Walldorf and shared them with many senior development colleagues – which resulted in the strongest growth phase for Labs India in the following three years.

Today, the executive board no longer needs to strongly support individual labs, as the hubs have matured. Thus, in January of 2009, the practice of individual board sponsorship was abandoned, and the responsibility for all Labs was moved into the area of SAP's COO, Ernie Gunst. With this change, SAP underlined that the focus would now be more on efficiency and consolidation than on hand-holding and support. Clas Neumann, the current global head of all labs, a position that requires all managing directors to report to him, reports to the COO on all Labs matters.

Lessons Learned

Top management support including a clear commitment from the CEO is utmost important for a young captive center or R&D hub. In the initial phase, there are many internal forces that work against the location – or want to prove that the concept of doing things so far away would not work.

As a location matures, this support is not required any more. The location has to prove itself against global corporate standards, and it does not need to be handled differently from other hubs. Constant improvement and competition among locations will then lead to further progress.

The Role of Labs Management

The **Board of Directors** at SAP Labs India is the official reviewing body of its business and has the authority to sign off its balance sheet and verify its profit or loss. This board is composed of the responsible board member, the **Global Labs Head,** and the **Managing Director**.

Role of the Labs managing director

- Represent the Lab to the outside world (customers, partners, community) and be its legal head;
- Plan and achieve the lab's budget / objectives;
- Develop and keep the overall framework of processes and policies, that make a functioning company out of a lab;
- Ensure compliance with SAP's corporate guidelines / strategy as well as with legal rules and standards;
- Align the different labs services, like Human Resources, IT-Services, Finance and Administration, to form one team that supports the location's smooth operation;
- Keep SAP Labs as 'top employer' on the list of the most admired companies;
- Cost control.

During the early days, the lab directors of Labs India spent quite a lot of time getting into the development of individual business units and in meeting the development managers, developers and the development teams. The business units were divided among the lab directors. The lab directors of each lab had regular face-to-face meetings and conference calls with the Line of Business (LoBs) they belonged to in order to align the activity of each Lab to support the growth of the Indian business units. Requests were constantly pouring in from every new business unit to increase the depth of and breadth of development. To support Labs India more efficiently, the co-directors divided the LoBs among themselves.

This part of the lab director role became increasingly challenging as the Labs itself grew from 100 to more than 4,000 today. In 2008, there were more than 300 different development teams belonging to more than 60 Lines of Business (LoBs) at SAP Labs India – it became virtually impossible for a single person to meet all of them in person to discuss individual grievances or development matters.

One of the major tasks of the Labs leadership has always been employer branding, because in a high-tech city like Bangalore, it has always been important to make sure that the young Indian workforce would never forget why they should choose SAP over other technology companies in India. Before the role of the Labs President was introduced, the lab directors were frequently playing the role of a host or a guest, either organizing visits from universities, government representatives, or SAP customers, or being themselves guests in industry groups, speaking on conferences, or talking to media. This also put a great deal of pressure on the Labs directors, as they had to make sure visitors got a good and professional impression of the Labs in order to maintain its corporate identity. In addition, an advisory group of senior managers was created to define the location specific policies, to review the status of the location, and to deliberate on the future direction of the Labs.

Lessons Learned

In a fast developing R&D center, the role of the MD cannot be constant over time. For smaller and remote location labs, the MD needs to be well connected both to the daily local work and to the headquarters. In this case, very often, the MD necessarily has to 'own' all service functions – either doing HR and administration by himself or having dedicated staff, reporting to him or her on these areas.

At a large or mature lab, the 'local kingdom' of a lab MD is not necessary anymore, because the need to be aligned is more pressing than independence. It can be replaced by control from global organization units, but the MD needs to be the local top manager to coordinate the different activities and take care for their local implementation.

How SAP Labs India and Its Internal Services Are Managed

Labs India, since being a captive center, used to charge all costs created at the Labs back to SAP AG on an 'arms-length' basis (current costs plus fixed profit margin). The business units at Labs India as described before (for example, Global Services or Product Development) work as parts of the global units, so the Labs management does not interfere with the project plans and deliverables of different units.

Nevertheless, until 2004, it was a good practice, when meetings for the key development heads at SAP Labs India were held together with the LoBs and the Labs India management, and the general annual goals of the company business and its products were shared, too. In this way, a consistent application of policies could be achieved as well as reliable process benchmarking and management practice was possible. However, this had to be stopped in 2005. On the one hand, there was growing reluctance from the Lines of Business to involve Labs management in the process, and on the other hand, Labs management added less value, as the lab had become too big for them to be involved in detailed assessment of output requirements.

Instead, since then, Labs management has been involved on an escalation basis by the local LoB heads or their global heads, very often on HR or attrition issues, but also when teams needed to execute on specific growth or consolidation plans.

One important function of the Labs management and the local services is, of course, to provide a 'home'. The global LoBs tend to restrict their interaction with the employees on LoB goals and execution plans, it is more and more the Labs management's role to explain the global strategy, SAP's value system and business model to the employees.

Global Functions versus Local Responsibilities

For the first five to six years, the Labs India service departments, Human Resources (HR), IT-Services (ITS), Training, Finance & Accounting (F&A), Public Relations & Marketing, have been managed by the Labs India management. Whereas ITS as a typical cross service low-touch function, requiring intensive support from Global ITS, became part of Global ITS in 2003, other functions continued to report to the Labs India directors.

In most of the labs around the globe, the organizational structure appeared as shown in Fig. 10. As one can see from the chart, the overall control of all service functions in one specific location rested with the managing director (MD) of the lab. He or she was responsible to drive all the cross projects like creating a new facility, run local events or get the employer's branding into the top ranks in a specific country. This had both advantages and drawbacks:

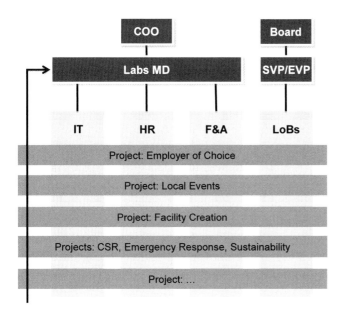

Fig. 10. Organizational structure of SAP Labs India and its service functions, during the initial years

Advantages

- Fast decision making process;
- Closeness of these functions to the 'customers' in the Labs, i.e. mainly the other business functions and the developer community;
- Strong sense of commitment to the Labs India goals;
- Sub-standard performance of local staff could be dealt with swiftly;
- High team spirit and positive interaction among the local service functions ('We are one team to build a great company').

Disadvantages

- Strong local focus – no consistent view what happens elsewhere;
- Only limited application of best practices;
- Inefficiencies in departments, due to the fact that needed capacity is built up locally, while it might be available somewhere else;
- Higher risks of opacity and failures to employ SOX compliance.

The disadvantages, however, never became so prominent, as the Labs India leadership always made the call on what additional competencies to build up locally and what competencies to request from the headquarters or other subsidiaries. Additionally, as it was in one of the world's most cost-efficient locations, the Labs' overhead has always been consistent and is a dependable asset.

Today, the situation has changed dramatically. Not only have all service departments become part of global business lines; all local department heads now report to colleagues who are *not* located in Bangalore. The local HR manager reports to the global HR function in Germany, the local facility manager reports to the global facility manager in Germany, the local training manger reports to a regional training manager in Shanghai, and so on. As said before, this requires very good networking and communication skills from the Labs management and the service function heads, as the alignments need to be achieved on multiple levels and in different directions.

In the new structure (Fig. 11), the MD of a lab is still responsible for the different cross projects, but now he has to align with local service functions on a 'goodwill' basis, which means forming cross-project teams out without formal authorization.

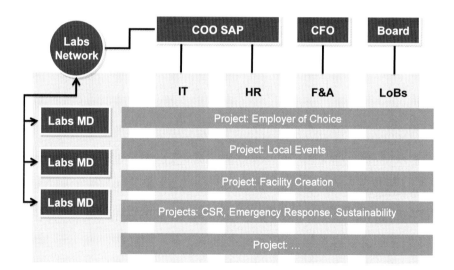

Fig. 11. Organizational structure of SAP Labs India and its service functions, today

The Labs' MDs did of course challenge this structure with the following arguments:

1. The local Labs management is responsible for cost control, attrition control, running the infrastructure, and both maintaining and promoting the Labs as a top employer in the Indian talent market. Without any formal power or lever to make the departments work appropriately, with regard to the Labs management's goals, this is a very challenging task. This kind of model needs a lot of goodwill from the local department heads to cooperate among each other and with the managing directors (MDs). And it builds to a large extent on the networking skills of the MDs, as they need to influence many stakeholders abroad to make things move in the right direction (or the direction they perceive to be right).

2. The decision making naturally becomes the slower, the more people are involved. Very often the local service colleagues may feel insecure about making decisions, ultimately choosing to defer to their German manager – and another day is lost. Here it is important to have a precise service catalogue established, defining which decisions made locally and which could be a global affair. Only then, this environment can work at a speed that is still fast enough to keep a location like Labs India moving. Management should avoid allowing too many issues to become mired in frustrating stages of discussion. This would not only be inefficient, but could give the impression that those discussions do not add any value to the final decision.

3. The local managers can easily 'escape' a real assessment of their performance. It has been commonly observed in engineering departments that external/remote supervisors tend to 'pamper' their subordinates and to give them excellent ratings without any knowledge of they are really doing. This is exactly the opposite of what SAP Labs wants to achieve as an organization with high standards for performance. In locally managed areas, there is usually a 70/30 split of ratings like 'meets expectations' and 'exceeds expectations'. Interestingly, this does not hold true in areas where people are managed from outside – in this context, a ratio of 100% 'exceeds expectations' is usually reached.

   Therefore, it is important that for functions like HR, Training or Finance, a second local assessment line is formally established – in order to give input as well on the local level. This is absolutely crucial; otherwise 'happy mediocrity' will sooner or later kick in.

Those who like to perform and get feedback and rewards for their exceptional performance will be frustrated and leave; whereas those who under-perform will find a cozy place to survive, as their boss is 5,000 miles or more away.

4. It is most important to keep a sense of teamwork among local departments despite those global silos, which do not plan / provide for incentives in that field. This can only be done by the MD or president of the company, as one cannot really expect that the global head of Knowledge Production Services, of HR, IT and Facilities get together for one hour in Walldorf to discuss the structure of future events in India, where all these services are required to work seamlessly together.

In such environment the Labs' MDs must be careful not to end up running a machine that keeps raising escalations or keeps accepting mediocrity. Actually, in neither of these situations can the MD actually steer the organization in the direction that he or she believes is right, if he or she lacks the tools (e.g. direct top management access) or the right contacts (knowing a few global stakeholders really well).

On the other hand, the local service head (like the VP HR India or the CFO India) may find it better to be part of a really global team, since this opens additional (HR specific) learning opportunities and new career perspectives. So not all local service heads are unhappy to report to someone outside the country.

As the Labs network ventured into 2009, the global structure was established for all support functions. It is now up to those global and regional stakeholders to make it working together. For a final assessment on the success or non-success of this restructuring, it is too early to tell.

Lessons Learned

In any captive center, the success is based mostly on the hands-on involvement of local management. How much control is given to the local management besides the global departments, is a key question to be carefully evaluated. The main factors to consider include the overall complexity of the global set-up, the established trust level, the local onsite capabilities, and the size of the local organization.

Shared Services as a Part of Labs Operating Environment

Shared services are a positive development, if implemented appropriately and quickly; many global companies have already proven this fact.

A good example of an excellent shared service organization at SAP is its 'Global IT'. Global IT found the right balance between keeping local accountability and importing global expert support from other locations like Singapore or Germany. It was implemented in such a way as to enable some local colleagues in India to advance due to the additional responsibilities they received in this shared service environment. For example, rolling out IT initiatives and products in the Asia-Pacific region. Additionally, this kept the costs at a minimum, as the services are provided from the most cost-efficient location. During the change from the local model to the shared service model, not a single IT employee left Labs India.

The HR shared service operation was put up in Singapore, and all execution power in the areas of mobility, recruiting, and training operations were concentrated there. At the same time, those functions were stripped off their responsibilities in India. However, the shared service center still has people locally in India, while the different heads for the different HR service lines are all located either in Singapore, China or Australia. The local Labs HR manager is no longer accountable for the hiring process and its execution – it is now handled by specialists from abroad, who come two to three times per year to oversee what is happening.

The implementation of the HR shared services was not easy for Labs India. First of all, there had always been strong resistance in the management and among the employees to accept services delivered from Singapore or Shanghai. Initially, the added value of this model was not transparent at all – it was merely seen as expensive overhead caused by the very limited knowledge of local needs. The shared service structure was tried for the first time in 2004 when the former HR head of Labs India, Bhuvaneshvar Naik, came back from one and a half years at the global HR headquarters. He got the job and budget to establish a new shared service center for Asia Pacific, but he became stuck with the different regional and local Indian stakeholders, and he finally left the company.

A second try was initiated in 2006, when the joint managing director of Labs India, Martin Prinz, left for Singapore to run the HR services from there.

Knowing India, he did not apply a bulldozer method, but offered his group's services based on clear Service Level Agreements (SLAs) to Labs India. Today, services like HR Direct (a hotline for employees), mobility, and recruiting are delivered from that shared service center, either via employees working from there or local employees in India, belonging to the center. Of course, such a model has many benefits, and better and faster service should be priority one when establishing such a shared service center. If employees feel that everything goes slower or is getting more complicated than before, the concept will immediately lose its credibility – which will be very hard to regain.

The operating environment with so many different reporting and controlling lines outside the Labs has both – challenges and opportunities for the colleagues working in these areas. A challenge is certainly that groups and teams become segregated. Let us take Training / HR as an example: in most companies, there would be one team, with different career path options for colleagues to pursue, including lateral moves or rotational assignments. These increase job satisfaction and exposure, but if this team is now distributed into Training Center of Excellence (CoE), Knowledge Production Services, Global Mobility, HR Business Partner Organization, Recruiting Services, Payroll, HR Direct and HR Operations – it will become challenging for the colleagues to realize their personal career path. And it will become challenging for SAP Labs employees to know whom to talk to for a particular issue they might have. In addition to that, the new shared service model has led to high attrition in HR and training functions; many could not find themselves in suitable positions after the change.

On the positive side, one has to acknowledge that in some areas, the service has certainly improved. It is definitely better for colleagues to call one central number, if they need support, than having to figure out whom to talk to in HR and then trying to get into a working relationship with that person. And for the colleagues working in service functions, there are of course many more learning opportunities, as their exposure to international colleagues and practices becomes much stronger. However, this requires the right employees to make use of those opportunities – not everyone has the attitude or skills to use these chances in a positive way and to really add value.

4.7 Key Challenges of the Operating Environment

In summary, the Labs' operating environment has changed dramatically in 2007 and 2008, due to the globalization of practically all service functions at SAP, like HR, Training, Finance or IT-Services:

- Labs' Management faces new communication and networking challenges, due to the trend that global departments (HR, Finance, Facilities, IT) influence many processes at the Labs that still need to be aligned locally.

- Most processes have changed, as the decision power with regard to staff and budget is now located outside of India. This made it extremely relevant to manage cross departments and functions without formal authority, but with convincing arguments.

- Global shared services are here to stay, as they have been implemented, to eliminate the need for every location to have these services functions. After having delivered mixed results initially, in terms of implementation speed, costs, and quality of output, they were perceived mostly positively in 2008.

- The global service organization and the product development organizations receive very different requirements from SAP Labs India, and it is becoming increasingly difficult to fulfill these requirements with a 'one-size-fits-all' approach.

- India is a rapidly and constantly changing environment. This situation requires very flexible local measures and empowerment to make and execute decisions quickly.

- In order to sustain high performance within the organization, SAP Labs needs to attract outstanding talent, not only in its engineering departments, but also in the Labs' service functions. A completely globalized structure bears the risk of not acting appropriately in the tight Indian talent market where top people have many other job options.

- Any company needs to find and develop a framework or organizational set-up that allows a wider spread of local policies and procedures in order to get closer to what the internal customers really want.

- On all levels, SAP Labs is still absorbing the 100 % growth over the last two years and the change from a local operation to a part of a globally integrated unit. Managers on all sides have to learn how to operate in this environment. Many new relationships have been established, either via new assignments or via new reporting lines. Those are to be strengthened, and the necessary trust level has to build up.

- Even though reporting lines have changed, the core task of the Labs' management still is to align local service departments in order to guarantee smooth execution and best-in-class processes. Through Six Sigma projects in the past, many bottlenecks have been removed successfully.

The factors which led to the fast initial success of SAP Labs India, for example a high motivation to deal with the typical growth challenges of a young organization, the will to build trust and to learn in a global environment, and a motivated management and staff have become less relevant in today's situation.

SAP has taken bold steps in bringing local managers of all levels into global reporting lines. Even though some departments may have confused globalization with tight control from the headquarters, there is no way back. Today, the operating environment on the local level is very complex. Highly skilled managers are needed to understand this complexity and to deliver good results. It is to be expected that not everyone is made to work in such environment – SAP Labs India sees this when new hires leave soon after their appointment, or do not accept offers to on-board, as the applicants feel insecure working in a long distance relationship with their boss.

Today, too many people still need their boss to pass by every day; otherwise they may not feel recognized or, even worse, would not see a reason to work at all. These cannot be the people one wants to employ in a global company. On the other hand, the ones who understand the environment and are able to operate in it without any problems, are a really rare breed – and difficult to find. This will be a major challenge for SAP Labs India: to find the right people and to get them into the right jobs – employees and managers who know where to draw the line; where to accept accountability and where to feel empowered to make decisions; people who do not hide behind some authority abroad but who are real team workers regardless whether the team members are local or from a foreign organization, country, or culture.

Another point is that global functions also offer global opportunities for colleagues on all levels. This includes transfers to other locations, but more important, it provides opportunities. For example, a local Indian HR manager could work on a global talent management program for all 50.000 employees of SAP.

With its consistently global structure and restructuring, the company is definitely on the right track, but since (many) people are involved, this journey will take some time.

At the same time, SAP needs carefully implement globalization in the right manner: as a multilevel, give-and-take collaboration, based on mutual trust and shared responsibility, not as a micro-managing behemoth that clumsily and inefficiently controls its global operations.

4.8   How SAP Operates Product Development from Labs India

Product development is all about engineering on existing and future products and solutions. Initially, only smaller parts and projects were delivered from SAP Labs India under very close guidance of senior colleagues from Germany or other locations. However, as the Labs grew, trust also grew with its capabilities, and larger projects were delivered by it. Today, major solution and product decisions are made elsewhere, for example, in Germany or Palo Alto, whereas the execution responsibility for complete solutions (such as for many industry solutions or for ByDesign) is given to India.

The delivery model has emerged from the initial close guidance model to really independent, decentralized development. The quality standards and the delivery time are the same, taking into consideration the much younger engineering staff.

The core product development units have very specific requirements when it comes to their engineering capabilities. First of all, they are much more concerned about stability than service teams usually are, as it takes some years for an employee to become fully productive in product development. Consequentially, those departments monitor attrition very closely. They want to keep their engineers challenged and happy, so they must usually spend a reasonable amount of time in thinking about what pieces to build in India and how to distribute the work in a fair manner between India and other locations. Third, a strong innovative spirit is necessary for product development teams, since very often, they are facing challenges on the technological side, which require some creativity to solve. And finally, they want the job to be executed, so they are always looking for managers who are excellent in project execution and who are good leaders for their teams.

Looking at these challenges, it is clear that the requirements from these units are quite special compared to other departments. It is obvious that the baseline is flawless, which mainly means the work of HR, Training, ITS and Facilities / Administration. On the other hand, cost does not play the same predominant role as in the services, since the Key Performance Indicators (KPIs) of these units are different. They are generally measured in terms of product delivery (time, quality, and scope) rather than in terms of cost. So more often than not these units demand greater monetary expenditures on people than other departments that cannot do without harsh cost cutting control measures. In this area, attrition control is the key!

At the same time, they expect that Labs India creates an operating environment that fosters innovation, and that actually enables people to be creative. This requires space, excellent IT and recreation policies, and facilities that match international standards.

With respect to talent in the field of engineering, SAP Labs India competes much less with external vendors in India, than with opportunities abroad, be it within SAP (Labs Palo Alto and SAP AG in Walldorf are the preferred locations) or outside SAP.

In terms of getting attractive projects, for most of the projects executed at SAP Labs India, there are no external vendors who would be able to handle them. Thus, they are done in-house. Of course, Labs India has to compete with other SAP labs, namely in Eastern Europe, Canada, and China.

Excursus: How SAP Manages Global Services from Labs India

Many of the SAP labs around the globe do not only develop software products, but also maintain those products. This maintenance is either the result of additional testing or is requested by customers who discover inconsistencies or even bugs. So servicing software does very often include hands-on coding, which requires business and analytical skills. All those customer centric activities are bundled together in SAP's service organization.

SAP's business model relies heavily on the delivery of fast, reliable and dedicated services to its customers. They are a backbone of its annual revenue, and their share is rising constantly.

Labs India has always been a major hub of the SAP's global service organization. Currently, close to 1,100 people in Bangalore are working in this area.

The KPIs for these units are rather simple, mostly relying on closed customer queries and requests, customer satisfaction and feedback and number of problems solved. Therefore, the nature of the job comprises a good customer touch, a strong commitment to delivery, high execution capabilities and of course, the principle agreement on work that is challenging, but may not represent the cutting edge of technology.

From an organizational standpoint, SAP Labs India measures global services in terms of timely output and cost. Overall, this is about the bottom line. Therefore, it is understandable that managers of the global service organization are always very keen to understand cost projections, the impact of attrition on the output and cost, and movement in the job market. Accordingly, they assign (or do not assign) jobs to Labs India. Their expectations from the Labs India management are clearly to keep the cost under control, to support them with specific incentive systems (which differ from the product development departments), to provide the necessary environment, such as infrastructure or ITS, for a flawless execution, and to bring colleagues aboard. They wish to have 'peace of mind' regarding such points.

In the end, the service units at SAP Labs India compete with other, external IT service vendors in India, in terms of delivery and cost – so the direct competitors are companies like Wipro or Infosys. This is important to understand, because those companies usually have a lower cost structure than a captive center of a multinational company. Even after adding their profit margin, they might charge lower project costs than SAP would have to spend, if the same work was done in-house at Labs India. In 2008, some IT service companies were offering trained SAP ABAP programmers to Labs for the cost of just 80 Euros per day! Therefore, SAP constantly evaluates which projects might be better and more effectively outsourced to another company and which ones are needed to be kept in-house.

From an organizational perspective, the product maintenance departments (Global Service teams) are organized similarly to the core product development. Thus, in the following chapter, we will describe the organizational set-up of product development and services at SAP Labs India. To make this easier to read, please note that wherever we write 'product', we mean 'products and services', as the structures are the same.

Lessons Learned

Running distinct different units like Product Development and Professional Services in one organization is only possible, if the policy framework is flexible enough. Innovation and effectiveness are not naturally exclusive and both areas can learn a lot from each other. To keep the organizational walls open and to encourage transfers, has helped SAP Labs India a lot to retain the 'One SAP Lab' feeling.

4.9   Product Development Organization at SAP Labs India

Labs View of Development Organization

In the sections before, we have described the global service functions of the lab and the key challenges of the Labs managing director to make the lab function as a unit.

Towards the product development, such as with the Lines of Business (LoBs), the Labs management has a clear mission – support them so they can operate smoothly. The LoBs have to run a business – and the local labs management has to provide a well-working environment for it. The related service levels are scaled up or down depending on the development activities currently happening at the Labs. The development manager in the Labs, for example, Senior Vice Presidents (SVP), Vice Presidents (VP) or Developing Managers (DM), coordinate their needs and forecast with the lab director. Typically, they would discuss recruitment needs, their growth plan (space constraints), their need to house third party developers or specific training needs. The lab director and the service teams now act in a customer-supplier relationship, trying to meet the demands of the different development teams.

Of course, this coordination cannot always happen free of conflict, as the requests are usually urgent, while the response is often perceived to be too

slow. So it is always a matter of negotiation, agreement, and then fulfill-
ment of such agreements that forms the basis for the relationship between
the development management and the Labs management. It is the responsibility of the lab director to ensure a smooth functioning of the location, so
that different Lines of Business can execute their development tasks and
meet the overall organization goals. Besides this support, Labs management
has two important governance roles to play: to ensure legal compliance, and
to manage compensation according to the local market conditions.

Compliance Adherence

The lab director has to make sure that the different Lines of Business ad-
here to the relevant legal and corporate policies. So the Labs management
has to manage the balancing act of being, on the one hand, the supplier of
the development teams, having to keep its customers happy, and on the
other hand, 'policing' the Lab, which governs the local norms, laws, and
guidelines. Terminations because of violations of the code of conduct are,
for example, usually triggered by the Labs management.

Compensation

The compensation and benefits offered by the Labs are a very local matter,
in which the labs management plays an important role. The compensation
is administered by the Labs in close association with the Lines of Business.
It is the responsibility of the Labs management to ensure equality in terms
of compensation across the different lines. In a country like India where
the inflation is high, the annual salary increases are mostly in the double
digits. As the professional environment is highly competitive, salary increases can become a contentious point. Employees discuss their salary re-
visions most often with their peers and even decide to quit if they are not
satisfied. Hence, it is important to reward good performance and also to
ensure fairness as perceived by the employees.

The Role of the Line of Business and Services

At the top of SAP AG's organizational structure, the executive board
members used to take responsibility for broad product areas, application areas, industry solutions, and country versions. Further, these broad product
responsibilities were subdivided into main product areas which are assigned

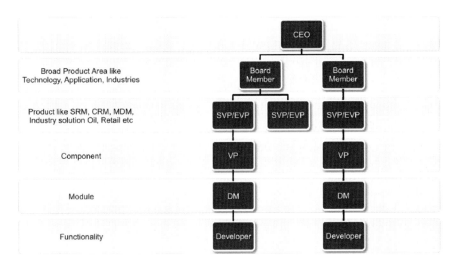

Fig. 12. Organizational structure of product development at SAP AG

to Senior Vice Presidents (SVP) or Executive Vice Presidents (EVP). Each of them is supported by Vice Presidents (VP), Developing Managers (DM) and Developers.

In 2009, all product development was assigned to one board member, Jim Snabe. He named this unit 'Business Solutions & Technology', which included all core products (like ERP, CRM), industry solutions, and the technology offers (like SAP NetWeaver). The global service organization was assigned to the board area of Gerd Oswald.

The **LoBs** have the total responsibility for research, development, and support of their respective product areas as for example CRM or SCM. Their role is quite important from the product development point of view, as they define the product strategy and the roadmap of their respective product areas. On the whole, they are responsible for product planning and execution as per their commitment to SAP's 'Strategic Business Plan', since the on-time release of innovative solutions is of paramount importance for meeting business goals. They need to come up with innovative new products and also maintain existing products within budget constraints.

On the organizational side, the LoBs usually decide where they build up their teams (of course within the given budget) and which location gets which part of the solution to build. This distribution is a very important part of their role, as the design of the distributed network within their own area of control will trigger the main cost and efficiency gains they are able to achieve – or the other way around: if the network is not well aligned, they might run into tremendous challenges to keep the organization going for the same goals and to execute their projects consistently according to plan.

Usually, the LoBs divide their product responsibilities into subareas or components, and they assign them together with related resources to Vice Presidents under them. Accordingly, it is the responsibility of the **Vice Presidents** to cooperate with their peers ensuring the final delivery of the product. Their responsibility is further divided and assigned to the **Development Managers**, who are responsible for smaller development areas or modules and for the guidance of the developers in their teams. **Developers** have highly empowered roles within the product development organization. Their work can range from an isolated functionality, which is only used in one particular module of the product, to a very complex functionality, which is heavily dependent on several other components within the product. At times, there are also instances in which the component dependencies span across multiple products. The words of Henning Kagermann help to concisely summarize the role of developers at SAP. In a shareholders' meeting in Mannheim in 2006, he said: "SAP needs employees who can combine both technical and business know-how with the right portion of creativity and ability to innovate, but also with an understanding of what can be executed."

The Local Branch of the Line of Business Development Organization

Today, it is more the rule than the exception that product development groups work with distributed teams or resources across the globe. Sometimes, the network of groups is designed in order to be close to certain key knowledge holders, to important customers or to specific teams one needs to collaborate with. But very often, the distribution is also a consequence of reorganizations, mergers, break-ups of teams, or cost considerations during the expansion phase of a group.

The distribution of work within a specific LoB requires special consideration of processes and organizational aspects, as the people need to work efficiently across different locations, time zones and cultures. The LoB heads take responsibility for allocating individual focuses and tasks to different locations and for ensuring the quality of the end product. Tasks are distributed

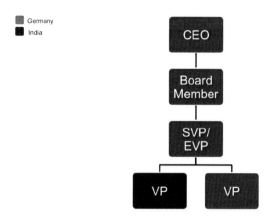

Fig. 13. Location view of the organization structure at SAP AG

with a long term perspective on developing specialized skills in their re-spective locations. Additionally, LoB management has to make sure that, regardless of the specific location, the global SAP processes, quality guide-lines and standards are followed within all units. The development process, the practices and the policies of the involved development locations also help to guarantee the quality of the product, because in the end, the cus-tomer only cares about the final result and does not bother too much where the product has been produced.

However, things become a little more tricky, when it comes to people re-lated policies and standards: on the one hand, LoB management should be aware of local policies and practices with respect to the handling of people. The labor laws and regulations might also vary depending on the geo-graphical location from which the employees are operating. Therefore, the hiring and promotion rules are normally defined by the individual SAP Labs organization. On the other hand, SAP also has global HR policies, like talent management, standardized training, distribution of stock options or employee surveys, which need to be administered on a global level.

A well designed organization is required to have enough reach into every team around the globe to execute the global processes, but at the same time to have a local management that the SVP can trust without having to famil-iarize with all the details of local norms.

A typical example for this complexity is the appearance of a sudden emer-gency situation that requires a significant part of the organization to work for one or more weekends in order to meet a critical deadline. In India, consistent information to the affected colleagues would be enough, including information on why overtime is required. In the end, it is up to the local management to demand overtime for colleagues. However, in Germany, an approval by the Workers Council is needed, which requires a certain minimum lead time and, of course, bears the risk of not being approved, in case the council is not sufficiently satisfied with the reasoning. These kind of implications need to be thought through, if the responsible manager is located in the U.S., but his teams are working in Germany and India.

Another example is the predictable stability of a group. In the U.S. or in India, developers can resign within 1–3 months of notice, depending on their contract. In Germany, this period is 6–12 months. So the situation of having vacancies is a regular problem to be managed in India for any manager, because usually, the resigning colleague has left before a replacement could be hired. In Germany, however, the replacement is very often already in place before the other colleague finally leaves.

Regional festival seasons also play a role that needs to be factored with a long lead time. One cannot count on 100% attendance during Christmas in the U.S. or in Germany, during Diwali in India, or during the Spring Festival in China. This fact is often forgotten and then the shock hits, when an SVP all of a sudden discovers that next week, only half of his capacity will be on duty. This kind of awareness is needed in a global context – in order to plan realistically and to not demand impossible things at the wrong time.

The Evolving Organizational Structure at Labs India

Typically, the development organization of SAP Labs India has evolved over the years according to the subject knowledge and the size of its teams. As the teams matured in terms of development expertise and networking they started becoming increasingly independent. Labs India took a pragmatic view of this evolvement and fine-tuned the organization. The structure of the development team at Labs India went through three distinct stages:

The Startup Structure

From 1999 to 2002, the headcount of Labs India increased to 506, and the teams focused mainly on the areas of localization, industry business units, CRM, and tools development. The team sizes varied from 15 to 30 and followed a typical start-up organizational structure. At least for the first four

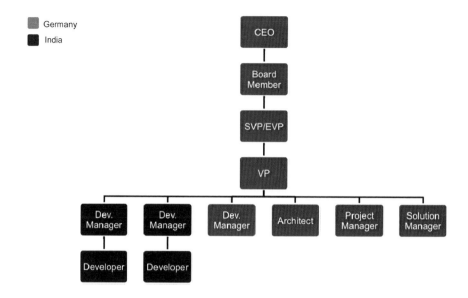

Fig. 14. The startup structure of development organization at SAP Labs

years after the inception of the Labs, no VPs or SVPs were established in the development organization of the Labs in India, and it was extremely difficult to coordinate with the variety of stakeholders to ensure a healthy growth of the location. On the one hand, it was required to hold the hands of the young Development Managers (DMs) to execute tasks with the right focus, but, on the other hand, it was also important to engage the whole ecosystem to ensure the long-term survival of the Labs. During these days, managers were allocated a budget and responsibility for realizing the requirements a functional module together with their small teams. Usually, people management and project management were all on one side. The local development managers only reported to Vice Presidents in Germany or Palo Alto. The main challenges for the development managers were hiring new team members, aligning them with the overall product development goals, and then delivering the assigned topic and functionality. The small team sizes involved typical start-up advantages: the team members were enthusiastic, and they came up with innovative technical solutions to complex business problems. They took the opportunity to enhance their functional knowledge, to learn to deal with the complex challenges of product development and to get familiar with SAP's product development process.

Since the experience of the team members was low – and SAP mainly hired people without prior experience in SAP technologies and products – these team members needed broad guidance and coaching from senior colleagues: solution managers defined the requirements, senior architects contributed high level architecture proposals, and the project managers came with detailed project plans that kept in mind the overall master plan and ensured alignment between related project plans. During this period, the development managers were mainly involved in breaking down the work packages into detailed tasks and activities. They would then assign those tasks to the appropriate individuals and ensure the quality of the delivery. This period typically lasted one or two years, depending on the complexity of the area. Once the team became experienced and knowledgeable in a product area, they were seen as mature and ready to move to the next organizational stage.

At the beginning of the SAP Labs operations, the Indian team strongly depended on expertise coming from Germany or the U.S., and it was always getting instructions or task descriptions. One of the main reasons for this close guidance was the lack of functional knowledge. While the Indian technical graduates and employees are quick to learn new technologies, they usually enter the workforce without any prior working experience in any other industry. Hence, most of the developers have never seen a manufacturing facility, sales office, or a finance department in their professional lives. Therefore, SAP devised several methods to train its new employees, starting from giving sessions about industries on video, to customer visits to help them understand the 'real life' challenges faced by the end users.

Additionally, development managers at SAP Labs India participated in several other activities. For example, it was made mandatory for the Labs' managers to participate in hiring activities, conduct road shows to popularize Labs India, organize developer-to-customer programs, execute programs reviewing SAP's quality management, arrange programs for inducting new employees into the company, write job descriptions, define policies, carry out audits reviewing teams, and to spread best practices across the teams.

A special program during those days was the so-called 'Team Info Days', during which, week by week, different teams would build stalls in the cafeteria and present what they were doing – to help other employees across the lab to better understand the big picture. It is notable that in those years, most things worked across the Lines of Business, and nobody behaved as if they were isolated. As the LoBs in India were all in the same situation, facing the same challenges, the willingness to support each other was much higher than in more advanced organizational stages. More often than not, mature LoBs only look upwards to get guidance and restrict support to only their own teams and members. However, looking back, this was certainly matter of size, since, until the Labs crossed the 500 employee mark, all 25 – 30 development managers knew each other, and there was a strong bond among many of them. Ramesh B.G., a development manager at that time recalls: "The flat organizational structure of that time helped us tremendously. Most of us managers were reporting to executives in Wall-dorf, who directly reported to SAP's Board. At Labs India we knew each other very well and the sense of teamwork across the Lab was never as strong as then."

At SAP Labs India, the developers were young, and in most cases, they were good technical or functional experts, but, due to the organizational circumstances and peer pressure, they were also forced to aim for a position as development manager. They were new to product development, project management, distributed development, and to SAP technologies and products. Hence, this form of 'guided organization structure' helped them to learn more from their colleagues in other locations. It also gave them the opportunity to manage the expectations of young software engineers. Overall, one can say that one of the biggest challenges was the transition from the first stage of the organizational structure to the next stage; if this transition was not successful, the team would become a big burden for the remote location that provided the architects, solution managers, and project managers.

Lessons Learned

A flat two-level hierarchy delivers excellent results locally, if there is strong senior management guidance from abroad. For a company size up to 300 – 400 employees, this structure is ideal, if the teams use the small size of the company productively, and substitute high levels of energy and willingness to collaborate for experience.

The Growing Structure: Project-Based Organization

Between 2003 and 2006, the headcount of Labs India increased from 748 to 3,230; the organizational climate was triggered by two main organizational changes initiated at the global level under a project code-named SCORE (Strategic Cross Organizational Realignment). The first change was the formal split of development into Installed Based Development (IBD) and New Application Development (NAD) in September 2003. The second was implementation of a project based organization in early 2004. Prior to these reorganizations, development teams or even individual developers at SAP had managed both installed based development (maintenance support of already released products) and development of new applications (products that were still in the R&D stage and not yet released to the market).

When both IBD and NAD were done by the same teams, there was, in most of the cases, no clear internal decision on how much effort should be spent on support. This situation did not allow for the resource optimization needed for support activities. In addition, it often happened that teams were working day and night to solve customer messages and to work on bug fixes, so they had never the time to work uninterrupted on new concepts and functionalities. This, of course, was felt as a disadvantage for turning innovations into products. And finally, even though having the same person do software maintenance and new development, has some advantages (for example, get closer to the real customer needs, fix the problems one has created oneself, and prevent them in newer releases), it also involved less than optimal assignment of talent as there are individuals who excel at the customer's site and others who could do great things in new concepts and developments. Putting too much work on people that they do not like would be a waste of their talent.

Later, when SAP brought together all the development support colleagues in one team, the overall efficiency was increased significantly, because product support synergies were created. During this period, SAP Labs also got its first Vice President in the area of industry solution development, Jayaram Srinivasan.

After the split of the development teams into IBD and NAD, NAD was redesigned as a project organization. Prior to the reorganization, development managers had taken care of both people and product areas under their responsibility. This had restricted SAP from juggling the portfolio and moving people across projects. The new project based organization forced the development organization to split responsibilities into development management and project management. The development managers focused on the competency development of their people, mainly developing their abilities and skills to execute. The project management colleagues focused on the execution of projects as per the product development master plan. This way, team members always had a home team that provided the stability of one development manager; they used their home for competency development in areas like mobile technology and demand planning. The projects were transient in nature, and the project managers used resources from different competency areas to execute their projects. This provided maximum flexibility for the development organization to mix and match the resources based on the crucial requirements of the projects.

Ramesh B.G., Development VP, adds: "Not everyone liked the split between project responsibility and people responsibility. Though it was not executed in the same manner in all lines of business, many managers had to do a call deciding on either way. The problem in India was that the development manager, who had the people responsibility, was seen as the more 'glamorous' job, with respect to title and responsibility. Therefore some of our best managers, who were excellent in handling projects, chose to become pure people managers – it took them some while to realize, that by the end of the day that was not what they wanted. In the end, some of them swapped their roles back to Product Management (PM)."

As this was a period of rapid growth at Labs India, the project based organization supported growth by banking on the functional, architectural and

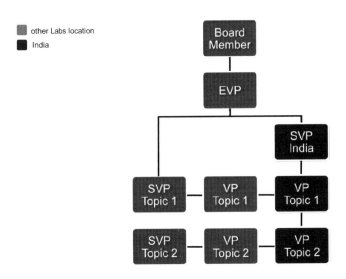

Fig. 15. The project structure of development organization at SAP Labs

project management skills of the experienced German team. This enabled the vice presidents and senior managers to contribute on a much higher level and to deliver on a much larger scale. Through its new organizational structure, Labs India could increase the breadth of its operations, and benefits arose from the larger development teams. The development teams witnessed several large scale innovations during this period, which accelerated their learning and contribution from India.

Of course, the typical matrix problems appeared, the 'battle' for resources among development managers and project managers, but with all of them reporting to the same VP, this problem was solved to a certain extent.

Lessons Learned

In an environment of strong growth, it is important to establish more roles, like project management, people management, and technical management. This creates growth opportunities for the individuals along with organizational growth.

Furthermore, the establishment of a matrix organization along with the split of the teams into customer facing groups and core development groups has been proven to be successful. This structure offers flexibility for companies to strike a balance between local freedom and global standardization.

The Grown-up Structure

Finally, from 2006 to 2008, the headcount of Labs India increased from 3,230 to 4,073, as the teams were already operating on a large scale, the annual growth rate slowed down year by year. On average, SAP Labs India grew by only 10% p.a. in those three years, despite acquisitions. The location in India became more mature and self-sufficient in terms of knowledge, and it reached a stage where four SVPs and more than 30 VPs were working in development in India.

During this particular period, Labs India had large development groups with knowledge in SAP NetWeaver, in the areas of the Business Process Platform (BPP), mid-market solutions, and large enterprise solutions, such

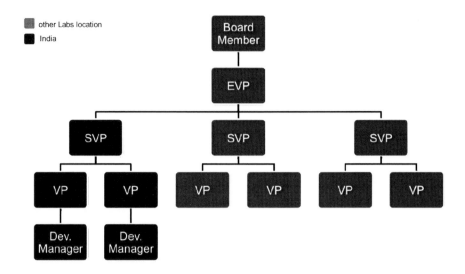

Fig. 16. The grown-up structure of people organization at SAP Labs

as the business suite and industry solutions. Another large team provided mission critical development support to several customers around the world. There were also teams with knowledge about system landscape and build, as well as pre-sales demo development activities. This provided an ideal ecosystem for Labs to execute projects on a truly global scale.

In mature areas, the organizational structure in India is now similar to the structure in other locations. The knowledge and expertise in Labs India is at a high level, and its development teams collaborate across teams and locations as equal partners.

Many development teams at Labs India now have their own product management, project management, and architectural capabilities, and they work independently on business cases approved by senior management. According to these, the project teams provide several proposals on an ongoing basis. The teams in India have developed comprehensive expertise across all lifecycle stages of their projects. Accordingly, development teams in other Labs locations also became increasingly comfortable with the distributed development process which progressively became a way of life. There were several developers, managers, and vice presidents with long time experience, and this helped them to tap into SAP's informal global network. Indian teams now started to actively participate in collaborative product planning exercises and executed projects together with other locations on a global scale. During this period, SAP Labs India also developed deep expertise in working alongside contract workers from leading Indian software vendors like Wipro and TCS. On average, there were about 1,000 contract employees, working along with 4,000 permanently employed developers at Labs India. As Georg Kniese, former managing director of SAP Labs, recalls: "At the end of 2004 we had about 150 to 200 contract employees out of our total strength of 1,300. At the end of 2007 we had more than 1,300 contractors out of overall 4,300 people. We trippled the labs strength over those three years, but to manage the fast growth effectively we increased the share of contractors over proportionally. While scaling up, we managed to improve our overall process stability and quality, and that is the real accomplishment."

Development teams in India used third party resource capacity to effectively orchestrate development, on the one hand, and to increase the scale on the other hand. This further enhanced the flexibility of the product areas and took the overall efficiency to a higher level.

Starting from the 4th quarter of 2008, SAP felt the global impact of the economic crisis across nearly all sectors of business. In order to reduce variable costs as fast as possible, many of the contracts of many IT service providers were not extended further into 2009. This brought the number of contractors down by 50 % and proved that it was right to use this workforce as a balancing factor for peak times.

Lessons Learned

In a state of slow or zero growth, it is important to have a critical mass, as smaller organizations may not be able to survive due to missing perspective of the individual employees.

With more than 4,000 employees in 2009, SAP Labs India could establish structures from the 'fresher' up to the Senior Vice President and could get responsibilities coming to India along with these structures. This enriches the job opportunities of everybody.

Very small R&D hubs would be rather hard to sustain, if there is no growth opportunity for the organization and the individuals.

4.10 Factors Influencing the Organizational Structure

Besides the maturity stage, there are some equally important factors that have influenced the organizational structure of SAP Labs India:

1. The most influential factor is the question of what to develop and where to develop, as committed in the Strategic Business Plan (SBP), which is derived from SAP's Strategy 2010. It defines the core investment areas of SAP for now and the future, for example areas like Business User Applications, the small and mid-size market products or the Business Process Platform. Besides this, it defines the fields in which SAP wants to remain the global number one software vendor, such as CRM, SCM, SRM, or in its Industry solutions. As a result of the SBP, the product portfolio of SAP is planned and the needed capacity is aligned according to the budget plans.

   An important step in this process is the question, how and where a product should be developed. This is mostly decided based on the availability of skills and the necessary ecosystem requirements like partners, research institutions, and first pilot customers for executing the strategy. But, of course, cost does matter as well. So depending on the business plan, there might be as well a more general condition that the development should happen in one of the locations, where the costs per developer are below a certain threshold.

   Solution managers at SAP Labs come up with high-level design and boundary conditions of the product. These high level requirements are created along with architects who provide key input in terms of the technology innovations that can be productized. To develop skills and to translate the same to value, developers at SAP Labs need focus and investment. The focus helps to decide on topics like SOA and Business Process Platform, while investment comes by committing resources for a specific period of time. Of course, not in all development areas, the solution management, the architects and the project managers are co-located in the same Lab.

2. The focus of the Lab matters. As it takes very long to build up necessary skills, Lines of Business usually look for teams that can be used as the nucleus for their next project. Results from newly established development teams may not be evident after one or two quarters, and at times it will take one or more years for them to deliver

high quality software. Consequently, it is important to develop a focus for each lab and to align the focus of specific development teams with the lab's center of expertise. This is an ongoing process, because in times of strong growth the scale matters more than the focus.

3. The overall location strategy in a Line of Business plays an important role. It is of paramount importance to define the overall location strategy before getting into the details of an organizational structure. Therefore, the organizational structure should never be decided with regard to one sole location; the global strategy should rather be taken into consideration. For instance, for a successful Indian location, it is necessary to have an enabling structure in Germany and the other way around. Nevertheless, the structure should also provide opportunities to the workforce to engage in assignments that help them to achieve their personal goals. Hence, it is important to work on synchronizing organizational goals with the goals and aspirations of the workforce. Another important point is SAP's global location strategy for its labs, which might be different from the one a specific Line of Business wants to pursue. Whereas each LoB would try to optimize its own productivity across the globe, the cumulative impact on their location strategies could lead to a scenario at a specific location (like India) in which the demand for growth and infrastructure could not be fulfilled. Or a lab could even be jeopardized, if some LoBs decide, at the same time, to withdraw from that location.

4. It is very important to ensure a fair distribution of tasks across the locations. Most of developers dream of working at the cutting edge of technology. It is also a natural aim for team members to prefer working in highly visible projects that are of interest to the top management, in projects with the most important customers and in areas of strategic relevance for the enterprise. And developers are always curious to move into assignments in which many top talents are engaged, as these projects are always perceived as the area that provides maximum opportunity to learn and grow. Therefore, tasks should be assigned to locations in a way that developers get to share both volume and value tasks. Volume tasks are those that are required for the enterprise to deliver its products, and value tasks are those that provide opportunities for acquiring rare skills, which are of high demand within the organization and in the market.

5. Cost considerations also influenced the choice of the development location in India. The headcount should be acquired and tasks should be distributed depending on the availability of talent.

6. The LoB needs to be 100 % sure to have appropriate management capabilities to manage a remote location. Did we find the right local management and leadership skills? Does my team at another location have the experience to work with remote teams? Do we have enough people who are flexible enough to spend a considerable amount of time in the other location? These are questions that need to be asked – otherwise the whole organizational sep-up may fail.

7. The distribution of topics also depends on the ability to divide tasks into discrete modules. Over the years, technological innovations have helped organizations to do this in several ways. For example, in the mainframe days, it was impossible to split the software into user interface, business logic, and back end logic, but with the arrival of concepts like Model View and Controller (MVC) architecture, SAP is now able to develop the user interface in one location and the business logic and database modeling in a different one. With the Service-Oriented Architecture and Enterprise Services as well, SAP provides great flexibility to managers to distribute tasks. SAP Labs has to make sure that the tasks are bundled into large logical pieces since too much distribution would only erode the benefits arising from distributed development. It is very easy to structure the organization either to meet short-term goals or to achieve long-term objectives. The challenge is to structure the organization to achieve long-term objectives without compromising on short-term goals. The organizational structure should always an embed attribute that reflect priorities and eliminate short-term risk.

4.11 Challenges of SAP Labs India's Organizational Structure

While the systematic growth of the development teams has helped Labs India to increase its innovation and efficiency in an revolutionary way, this did not happen at no price. New challenges were encountered at every step, but the development groups always came up with innovative approaches to overcome the same.

1. During every stage of growth, the biggest concern has been to grow without compromising on the overall quality. When the distribution of tasks, the complexity of the stack, and the number of players in the game increased, SAP also had to upskill key players in terms of quality management or operational staff. Accordingly, in the initial years, a small, but efficient central quality team at the lab played an important role for the success. As the individual teams were often too small to have even a single dedicated 'Q-Person', the central team provided guidance on the standards, organized quality audits for all teams, and pushed the exchange of best practices across the teams. The lab directors supported these activities top-down and ensured that the quality audits were taken seriously by the different development teams.

   Over time, the lines of business grew and installed their own quality teams, and at the same time, they accepted accountability for their product quality. So the central quality management unit was dissolved.

   During the 'start-up phase' of the organization, the focus was on learning more about SAP's quality management process, during the 'growing up phase' the teams focused on following the product innovation lifecycle, and in the 'grown up stage', new processes like SAP Sigma were introduced.

   Until today, consistent quality demands continuous attention, specifically for younger teams, as the guidelines became more extensive and the technology stack more complex.

2. Simple issues, like the language to be used in meetings and documentations, were initially a problem – as traditionally the official development language at SAP was German. Soon after the establishment of Labs India, SAP mandated that all the coding and documentation should be done in English and that a translation into German and other languages would only happen subsequently. This was discussed at the highest organizational level in the product and technology council, and all the senior executives committed themselves to this decision. However, it involved the challenge of inconsistent English skills around the globe, of course. Even apart from the different language skill levels in the U.S., in India, in Germany, or in China, a consistent terminology had to be developed that could be used by thousands of developers in an ever changing environment.

3. Another big challenge is to handle reorganizations and the changes of responsibilities of different executive board members and Senior Vice Presidents. Everyone knows that organizations do not only thrive on structured networks, but also on informal networks. Therefore, any reorganization or disruption of the informal networks will reduce the productivity. Additionally, new heads in the development areas brought new perspectives or gave new impetus to slow running projects. At times, it took several months or even up to one year for the organization to stabilize after a major restructuring. While this had always been evident in a single location setup, it had an amplified effect for the distributed teams. New heads of development and senior members of the management team had to travel extensively during these times in order to have face-to-face meetings. The heads of Development made it a rule to visit Labs India after a major reorganization to explain its purpose and to reassure commitment from the location.

4. It has always been a challenge using globally aligned tools for supporting the development process. These are development tools and communication tools. SAP Labs India has constantly been innovating new ways to support the technical infrastructure through the introduction of applications like Netmeeting, Wide Area Network (WAN) phones, videoconferences, Interwise internet meetings, SAP Connect, telepresence, and other tools. These services are available for all employees to make working in different teams on different continents easier, and they provide close contact and connection. In addition, global events are telecasted live, and this eliminates the need to be present during such events. In spite of all those well chosen technological innovations, it is still extremely challenging for SAP Labs' employees to participate in a brainstorming exercise, a customer workshop, or an architecture discussion from a remote location.

5. There is the problem that senior managers may have only limited experience in organizational design or re-design. It is always easy to draw a few boxes, put names in them, connect them with some solid and dotted lines and call this a new organizational structure. The SAP Labs India management has always tried to influence the process, in order to advise LoB managers to ask themselves the most important questions in this context:

– *Does the structure meet the organizational design criteria?*

A design criterion could be to have an efficient development service organization, another one could be to have an architecture team that plays an important role as a knowledge hub – two completely different things that need to be handled differently.

– *Does the structure create power imbalances?*

For the first 20 years, the powerhouse of R&D at SAP has been in Germany, and later it was in the U.S. as well. Nevertheless, it is important to also structure the team in India in a way that acquires the necessary opportunities for decision making, which on the highest level will usually not happen in India.

– *Does the structure support the work flow?*

Every organization has a specific work flow. For example, it is not sufficient to establish a team in India and call it "Development of xyz Product", if every single developer has to get necessary information from three different locations to do his or her job. How does information flow? How do we enable people to communicate in this structure?

– *Do we have the right amount of complexity?*

Some people tend to make things overly complex; others make them too simple, without taking all aspects into consideration. The organizational structure must match the complexity of the different R&D centers that are included in this structure. The number of interfaces has to be high enough to enable communication with all those who provide necessary information, but, on the other hand, if a certain number is crossed, the design ought to be reviewed for possible overhead. It is very important to establish an appropriate number of review/steering boards and alignment meetings to give teams in India the right amount of influence and visibility, while not making the process overly bureaucratic.

– *Is the organizational culture congruent with the design?*

SAP is used to matrix structures and also organizations spanning several continents. Besides openness and a low degree of hierarchical thinking are important elements of its culture. Thus, the organizational design should not be in sharp contrast to the traditional culture of SAP.

The only thing that is constant is change: Organizations and processes are designed to increase efficiency and to achieve speed. SAP Labs finds itself in a dynamic market environment where expectations are constantly increasing. The market conditions are turbulent and the state-of-the-art technology of today might be obsolete tomorrow. Mergers and technology decisions that have long-term impact are encountered on an ongoing basis. Organizational priorities and strategies keep changing, and structure, too, changes with strategy. By being aware of the opportunities and challenges of distributed development, SAP Labs India is more confident today than ever, to be able to handle these challenges.

Lessons Learned

Even though the 'right' organization does not automatically guarantee success to an R&D location, one can hardly spend too much time on thinking about the organizational design.

The local management must be included into organizational considerations, as the global heads of business lines cannot oversee the impact of their decisions in the local subsidiaries.

Organizations in a volatile environment like India will never be static and will have to change over time. The advantage of India is the flexibility of all stakeholders to support change once it is discussed and agreed, and not to waste energy on resisting it.

5   Product Development and Innovation

Developers at SAP take immense pride in the work they do. Development groups are considered special, and the title 'Developer' is revered inside the organization. Engineering excellence and admiration for craftsmanship are part of the company culture and are generally expected from a German company.

From the early days onwards, Labs India focused creating a location that lived and breathed the same engineering culture as in Germany. Development tasks were done in taking into consideration every activity in the software development lifecycle. In this way, developers could gain comprehensive knowledge of the customers' trouble points and develop deeper insight into the challenges faced by end users.

The chart shown in Fig. 17 provides further information regarding the Labs India headcount split: Research and Development constitutes 60% of the work, 27% go to maintenance and support related activities, and 9% of the headcount work in Customer Solutions & Operations. Following a strict separation of new application development and software maintenance and

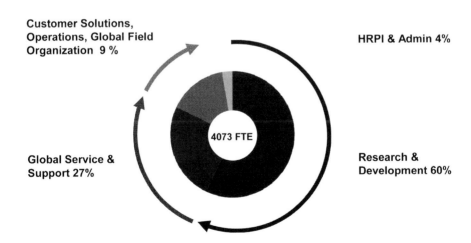

Fig. 17. Split of headcount at SAP Labs location (as of Q4 2008)

C. Neumann and J. Srinivasan, *Managing Innovation from the Land of Ideas and Talent: The 10-Year Story of SAP Labs India,* DOI: 10.1007/978-3-540-89283-0_5, © Springer-Verlag Berlin Heidelberg 2009

support, it was made clear that support groups should work with a strategic focus on providing best-in-class customer service, while Research and Development on the other hand, should be responsible for delivering innovative products. Development tasks include both new innovations and continuous development of newly developed products based completely on customer feedback.

The Customer Solutions & Operations (CSO) team cooperates with the sales department to position products in the market. It therefore works closely with development groups to provide demos and consulting support, and to provide further information regarding already developed products. Research and Development works closely with other development groups and support staff around the globe to learn from customer experience. In addition, they provide deeper technical knowledge in support to other teams whenever required. Global Service and Support communicates with consultants at customer sites, with customer key users and developers inside the development organization.

In May 2006, at the annual shareholders' meeting in Mannheim, Henning Kagermann said: "Knowledge, innovation and capital are the only raw materials on which SAP's financial performance depends. It is critical to us how well and quickly the organizational intelligence of a company can be integrated into software with expert knowledge and how quickly this software can then be made available to customers worldwide. We therefore need the right mix of talent."

At SAP, technology has always been seen as a instrument to solve end user challenges, but not as an end itself. Experts from diverse functional areas such as Sales, Manufacturing, and Finance often sit together deeply discussing business challenges in order to develop innovative solutions to satisfy end users' needs. Even when the developers design large scale enterprise solutions to solve the pressing challenges of global multinationals, the focus for developers is always the end user. A recent article from *BusinessWeek*, 'How SAP Seeds Innovation', captures this attitude very well. The authors John Hagel and John Seely Brown write: "SAP went further— it focused on the needs of individuals, not just companies. Even though most of its customers and partners are enterprises, SAP recognized that participation ultimately is by individuals. It designed its various collaboration platforms with the goal of making individuals more successful in their daily roles by helping them connect more effectively with the specialized resources most relevant to them" (Hagel / Seely Brown 2008).

Developers at SAP always work towards enhancing their technical skills, their business skills, and their soft skills in order to mature into a full-fledged professionals. Technical skills help them use the most powerful technology innovations to solve end user challenges. Business process knowledge enables developers to empathize with the end user challenges and to design better solutions that solve the real problems an enterprise faces. Project management skills are necessary in order to handle complex matters, to detail them into an actionable plan, and to get to the expected end-result. Well trained soft skills such as communication and presentation skills support developers in explaining complex and abstract problems in a simple way and in documenting and communicating them to fellow developers in other locations.

The presence of development groups across different lifecycle stages, from Research to Customer Solutions, also help developers to switch functions over a period of time. This provides them with the opportunity to start developing innovative solutions in the research team, and then move to product groups where their focus is working on adjusting and scaling the products to match certain customer needs. When the products become successful in the market, the developers are able to move on to global service and support, where they support customers to derive maximum benefit from their investments. Developers with expert knowledge regarding specific customer challenges can in turn use their expertise to focus on creating new innovative solutions to end user challenges, and they are well qualified to move on to Research and Development.

5.1 Development Process in SAP

The first formal description of SAP's software development framework dates back to 1994. This first framework, named 'HORIZON', focused on the core software development process from specification to test. HORIZON was used by software developers during the late 1990s and was also used by SAP developers in India during the early days of distributed development. Extensive training for Labs developers was provided to ensure the compliance with HORIZON. Together with document management, this framework responded to the ISO 9000 requirements. The Solution Development Lifecycle (SDLC) was introduced in 2000. It offered product-level planning as well as processes to support the market introduction of new products. In 2003, SAP launched the Product Innovation Lifecycle (PIL) to provide a consistent approach to company-wide quality standards.

At the same time, by pushing all development areas to follow the same processes, standards and quality guidelines, SAP moved the responsibility for quality back to the respective development teams and closed the central corporate-wide GQM team (Global Quality Management). PIL focused on the early stage of product lifecycle, including portfolio planning and product definition. Its goal was to provide a consolidated, cross organizational demand for all development units. The latest version of PIL, PIL2.0, enabled a more flexible and agile approach that improved SAP's ability to develop an even greater variety of products.

Quality at SAP is not negotiable, and it is a prerequisite for meeting and exceeding the customer expectations. For this reason, SAP decided to define principles of quality as a part of its global policy. This policy underlines its commitment to excellence and describes the core principles that globally guide distributed development activities. Without such a policy, it would be impossible for the different global development centers to work simultaneously on those products. Distributed development demands a clear direction and a shared understanding of roles and processes. SAP provides this with its Product Innovation Lifecycle (PIL). This scheme is

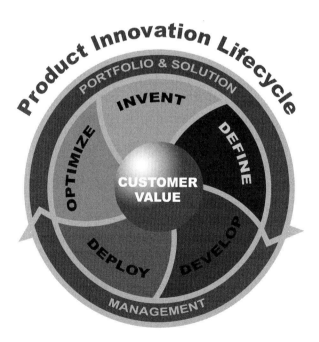

Fig. 18. Product Innovation Lifecycle (PIL)

one of the major pillars of SAP's quality management system, and it provides the framework for the developers to operate in a distributed environment without compromising on quality. PIL tries to ensure room for innovation and agility, and at the same time serves as a planning and execution framework to ensure product quality by design. It contains both a basic set of rules that includes product and process standards and a set of various best practices. PIL ensures proper documentation across different phases of software development and thereby eliminates uncertainty that arises due to global distribution of activities.

Overall, SAP uses PIL to plan, manage, and monitor its product lifecycle to ensure quality. PIL describes how to convert market opportunities and the company's general strategy to software products that add value to our customer's business.

PIL at a Glance – Challenges of Providing Complete Software Solutions

SAP faces many challenges in developing its wide range of business software, which includes industry solutions, fundamental enterprise software applications, and specialized business solutions and services. This software represents an open platform that responds to the quickly changing business requirements, such as legal regulations and industry standards. Other external challenges are business related. They comprise upcoming market opportunities as well as general challenges related to producing standardized software solutions. All those challenges are intensified by the fact that SAP is fundamentally committed to the customer's demand for high quality.

As displayed in the PIL process map, PIL is structured into five phases: invent, define, develop, deploy, and optimize. Horizontally, PIL is organized into four layers. These include a product portfolio layer, a program layer, and a project management and methodology layer. Each process within the process map belongs to both a layer and phase. Additionally, mandatory handover points called **Quality Gates (Q-Gates)** are an integrated part of PIL.

Invent and Define

In order to begin the **Product Portfolio (PP)** management process, it is necessary that long-range strategic business goals, as defined by the SAP Executive Board, and approved by the CEO, are determined and prioritized.

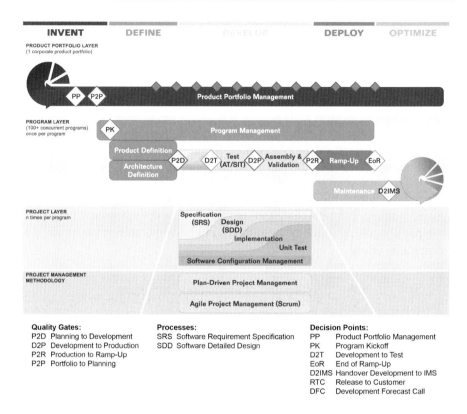

Fig. 19. Process map of PIL

This order of priorities takes into account the three-year financial roadmap and revenue opportunities. The resulting prioritized portfolio articulates SAP's product strategy in an efficient format, helps to prioritize all investment clusters based on their strategic fit, and is available to SAP's senior management involved in corporate strategic planning.

In the **Portfolio-to-Planning (P2P) Q-Gate**, the SAP Product Portfolio Council decides upon the entire SAP product portfolio. This decision initiates all the development programs needed to create the portfolio. Development Forecast Calls (DFCs) are set up every four weeks to continuously define, approve and manage SAP's product portfolio.

During the **Program Kickoff (PK)** phase, every new program at SAP is officially listed in SAP's program repository. This phase has to be completed by filling in an online form called the 'program birth certificate'. Once a new development program is approved and stored in the program repository, different workflows are automatically triggered. These include the assignment of a release master plan (for milestone maintenance), the creation of a program project blueprint (a master list of all core deliverables associated with the program) and the communication of the new program to all service units within SAP.

Between the Invent and Develop phases, the **Product Definition** process details the major investment decisions for new products and enables the beginning of product execution. The successful completion of the Product Definition process is formally decided and documented in the **P2D Q-Gate**. On the other hand, the program architecture should align with the overall SAP architecture scheme, ensuring harmonization from a technical point of view. Special technical topics such as scenario architectures are described in an Engineering Response Document (ERD) that is also available in the 2D Q-Gate for some special topics.

A Collaborative Architecture Resources Commitment tool (cARC) is a central tool for portfolio management and product definition in the invent and define phases of PIL. It is used by the project requestor and developers to exchange information. It also provides functionality to link individual requirements to a portfolio case and subsequently to track the status of implementation.

Develop

Turning high level requirements into ready-to-market software solutions requires a multistage process of decomposing and refining the high level information. This is done within the **Software Requirements Specification (SRS)** process, which aims at translating requirements into development language and providing a common understanding of the business and technical scope of the software solution in question. SRS serves as a basis for subsequent processes and activities, such as design, implementation, and product documentation. SAP's User Centered Design (UCD) process focuses on the early and regular involvement of end users throughout the complete SAP product design and development process.

A 'software requirement' is a single logical statement that follows a predefined pattern. It describes one single behavior or attribute of a software component. It should be clearly understandable and unambiguous. In order to be verifiable, it should have a cause and effect. A software requirement can be used to describe both the functional and non-functional behavior of the software. Functional behavior represents the 'what' of the software, whereas the non-functional behavior relates to SAP product standards such as security, performance, and usability.

The Software Detailed Design (SDD) process guarantees a precise and complete development response to requirements. It ensures high quality and efficient implementation based on defined SRS requirements. Once the completed SDD has been reviewed by design experts and is available in its final version, the transition to implementation and unit test is performed. All necessary documents must be checked into cProjects, the project repository, to comply with Intellectual Property (IP) requirements. All the projects created in cProjects are assigned to project leads. These leads are expected to report regularly on the progresses in cProjects.

The Implementation and Unit Test (I&UT) process guarantees the precise and complete development and test of individual software objects. At the end of a development process, the test range increases, and a Module Integration Testing (MIT) is performed.

Acceptance Tests (ATs) concentrate on processes, while **Scenario Integration Tests (SITs)** focus on scenarios. These tests ensure that each new function is implemented completely, proceeds according to its specifications, and cooperates both with existing and other new functions. The final result of such tests is a key part of the information presented in the **Development-to-Production (D2P) Q-Gate**.

All test cases and test results are systematically captured in the General Test Catalog (GTC) system, which, along with the test workbench, is used for storing test cases, test plans, test catalogs, and test packages. Feedback regarding the tests is also captured here, and the creation of problem messages is linked to the test cases. GTC is also used for reporting and analyzing test results.

At the end of the development phase, the Assembly & Validation process simulates the customer experience associated with every new SAP solution or product. During this process, the new solution or product is installed using only the tools and documentation that will also be available to the customer. The configuration is completed according to the documentation, and the most important business scenarios are tested as samples. The decision to release the product is made during the **Production-to-Ramp-up (P2R) Q-Gate**.

Deploy and Optimize

The Ramp-up process is SAP's standard market introduction process. During Ramp-up, the solution is installed at a number of customer sites so that the solution can go live, and the customers deliver proof of successful reference projects. Those ramp-up customers are carefully selected, and at this stage, the maintenance and release (including customer message handling) is done by the development team. Corrections are delivered in support packages which are available for all customers involved in the SAP Ramp-up process. This phase ends with the **End of Ramp-up (EOR)**, where the feedback from the ramp-up customers is collected, documented, and measured against Key Performance Indicators (KPIs).

The final stage of PIL is the handover from Development to the **Installed Base Maintenance and Support** team **(D2IMS)**. After this decision point, the product is in mass shipment, and the IMS organization assumes the formal responsibility for handling customer messages.

SAP has developed a '5-1-2 maintenance strategy'. Based on this, it supports all core applications throughout the maintenance phase over the following periods:

- Five years of mainstream maintenance;

- One year of extended maintenance at an additional 2 % fee;

- Two years of extended maintenance at an additional 4 % fee.

The overall goal of the Q-Gate meetings is to provide a high degree of transparency regarding the product status to all concerned parties. Q-Gate meetings must end with an explicit go or no-go decision on critical issues. In this way, the Q-Gates ensure that the decisions are made on time and that the status is periodically reviewed. The SAP Repository, the Collaborative Architecture Resources Commitment (cARC) program, the Collaborative Projects (cProjects) suite, the General Test Catalog (GTC), and the test workbench tools jointly provide a comprehensive environment for development groups to stay aligned and to ensure transparency for all stakeholders.

SAP has to deal with internal and organizational challenges, because it develops its software collaboratively in many locations worldwide. The challenging implications of distributed development on a global scale include managing differences in culture, language, and time zones. Moreover, SAP closely collaborates with a great variety of partners. PIL provides the necessary framework for developers to distribute tasks around the globe and to deliver on the commitments without compromising on quality.

5.2 Development Tasks in Labs India

At SAP, development can be viewed in many different ways, depending on how it is classified internally. Programs and projects are created according to these classifications, as the skill requirements for their execution varies based on the type of development. Several technical components are developed once and reused many times in different applications. For example, applications such as Finance and Human Resources may be the same for different industry solutions, and are therefore reused in different industry solutions. Functions that are built for one specific industry are also at times reused for another industry, for example, retail applications are also used in the Oil & Gas industry solution since service stations have convenience stores attached to them.

All development groups at SAP Labs India have either a specific market focus, a technology / application focus, or they focus on a certain stage of the development lifecycle. Development groups with a market focus are formed in line with the broad market segments of large, mid-size, and small enterprises. This is usually done for the ERP suite. SAP offers 25 different industry solutions, and specific development groups inside SAP are structured with those solutions in mind. Country specific and customer specific developments are developed at the same time. With its country specific solutions, SAP tries to address the language and legal issues apart from handling country specific business practices. Customer specific developments are normally carried out when customers have unique business processes that provide a competitive advantage to them.

Development can also be categorized according to different solutions offered by SAP, including Customer Relationship Management (CRM), Supplier Relationship Management (SRM), Supply Chain Management (SCM), Product Lifecycle Management (PLM), Human Capital Management (HCM), and Financial Capital Management (FCM). Apart from that, development is sometimes also classified by the layer of the software architecture such as Technology, Business Process Platform, Application Development, and Application Content Development.

Classifications based on the development lifecycle such as Research, Development, Development Support, and Customer Support is also common, as challenges are different in different stages of the software development lifecycle.

Overall, the development groups at SAP are structured according to the global corporate strategy and are reorganized from time to time to reflect the market realities. During reorganization, special care is taken to ensure that the value of existing knowledge expertise is not destroyed during the process.

Development investment is normally highest at SAP during the production phase, followed by service and support, and then research. Research groups work with minimum budget to bring out the next big innovation to the market. Once an idea is accepted by the market, the related product goes into a production phase, during which it is made ready for the mass market and is continuously enhanced based on the feedback from key customers and other stakeholders. In the next stage, customer support teams work closely with customers and provide necessary product support. This is important because customers will only get maximum value from their investments when they run their operations with SAP products for a long time, without disruptions. Let us now dive deep into different areas of development at SAP Labs India, understand how the teams have evolved over the years, and also learn in detail about the opportunities and challenges of software development in India.

NetWeaver Development

SAP NetWeaver is an open integration and application platform that aligns people, information, and processes. It provides both the design time environment for SAP developers and the run time environment for SAP applications. This technological platform is used by SAP's large and mid-size enterprise applications. Most of SAP's development locations participate in the development of NetWeaver, with significant contributions coming from Germany, India, and Israel.

Development groups inside SAP are 'customers' of the SAP NetWeaver team. The application teams receive their requirements from the market and raise internal requirements to NetWeaver teams. This process ensures requirements are collected, consolidated, and analyzed, to design a single robust application that can be reused by all the application teams. Apart from this, the NetWeaver team also incorporates new technological inno-vations such as RFID (Radio Frequency Identification) on an ongoing ba-sis to keep the technology platform up-to-date and to maintain a techno-logical leadership position in the market.

The history of technology groups in India can be traced back to the mid-90s, when the K&V teams started working on the framework required for their Sales Force Automation (SFA) tool. During those early days, the teams acquired knowledge mainly in the areas of mobile technology, syn-chronization technology, and framework development. After the acquisi-tion of K&V, these groups became part of SAP basis development, and then went on to slowly spread their wings into areas such as SAP Portal, Middleware, and Business Intelligence. Technology teams were also formed during the split of New Development and Installed Base Develop-ment to maintain parts of ABAP workbench.

Today, a significant portion of the SAP NetWeaver development happens in Labs India. The contribution of Labs India to the NetWeaver stack fur-ther strengthened with the acquisition of Yasu Technologies and Business Objects, as these companies maintained a large presence in India before being acquired. Development groups defined the location strategy, clearly categorizing different development topics as major topics or minor topics for every location. Every location identified the major topics to which it could contribute and drive decisions, and minor topics in which it could support other teams in their development. Accordingly, major areas in In-dia are: Composition Environment, Process and Event Management, and Lifecycle Management. Minor areas include: Enterprise Information Man-agement, Service Oriented Architecture (SOA) – Business Objects Infra-structure, and SOA runtime.

A typical development cycle in NetWeaver starts with the **PDEF (Product Definition)** when the development groups define product strategies and roadmaps, and start prototyping based on the feedback coming from cus-tomers, the sales organization, and internal development groups. Long-term product goals and extensions to the existing programs are defined, and new programs are identified. The development groups get involved during the early stages of the planning process, to define the scope of the next upcoming release. All demands are captured as discrete requirements in cARC and are grouped as a part of an individual project. During this stage, product managers take responsibility for executing the project within its scope and timeline, and to deliver it within the given budgetary constraints.

In addition to that, the presence of large application teams and support teams in India help the NetWeaver teams to a great extent, as the requirements are communicated in face-to-face meetings, and the feedback coming from the customers is also passed to the development teams on a periodic basis. This greatly helps to improve the overall quality of the solution and provides the developers with a deeper understanding of the end user's difficulties. The NetWeaver group also has a large offshore test center in Bangalore operated by Cognizant; it provides feedback to the development team, based on the results of intensive testing.

Business Process Platform and ByDesign Development

In 2004, SAP started a new research program named 'Vienna', with the double focus on firstly developing the business application platform and on secondly developing the mid-market suite on top of the business application platform. Later, the mid-market application was codenamed A1S before SAP announced it as **Business ByDesign** on September 19th, 2007, in New York, USA. To put it in a nutshell, the **Business Process Platform (BPP)** comprises an SAP application platform and an SAP technology platform, supporting the creation, enhancement and execution of business processes. From the early days of this project, developers in Labs India have participated both in the development of the Business Process Platform, and in the development of the mid-market suite.

The Business Process platform contains a set of logically related business activities that produce a specific business result and provide value to the customer. The Business Application platform was based on the principles of SAP's Enterprise Service Oriented Architecture (ESOA), and it used the latest tools delivered by NetWeaver for development and deployment of SOA-based applications. Business ByDesign is business software for mid-size companies, and it was developed on top of the new BPP. All layers of the stack starting from SAP NetWeaver as the technology platform, the BPP and Business ByDesign were developed in parallel. This project was distributed among several locations. Germany, India, Israel, and China were the major contributors, but about 14 different locations participated in different ways in this most ambitious SAP research project.

The first developers of the BPP group in India came from different mature application teams. Their focus was to develop core business objects in different application areas such as CRM, SRM, FIN, and SCM, apart from focusing on reusable cross application foundation components, and finally the testing of the platform itself. ByDesign developers developed the suite on top of the BPP by orchestrating business objects from the underlying BPP and bringing together new technological innovations from NetWeaver for developing a state-of-the-art user interface and reporting feature. As the architecture and technology were new, several groups traveled to headquarters in Germany where they would define core architectural principles and development methodologies before finally traveling back to their home locations for implementation. In spite of virtual communication technologies such as videoconference and net meetings, it was difficult to plan complex development like this remotely. Planning days were organized at headquarters, and this helped different teams to participate, ensure alignment, and contribute effectively.

The developers responsible for product definition were located in Germany. Major product definition and design activities were coordinated by them. This facilitated parallel development of the technology, business process, and application platforms. Several tools were developed to decouple the development and simulate the availability of dependent layers to facilitate unit testing. Once components had been tested as individual units at certain milestones, all the components were brought together to work as a single large unit. This reduced the overall development time significantly and also ensured that the groups were working without too much interdependency.

Apart from this, the new model view control architecture allowed groups to achieve the required separation of concerns, in terms of user interface design and backend implementation. The proximity of the NetWeaver teams greatly helped in this research topic, as most of the technology components were also developed by groups in India.

The abundance of mid-size companies in India made the developers understand and appreciate the unique challenges of mid-size companies. During this period, the management initiated a developer to customer program and provided opportunity to the developers to visit mid-size companies in India and directly learn from them. Additional development was carried out in short sprint cycles; this provided the opportunity to build and test frequently and eliminated the risk of learning the major errors late in the development process. Nevertheless, this development was challenging as large-scale parallel development in iterations across the globe is generally not an easy task. The verdict for the newly launched Business ByDesign is still largely open in the market, but SAP is well equipped to leverage the collective intelligence of the colleagues spread across the globe.

Localization Development

Localization starts with the translation of a solution, followed by addressing country specific legal requirements and best practices. This provides opportunities for SAP to improve its footprint in the local market and also strengthens its core product. Localization is mainly done in the areas of Logistics and Human Resources (HR), making the business solution compliant with the local labor laws.

One of the main drives behind Labs India is its proximity to the Asia-Pacific market. Therefore, many localization solutions for different countries in Asia-Pacific, particularly in the area of HR and Logistics, have been developed at SAP Labs India. Localization development had started in Asia even before the Labs was formed. The developers localized SAP HR to meet the country specific requirements of Singapore, Indonesia, Malaysia, Thailand, Australia, and New Zealand. Unlike the core development, in which the product managers are part of the development organization, the localization product managers are part of the sales organization of the country in question. They cooperate with key customers and consultants to define the scope of the localization solution. SAP developers work closely with the field organization to deliver country specific support packages and legal patches. At times, even country specific templates are created to reduce implementation time at the customer site.

The localization of SAP products first started for other Southeast Asian countries and then moved on with India when the SAP Labs subsidiary in India was formed. After having implemented localization for their own country, Indian developers went on to take over the localization solution developed by General Electric (GE) for Australia, New Zealand, and Fiji. After a few years, SAP decided to relocate all English language localization activities to India. During this wave, the UK, U.S., and Canada localization programs came to India.

Today, the localization team in India handles a wide variety of localization tasks including HR, Logistics, Financial legal reporting, Employee Self

Service, Industry Localization, and even localization of CRM and SRM solutions. Localization programs for many countries including the U.S., UK, Canada, Brazil, Argentina, Ireland, the Netherlands and all Scandinavian countries, South Africa, Turkey, and Japan are carried out by teams in India. They release regular support packs and ensure compliance with local rules and regulations, and they support the sales organization to achieve a deeper market penetration and a higher customer satisfaction.

Industry Solutions

Through its industry solutions, SAP addresses the unique core processes of more than 25 distinct industries. SAP's industry solutions are tailored to industry specific standards, best practices, and processes to help companies optimize their business processes and to help them quickly adapt to the changing market demands.

SAP decided to start teams with focus on four industry solutions soon after having decided to open the labs in India. At the beginning, the Industry Business Units (IBU) Hightech, Aerospace and Defense (A&D), Oil & Gas (O&G), as well as Apparel and Footwear (AFS) were identified as part of the first development set at Bangalore. The reasons for selecting these IBUs were different. The Hightech and A&D solutions were headed by Mayur Shah and Nils Herzberg from Palo Alto, and it was easy for Labs management to convince them to get involved, as they needed to expand. At a time (1999), the U.S. job market was depleted due to the Dotcom boom. Since there was a lot of demand for AFS and Oil & Gas solutions in India and the Asia-Pacific region, a decision was made to locate the development teams closer to the market.

SAP came up with comprehensive solution maps to address the needs of all major industries. These solution maps outlined the processes required by those industries, and they explained SAP's approach to them in detail. The required functionalities were either addressed by the standard SAP solution, by industry specific developments provided by SAP, or by complementary software solutions certified by SAP. This concept provided a clear road map to the customers with industry specific requirements.

Industry releases were always one step behind the standard ERP releases, and most of the time these solutions were developed according to a prioritization defined by the focus groups for every industry segment. Consultants from top consulting firms worked closely with the customers in the focus group to define overall development priorities. The development scope was based on the customer's prioritization. The requirements were then analyzed by SAP, and after intense internal discussion, a decision was made regarding whether they could be realized with minor modifications in the core product or by developing extensions to it. For the developers, it was easy to work closely with the focus groups remotely to finalize prioritization, but in some industries, it took years to completely realize the requirements and deliver the solution to the customers. The developers communicated with several development teams to agree upon the specific code area in which modifications could be carried out. The dilemma was that both options for realizing an industry specific requirement had their advantages: Changing the core product ensured that the industry solution was kept lean and that only minimum investment was required for maintenance. On the other hand, an industry specific extension was always faster to implement, but required additional investment. The core development groups also analyzed industry specific requirements to discover whether those requirements were specific to one industry or several industries requested for a similar functionality.

At one point, all the manufacturing industry solutions were developed in Bangalore, and also several other industry solutions such as the ones for banking and for the public sector. Additionally, SAP created large development groups to handle the Oil & Gas industry solution, and after a period of time, most of the downstream and upstream developments were handled completely by teams in India. Similarly, SAP initiated another project to manage the complete Apparel and Footwear industry solution from India. This project team acquired expertise over a period of three years and started driving the industry solution development completely from Bangalore.

When SAP took over Kymetrics, a company specialized in retail analytics, Labs India also started an industry solutions team in its northern hub in Gurgoan. Today, this team drives the retail solution's demand management functionality and has developed specialization in the area of retail analytics.

From the early days, Labs India has also contributed to a major share of the Banking industry development. This group worked on the core banking solution and the collateral management system. It helped SAP to achieve a leadership position in this market. The development expertise in this area was so strong that product management people often had to come to India to learn more about the banking solution.

Industry development teams work very closely with the Regional Industry Groups (RIGs). These groups have presence in all regions, namely the Americas, Europe, Middle East and Africa (EMEA) and Asia-Pacific. These regional industry groups work with the key customers and help the development teams roll in the requirements and roll out the enhancements. Today, most of the industry solutions are completely maintained by support teams in India, because of their strong involvement with industry solutions development.

ERP Development

SAP ERP is the flagship product of SAP, and it has evolved over the last 30 years. SAP ERP is a world class, fully integrated application, that fulfills the core business needs of mid-size companies and large organizations across all industries and market sectors. It helps enterprises perform all aspects of their business. In addition to increasing efficiency within the organization, SAP ERP applications also support extending end-to-end business processes to customers, partners and suppliers.

Labs India started working on the core components of ERP by first focusing on the HR functionality. As the teams in India had strong expertise in HR from localization development, this became a natural extension and topic of choice for Bangalore. Teams started working on standard HR functionalities such as Talent Management, Shared Services and Concurrent Employment. Apart from this, the development groups also worked on Service Procurement, Enterprise Asset Management, and Project Systems. Several topics in the area of Manufacturing like Production Planning and Detailed Scheduling were also developed at Bangalore.

Today, SAP delivers innovations through enhancement packages approximately every 9–12 months. Customers no longer have to plan for major releases. They can now choose to selectively implement the business functions that add value and choose the functionalities that matter most to their business. SAP uses enhancement packages as a new delivery methodology, to quickly and easily deliver business and industry specific functionality. This rapid, non-intrusive deployment of selected improvements allows all customers to innovate in the way they want and according to their individual timetable.

The definition and detailed scope of a product is defined for every enhancement pack. Inside the development organization, product managers identify several themes such as procure to pay and sell from stock. The main idea behind a theme is to address the customer's problems by looking at the solution in terms of business process and scenarios, rather than looking at isolated functions. Themes are further broken down into projects, and the projects are assigned to the locations as per their competency. For example, projects in the area of manufacturing, service procurement, PLM and HR are driven by managers in India. This approach helps the teams to specialize in specific topics and to take pride in the task executed by the teams. It also provides a direct feedback from the customers to the teams. Accordingly, the ERP product management team for certain specific topics is also located in Bangalore, which has further helped the Indian team to participate in the complete lifecycle of development. Development teams either work on functional topics or on cross topics such as usability and analytics. In some cases, the development teams contributed to the development of cross topics such as report development as they did not possess expertise in specific topics. This approach helps the teams to acquire expertise on one side, and on the other it provides staffing flexibility to the organization during project execution.

ERP development teams conduct several rollout workshops for the customers in the region, which help them to both explain the results of their development to the field organization and to get feedback from the end users. In addition to that, the sales organization of SAP and the partners greatly benefit from these initiatives and this results in a higher level of customer satisfaction, apart from accelerating the adoption of enhancement packs in the region.

Installed Base Maintenance and Support

Every customer has mission-critical applications in an increasingly complex solution landscape apart from having tailor made integration with legacy applications. SAP provides advanced support options that mirror growth in size and complexity. SAP Enterprise Support is a key enabler for large enterprise customer integrated and standardized end-to-end solution operations. The key focus of SAP Enterprise Support is the holistic application and lifecycle management of the customer's application landscape. This includes all levels of code: standard code, custom development code, customer-specific code, and partner solutions.

With more than 35 years of experience, SAP supports more than 75,000 customers worldwide, with 140,000 installations in 120 countries. The SAP code can be modified only by developers within the support organization. A highly efficient group of 1,000 developers manage this complex specialized task for the entire range of products, supporting customers all over the world. In 2003, SAP decided to split the development organization into New Application Development and Installed Base Maintenance and Support (IMS). At this point, SAP embarked on a major restructuring, collecting all the developers involved in support activities from every development group to a central group. During this period, SAP Labs India became one of the main support locations for SAP.

In the early days of SAP Labs, it was already decided to have support people all over the globe in every time zone, to help customers around the clock. Therefore, support colleagues work in tandem around the clock and live the principle of 'following the sun' to provide uninterrupted support to customers especially in times of escalation. Customer issues are first handled by the 'Solutions Support' team who maintain direct contact with the customers. At times, Solutions Support teams even send consultants to customer sites to solve a problem. Today, solutions support is provided from China, India, Germany, and the U.S. The next level of support is 'Global Support'. This department tries to resolve problems by referring to an existing note or by providing a new note. Today, Global Support teams are located in China, Malaysia, India, Austria, Spain, Ireland, and Brazil. The next layer is 'Development Support'. This team tries to simulate the problem and provides modifications to the customer. Development support is carried out from India, Germany, France, Czech Republic, Canada, and the U.S.

Over the years, SAP has continuously enhanced the support tools to capture customer problems and provide a 24/7 support. Customers, partners, consultants, and development colleagues collaborate across the globe using the customer support system. Customer interactions are captured in the Customer Relationship Management system. Tools provided to the customer like 'SAP Solution Manager' support seamless collaboration between internal groups and external experts, and are able to manage a solution throughout its lifecycle. Developers capture the key knowledge on a constant basis through internal wiki pages, which helps to integrate new colleagues and to spread the knowledge within the organization.

Today, Labs India support teams handle escalations and send experts to countries such as the U.S. and Europe. The presence of large support groups and development teams greatly enhances the significance of the IMS team in Bangalore, enabling the groups to deliver immense value to the customers. Labs India is one of the biggest support locations along with Germany and has acquired in-depth expertise in providing world class customer support. It has proven again and again that it can deliver solutions to the customers at the same quality and speed as any of SAP's other Service & Support locations.

Custom Development

In the majority of cases, SAP's large customers design their internal processes in a unique way that provides a distinct competitive advantage to them. SAP's standard business process did not cover these processes and its Custom Development organization closed the gap. Custom development opened the door for SAP to learn about niche processes. The Custom Development organization helps customers to quickly and safely leverage and build more complex composite solutions and customer-specific enhancements. Customers do not only benefit from its engineering background, project expertise, and global development model; they also benefit from its close working relationships with SAP business process experts.

In the early days of SAP, Custom Development existed in a different form: it was then called Strategic Development Project (SDP). These projects were fully funded by the customers, and experts from SAP worked closely with the key users inside the customer organization to deliver certain functionalities. This model of development guaranteed tighter integration with standard SAP functions and also ensured higher quality. Today, Custom Development provides delivery centers in low cost locations such as China, India, and Brazil, which has increased its ability to scale within a short period of time.

At the same time, developers traveled to Germany and participated in Strategic Development projects. These same developers later became the first members of the Global Solution Center team. This team initially worked on customer specific assignments and delivered customer specific solutions to large oil and automotive customers. Later, SAP Labs started expanding the team's activities and executed several projects for customers in Asia and Europe. The team developed expertise in global delivery and executed several projects in the areas of NetWeaver, CRM, HCM, and SCM. It also maintained developed solutions by offering custom maintenance service.

The Custom Development working model is different from the regular development. The Custom Development team's field engagement managers work closely with sales teams in the Americas, Europe, and Asia to identify opportunities during pre-sales and post-sales assignments. After identifying opportunities, field engagement managers, together with project managers and the software architects at the delivery locations, define the scope and finalize the contract with the customers. Unlike regular development, Custom Development works with clear profitability targets and defines its own quality process to meet the customer's expectations.

Operations managers and development managers work with field engagement managers on the deployment and redeployment of resources. Once a contract is settled by the field engagement department, Custom Development uses its global delivery model to execute the project from any of the global delivery centers. Formal sign off with different stakeholders during the lifecycle stages increases the transparency and ensures high quality and enhanced customer satisfaction. The proximity of core development and support teams greatly improved the quality of deliveries from Custom Development. SAP further augmented the staffing by working closely with Indian offshore service partners such as TCS and Satyam, which greatly enhanced its flexibility.

Development with Partners

SAP Labs India has worked with about 1,000 third-party resources, which have increased the execution capability and scalability of application teams. Development teams orchestrated the services of internal experts and external staff, and managed projects in innovative ways. The offshore NetWeaver test center is only one example of SAP Labs India's excellent cooperation with partners.

The decision to set up an SAP Offshore Test Center (OTC) was made to move towards a centrally consolidated quality control center. OTC has evolved over the years, and today it takes responsibility for planning, scheduling, executing, monitoring, and reporting to various stakeholders to various degrees for different releases of NetWeaver. Furthermore, SAP entered into a specialized testing contract with Cognizant to realize the objectives of the offshore test center. This support structure is a critical component in SAP NW OTC, and it provides a good quality check on the products released to the NetWeaver customers. Cognizant participates in the maintenance of all code lines during maintenance phases, and it also ensures that released support packs do not involve any regression leakage for both internal and external customers. Cognizant also performs tests for all code lines in the development and correction phases. Apart from this, tests are carried out in a customer-like environment, and performance indicators are defined to check the extent of automation of the tests. Furthermore, test cases are constantly refined, and additions, modifications and deletions are carried out in close collaboration with the regional industry groups and quality management. Several NetWeaver components such as Enterprise Portal, Business Intelligence, Lifecycle Management, and Process Integration are covered as a part of this special engagement. In addition, several Key Performance Indicators have been defined and are now measured on a periodic basis. Efficiency is monitored for automated tests as well as for non-automated tests, ensuring continuous improvement of the testing process itself.

Cognizant and SAP benefited from their partnership in several ways. While SAP has increased the quality of its products through intensive testing, Cognizant has learned about development and testing methodologies and has also gained in-depth knowledge regarding SAP's products, even before these solutions were released to the market. This has accelerated the rollout of new developments.

Certification of Partner Products

SAP integration certification ensures customers that a third-party solution is truly integrated with an SAP product or technology. SAP's certification process guarantees high-quality integration of third-party products and demonstrates to the customer that the solution allows a seamless flow of business data through SAP software and SAP components via open interfaces.

The Integration and Certification Center (ICC) offers several services to its partners. It supports the integration certification based on a variety of standard and custom integration scenarios, and for several SAP products it also makes hosting and test systems available to partners. Furthermore, experienced integration consultants provide assessment services to the partners to speed up the certification process. In addition, the ICC website in the SAP developer network offers certification-related information to the partners and enables information exchange among the independent software vendors (ISV) technical community.

The ICC team was established in India in 2000, and today it operates in different time zones running offices in China, India, Germany, Canada, and the U.S. The Certification Center has certified more than 200 third party products and has contributed to a great extent to increasing the partner community in India. The ICC team awards integration certificates such as 'certified integration with applications' and 'certified integration with NetWeaver'. Two additional certificates were also awarded for 'powered by NetWeaver' and 'certified integration via enterprise services'.

Overall, the ICC supports partners during the entire lifecycle of development, and thus guarantees the overall quality of the offered solution. High quality solutions increase partner satisfaction and in parallel, they reduce the Total Cost of Ownership (TCO) at the customer end. With its services, the Certification Center also accelerates the adoption of the NetWeaver technology platform by the partners and contributes to the growth of the SAP partner ecosystem.

5.3   Innovation at Labs India

For 35 years, SAP has consistently maintained leadership and has been in the forefront of IT innovation for business software / business control. For companies in the fast changing technology market, innovation is not an option, but a must for survival. Hence, every employee in product development is constantly challenged and encouraged to be innovative. Henning Kagermann, SAP's Co-CEO often refers to Joseph Schumpeter's words "Invention is the creation of a new idea or concept. Innovation is taking that idea, reducing it to practice, and making it a commercial success."

Innovation in India

If people discuss the most innovative places on earth, they might mention the U.S., Japan, or Germany – depending on the field they are discussing. But hardly anyone would have India on that list. Talking about India, there is a certain belief that the country has always had a surplus of cheap labor throughout many centuries (which is true as well today), so the need to invent new technologies and faster processes never existed. One could always put additional people on the job. To some extent, this perspective can be understood, if one compares the approximately 1,500 workers on a typical construction site of an IT office building (7 – 8 floors) in Bangalore to maybe 50 in such sites in Tokyo.

On the other hand, India is a country with nuclear capabilities, and it has even sent an unmanned mission to the moon at the end of 2008! In addition to that, innovation in India often happens in fields that many multinational companies are not aware of – for example, in the delivery of smallest packages of food to the remotest corners of the country. Or by developing a car that just costs 1,500 Euro!

The fact of the matter is that the Indian education system releases many top graduates every year who become successful both in India and abroad. Thus Innovation should only be a matter of good practice and opportunities, and less of a knowledge or capability issue.

Innovation in Labs India can be explained under three main categories, namely managed innovation, bottom-up innovation, and co-innovation. Apart from those, development teams are always on the lookout for increasing efficiency by way of process innovations.

Managed Innovation

Innovation happens everywhere, both in small and large companies. There are no fixed rules to achieve innovation. Stakeholders often expect market leaders like SAP to deliver innovations on a large scale. SAP has set a high standard for enterprise software, and there is an ever increasing demand for maintaining and improving the product standards. Employees might come up with stunning ideas here and there, but a framework is required to bundle them and to deliver a consistent message to the customer. Managed innovation provides such framework to the organization. It means innovating in a disciplined way, by working as one global team, by following certain policies, frameworks, tools and processes. Programs and projects are identified in a systematic way, and teams are supported to deliver continuous innovations on-time, in scope, in budget and in high quality.

Thomas Friedman, author of the book 'The World is flat' says: "We've created a global platform that allows more people to plug and play, collaborate and compete, share knowledge and share work, than anything we have ever seen in the history of the world". Today, SAP's development network is distributed across the globe; the development process both enforces discipline and provides necessary freedom apart from providing a framework to leverage expertise on a truly global scale (Friedman 2007).

Bottom-up Innovation

While managed innovation helps SAP to function as a large globally distributed multinational company, the well-defined development process at times stifles innovation and creates bottlenecks. Young colleagues who join SAP often need time to understand the challenges behind a mature product, process or the complete organization. Bottom-up innovation initiatives provide opportunities for Labs India employees to behave like small teams and feel free for innovative approaches. Special programs are created and provide the required opportunity to the employees to give life to their new ideas.

Bottom-up initiatives provide freedom for employees to break away from the water tight boundaries of the organization, its processes and policies, and they encourage them to think in an uninhibited way.

Labs India has a diverse workforce with significant advantages over other SAP locations. For example,

- The average team size of employees is around 25, and most of them have little or no experience – a fact that helps them to question and think out of the box.

- Employees often come with knowledge of open technologies, Java and Microsoft technologies, and hence they are able to critically evaluate SAP technologies and suggest improvements.

- The Labs India campus houses different technology and application teams. The employees network during training programs, over lunch and parties, and hence they are able to come up with innovative ideas.

- Most of the employees have friends and classmates from the same university who work in other software companies like Oracle, IBM, Microsoft or Google, and through these contacts they learn a lot about general trends in the industry.

Though the bottom-up approach builds on a maximum of individual leeway or experimenting aside from project control and design guidelines, it nevertheless requires some framework, in which the developers can operate. As mentioned above, it all starts with the opportunities: many start-up companies and even large IT giants like Google are widely known for their '20 % Innovation Time Rule', which means the principle right of all devel-

Table 6. A glimpse of bottom-up innovation programs at SAP Labs India

	Description	Aim	Results
Code Olympics (initially known as Code War)	A weekend of programming, during which people stay 48h continuously in the office to work on a specific development challenge. This task could be completely distant from ERP-related topics. The teams announce their ideas to the audience; final event on Sunday night for demo, rewards and party.	Provide the opportunity to solve a problem by programming with the help of any technology available (beyond SAP technologies); showcase individual and team strengths; experiment with new technologies; team-building.	Creation of a special innovation atmosphere; opportunity to think beyond the daily work; fun.
Impulse, Beyond the Barriers	India-specific project-based, annual innovation program, often hosted by one LoB (for example, ByDesign). These events focus on specific enhancements of one product line or the increase of productivity of either the customer or the developers themselves. Duration: 3 months, 20 % of developers' regular work time; the teams build business cases and prototypes; management and senior vice architects from an evaluation panel at different stages.	Improve the products, the development tools, and the processes; motivate colleagues by showcasing that their ideas matter and that they get room to apply them; dedication to these self-driven projects provides additional job satisfaction.	Very good results; many product features came into SAP products from these events; funding happens after the official event period is over; time-to-market approximately 12 months; very high participation, as the winning team gets to build a solution, and this drives the individual team members.
Inspire	Global program to bring ideas to market; individual ideas are selected by a central board. Small teams of 3 – 5 is provided with limited budget and entrusted to develop a prototype and introduce a product within 2 years.	Continually foster innovative ideas aimed at the development of new offerings or the enhancement of existing SAP products.	Some ideas from this program became products; the cycle until results can be seen is long, of course – it builds a lot on intrinsic individual motivation.

Table 6 (continued)

Jam sessions; board demos	On-the spot demos of great inventions (proto-types) in front of a relevant audience (board, employee meetings …)	Recognition, competition, event feeling, fun.	No specific additional outcome, as most demos are anyhow part of other initiatives or regular development projects –here showcased for the first time.
Idea Management	Regular global idea management – a typical coporate tool that aims to collect and reward ideas to make SAP's work environment better, including software tools and processes; not meant and used for new product ideas.	Provide a forum to employees to provide feedback on processes and submit their ideas on corporate initiatives or internal efficiency tools.	Very successful on a global scale, yields up to multi-million Euro savings per year due to increased efficiency in regular processes or better policies within development.
Patent Program	Global program to encourage indenture disclosure and patent filing; especially promoted in India through the Labs management; high incentives, if the patent application is accepted and the patent is filed.	Promote "inventor" feeling among employees – as having an international patent filed in one's own name amounts to big pride; shall protect the intellectual property of SAP and make employees aware of what can and should be protected.	Very positive outcome in India – in some years, the annual rate of patent applications per 100 developers crossed the numbers in Germany; solutions invented in India get usually protected, as the level of awareness of this program in India is high.

opers to use up to 20 % of their working time for their 'pet projects'. Labs SAP follows a different approach, creating special programs and opportunities to bring interested colleagues together at certain occasions to think about new processes, tools and products (cf. Table 6).

These opportunities are provided to encourage employees to either think on their own or form teams to develop innovative solutions. During the early stages of many of those corporate initiatives, a small evaluation team is formed by Labs India to analyze the ideas. The evaluation team provides necessary guidance and sponsorship to develop first prototypes. Innovative ideas usually go through a funnel of stages after initial presentation, business case presentation and prototype evaluation. The final winners have

Fig. 20. Logo Code Olympics project, 2007

the opportunity to present their results to executive board members, who routinely visit Labs India. These sessions help developers to get direct feedback from the executive board, and they also help the board members to learn directly from the young employees. Approved ideas are then realized through new projects or included as parts of existing projects. In cases of extraordinary opportunities, the investment arm of SAP, SAP Ventures, even provides necessary funding to encourage entrepreneurship within SAP.

Bottom-up innovation has been very successful in India over the last years. Actually, given the freedom to think and try – colleagues come up with quite surprising solutions to various problems. As long as promoted strongly by the management, the Labs India employees were able to contribute the highest number (relative to headcount) of ideas and innovative prototypes in the global systems such as Idea Management or the Patent Program. With the stronger role of the Lines of Business in India, the employees have nevertheless become increasingly focused on their product development – so their local development managers now have to play the role of promoters for such programs to encourage their teams to participate in them. One cannot leave it completely to the individual to fight his or her way through the different global programs and to fight with the manager for time and funding to further pursue an idea.

Co-innovation

Labs India has a unique ecosystem in Bangalore. Bangalore houses several software companies, and most of the multinational software companies such as Intel, Yahoo, Oracle, Microsoft, Google and Adobe have large captive offshore centers in Bangalore. Big IT service providers such as Wipro, Infosys, TCS, IBM and Accenture employ thousands of developers in Bangalore, and they work on several important projects for their worldwide clients. Bangalore is also home to several Business Process Outsourcing units, and these companies possess deep expertise and knowledge of large multinational business processes. Bangalore is also home to several new start-up ventures, and the activity in this area is still on the rise. Finally, the city has several top universities and educational institutions. All the above provide a unique ecosystem and an ideal environment for innovation.

Most of the large product and service companies are also partners of SAP, and this cooperation provides opportunity for SAP to collaborate and deliver value on a very high scale to its customers.

Such mesh-ups between local partners start-ups, faculties, and IT staff from other companies does of course not happen by itself. Therefore, SAP Labs has established different forums, centers, and programs over the time, either as part of global initiatives or as local ones, to make use of the local network.

COIL (CO-Innovation-Lab)

COIL is a global SAP program, for which dedicated centers have been created so far in Palo Alto, Tokyo, and Bangalore. It has a clear mission which is "to enable, enhance, and accelerate the collaborative development of innovative solutions and proof points and to provide opportunities to deliver rich showcases and demonstrations of co-innovation value". In other terms, real space of the highest IT standards has been created within Labs India, where today some of the Indian IT majors send their best researchers and engineers to build new solutions together with SAP Labs India software architects.

Currently, these solutions have a very strong focus on the acceleration of SOA (Service Oriented Architecture).

SAP Netweaver Center of Excellence

The SAP Netweaver Center of Excellence can be called the predecessor of COIL, as it had a similar focus and mission. However, the timing was not perfect: SAP had started the program before NetWeaver was really adopted by the local customer base and before its advantages were realized by other IT companies. Therefore, it got closed two years after its start – today, COIL has taken over those developments very successfully.

SDN (SAP Developer Network)

The SDN has been created to bring as many SAP developers and consultants as possible together in a virtual network to discuss new solutions of the SAP sphere in blogs and wikis. Participants help each other, providing ideas and solutions – even complete code is exchanged. The SDN is another global initiative of SAP. The overall SDN membership is nearly 1.5 million, but India has become the country in which the most participants have joined the network (around 295,000 in 2008 alone).

University Alliance Program and University Collaboration

The University Alliance Program at SAP Labs India was launched as part of a global program. It was active from 2003 onwards to quickly get most of the premier institutes aboard. As part of the University Alliance, the institutes get access to hosted SAP solutions that can be used for teaching and studying purposes.

Another major event happened in fall 2008, when the IITs (Indian Institutes of Technology) and other premier technology faculties were invited to present new innovations to the SAP Labs India management and to Corporate Research. This 3-day event (to which papers had to be submitted beforehand) took place on the SAP Labs India campus and generated a very positive response. Some of the papers presented were turned into projects planed as pilots for collaboration projects between the universities and SAP Labs India.

Process Innovation

One of the biggest challenges in large scale distributed applications is the division of projects and responsibilities across the globe. Distributed development also introduces additional communication challenges to the projects. Though the end customer does not care where their software is developed, it is extremely challenging to develop an integrated enterprise solution with teams distributed across the world. Hence, even a small change in the working model increases the overall efficiency. Managers and developers have introduced several changes to the working model during the last 10 years, and this is one of the main reasons behind the success of Labs India.

SAP's way of developing software has changed over the years, and the changes in technology, such as client-server, Model View Control (MVC) and Service Oriented Architectures (SOA), have created numerous possibilities to break gigantic blocks of code into several fully encapsulated modules.

New age integrated development environments provide state-of-the-art source code control systems that offer the functionality to create software builds by bringing together pieces that were developed in different locations. Highly structured customer support systems capture all the interactions with the customers and provide the opportunity to minimize solution times by working across time zones.

Apart from that, project teams also standardized on notations such as Unified Modeling Language (UML), swim lane diagrams, process and UI modeling techniques to align the communication among engineers and to minimize errors during the exchange of technical information.

Internationally known software development processes like Rapid Development, Lean or Scrum Development were evaluated and adjusted to the specifics of SAP's project structure. Development processes in the last 10 years were constantly changed based on feedback from practicing engineers and were enhanced to facilitate teams to work as one globally distributed development team.

Technology plays an important role in supporting these processes as well: Labs India was one of the first companies to implement Wide Area Network (WAN) phones that enable Indian and German employees to communicate through intra office desk phone numbers. Labs India has also worked constantly on communication tools such as NetMeeting, Interwise, WebEx, SAP Connect, messengers and collaborative rooms, smart boards, videoconferences and telepresence to capture and transfer the rich emotions during virtual meetings.

5.4 Summary of Development in Labs India

The above mentioned topics highlight the challenges involved in different types of development and explain the working model adopted to build expertise in these areas. The development areas mentioned are not the only ones that are present in Labs India today. There are several other interesting topics such as CRM, SRM, SCM and demo development activities, but we have touched on these, lightly rather than explain every topic in detail.

Over the years, SAP Labs India has acquired broad experience in different types of product development and has greatly increased the pace of innovation enhancing the execution capabilities of SAP. If one looks at the breadth and depth of knowledge hosted in Bangalore it is indeed true that 'Bangalore has grown to a mirror of Walldorf', as one German magazine stated. Labs India however did not stop here. It has cleverly leveraged additional factors such as the growing Indian market for business process software and the presence of a large community of innovative software companies, to further enhance its competitive advantage.

Peter Zencke, in a speech to SAP Labs India employees in November 2008, stated that with 4,000 people working at SAP Labs India, the limit of growth of the location was reached, but that there would still be ways to further improve and grow in the different areas inside the Labs organization, structure and product portfolio. To him, there are a lot of things that constitute the uniqueness of Labs India and thus should be further supported in the future to get the best out of the location:

1. the broadest range of multiple services and products;

2. the excellent customer focus;

3. the ecosystem between colleagues and friends;

4. the co-innovation initiatives (which only take place in Bangalore).

Kush Desai, Managing Director of SAP Labs India, adds: "We all need to make sure that what we have achieved in the last 10 years – which is building domain competencies, quick ramp-up, strong people and project management capability and the ability to work in a flexible multicultural environment – that all this is taken to a new height. This means we need to build far deeper business content knowledge. This can only happen when we first accept that customers are the best source for understanding the change of business processes and accordingly enable our employees to engage with the customers. This way a customer centric learning can be brought back into our business. We started with a focus approach in 2008 with close to 600 employees getting an opportunity to engage with customers and to gain business insights. Second, we should not hesitate to dream that the next element in the product chain can be conceptualized, designed and built from Labs India. We need to be the innovation hub of SAP. Third, we should be able to develop the next generation of thought leaders for SAP who are recognized both internally within SAP and externally. In a nutshell, SAP Labs India needs to be known for its innovation capability and its deep business insights. We need to demonstrate strong leadership and help SAP take the next big leap."

Lessons Learned

India can be much more than an excellent location for low-cost software development along given specifications or an extended workbench. If managed well, innovation can become the DNA of a development hub in India.

Many hurdles have to be overcome – the common Indian trust in hierarchies, the typical ways to excel by repeating exactly what one has learned or the 'lone fighter' attitude, which many colleagues bring with them when they directly come from the university.

The freshers that are hired directly from the universities often come from middle-class Indian families which prefer their kids to bag secure well-paid jobs. When SAP Labs created opportunities for them with appropriate incentives and recognition to try out new things in a 'secure' working environment this delivered astonishing returns to the success of the company – with respect to new products or processes.

There is hardly any piece of software that could not be developed in India today. This statement does not mean that it is also wise to offshore everything to India, but it shows the capabilities in principle. At Labs India, SAP research customer-focused development as well as new innovations and software maintenance– all of those can run successfully.

Key success factors are:

- well thought-through and documented processes that allow people from every corner in the world to participate;

- a clear and public buy-in from the top management and hands-on support from the middle management at the specific location abroad, to transfer knowledge;

- a careful start, early success stories and a well founded growth from there in terms of know-how and trust;

- individual budget planning for each new solution, including knowledge exchange by experts who come to India for some years or by local key developers who spend some years abroad;

- help employees to understand customer pain points and come up with innovative solutions rather than using the teams as an extended execution workbench.

6 People Management across Boundaries and Cultures

6.1 The Market for Talent in India

India is not only the country with the second largest population, but compared to the number one country, China, its population is still growing and getting younger year by year. NASSCOM estimates that the market for engineers and IT professionals in India is believed to be the largest in the world, with about 2 million engineers employed by IT and IT enabled services in the year 2008.

The strong growth of the IT and IT enabled services sector has ensured that those young engineers find a suitable position in a short time span, making salary raises in that specific sector faster than in other industries, even though the output or gains in productivity do not match the raise of the previous years.

By 2025, India's population is expected to grow to 1.4 billion. More than 67 % of that (nearly 940 million people), will be of the productive working age – a unique demographic advantage that will significantly drive India's growth. Unlike several other countries which will have an ageing population, India will be a young country, with 42 % of the people being below the age of 25. If the GDP of India continues to grow in the range of 6 – 9 % per year over the next decade, the GDP will range between USD 3 trillion to USD 5 trillion by 2025. The McKinsey Global Institute predicts the average household disposable income to almost triple by 2025 and it further predicts that India's middle class will reach 41 % of its population and grow to 583 million people. Additionally, NASSCOM estimates that solely in the year 2009, 464,000 technical and 2,503,000 non-technical young professionals will graduate from educational institutions, against an annual demand of 375,000 from IT companies. These numbers are the foundation of India's competitive advantage in global IT. However, one has to take a look beyond just the numbers to get a better understanding what they mean for the IT industry.

C. Neumann and J. Srinivasan, *Managing Innovation from the Land of Ideas and Talent: The 10-Year Story of SAP Labs India,*
DOI: 10.1007/978-3-540-89283-0_6, © Springer-Verlag Berlin Heidelberg 2009

The market for IT talent in India is not only big; it is also vastly different from any other talent market in the world. We see four distinct features of this portion of the Indian labor market:

1. **Mobility:** Indian IT engineers have always been a very mobile crowd, probably the most mobile knowledge workers in the world.

2. **Shortage situation:** In some periods (1999/2000 and 2006 – 2008), the demand for talent was much higher than the supply, leading to a shortage of IT engineers.

3. **Skill discrimination:** The skill level of engineers varies depending on the university they come from.

4. **Strong Preference for the IT Sector:** The strong preference towards the sector has led to a 'run' on engineering jobs, independent of whether the young students really find them interesting or in any way challenging.

Mobility

Indian labor has always been very mobile, stretching across the world. Indians went abroad to find work even at the beginning of the 19th century, when the destination was Africa or South East Asia. Today, Indians have communities all over the globe, ranging from the Middle East (where in Dubai alone there are some 100,000 workers) to the UK and North America. The jobs those expatriates are doing cover the full range of available job profiles – from most simple work on construction sites in Dubai to highly specialized jobs in medicine or research. There are also many Indians in the top positions of global business, like Indra Nooyi (CEO of PepsiCo), Shantanu Narayan (CEO of Adobe Systems) or Vikram Pandit (CEO of Citibank) – just to name a few. U.S. president Barack Obama also selected some India-born U.S. citizens for top administrative positions.

The knowledge industry with an estimated 70,000 Indian engineers and scientists working in the U.S. alone, followed by 30,000 in the UK, has always played a specifically strong role in the 'brain drain' from India. Some very famous academics include C.K. Prahalad, Amartya Sen (Nobel prize winner in economics) and Deepak Jain, the Dean of the Kellogg's School of Management. Besides these famous names, there are many more who are a little lower in the ranks, but nevertheless very successful in their jobs.

However, even within the country, the IT engineers have much greater flexibility when choosing their place of work than one might find in other countries. Bangalore, for example, attracts talent not only from South India, but also from all other parts of the country – even from overseas, where highly skilled IT specialists from the Indian Diaspora are always willing to consider a return to their mother country.

Mobility results in both opportunities and challenges for a company operating from India. SAP Labs India is present at job fairs and campus hiring projects all over India and is also present at job fairs in silicon valley. Today, more than 50 % of its hiring happens outside of Bangalore, despite the fact that in this IT hub alone, 800,000 engineers are employed. Young Indian engineers are also always willing to explore new countries, to gain new experiences – to just go abroad, which shows another positive aspect of the high acceptance of mobility in India.

SAP is faced at times with the situation that key software developers are needed to solve a customer problem on-site, something that cannot be done remotely. Before SAP Labs India had been established, this kind of situations was quite difficult to handle, since especially in Walldorf, it was not that easy to find colleagues with the appropriate skill set and the required flexibility to go to remote places like Siberia or Saudi Arabia for 6 – 8 weeks. Nowadays, SAP usually gets enough volunteers from India, who are willing to get posted far away from their home for a while – despite the fact that they have to tolerate a completely different climate and diet.

But on the other hand, high mobility can also cause disruption in the operations. Managing a team, one has to consider their wish to work on different projects and locations, and simultaneously to ensure consistency in the different software projects. Very often the drive to work abroad is stronger than the patience to wait until the opportunity arises within the company. As a consequence, employees resign and leave. In 2008 alone, more than 100 engineers from SAP Labs India were transferred to other SAP locations and at least another 100 resigned from the company in order to pursue other international opportunities outside of SAP.

The mobility within India is even higher. 10 years ago, there was hardly any other place in India besides Bangalore, where one could enter a national or multinational IT major and start one's career. Now, there are high-tech zones in many cities across the country, so very often colleagues have opportunities to get a job closer to their 'home town'.

Shortage Situation: "Demand Is Larger than Supply"

Despite the impressive number of engineering graduates in India, it would be wrong to conclude that there is always a sufficient quantity of qualified IT specialists for every job offer. Especially in 1999/2000, there was a severe shortage of graduates when many companies bought capacity from Indian companies during the Dotcom boom and the Year 2000 (Y2K) transformation projects. Even though the trend did not continue and the situation became much more favorable for the employers in the years 2002–2005, the situation began changing again in 2006. If the trend would have continued, the gap between the demand and the engineers leaving universities and colleges would have widened, eventually reaching 500,000 people by 2010. Half a million engineers short in a specific regional labor market can only mean one thing: rising salaries – and that is exactly what the industry has been observing since 2003. Every year there are double digit hikes, ranging from 13% to 20%, depending on the skills of a specific employee and the value he or she adds to the company.

One question that is often asked is: how long will these salary increases be sustainable? There are different views. Going with NASSCOM's perspective of a linear growth rate of the sector till 2012, it will definitely go on for some years. There is of course those who argue that companies (local and multinational ones) will not see any more comparative price advantage in the long run and therefore start moving out of India. On the other hand, there are two counter-arguments: Indian engineers on an average, cost around $8000 a year and an engineer in US or Europe would cost about $45000 a year. Even if Indian salaries would rise 12% and US salaries 3%, it would take 20 years for both to converge. Costs have been relatively stable in Indian companies in-spite of the yearly increases also due to rapid growth in the entry level positions. The other argument is that most companies have no other alternative, since their operations in India are just too big to close down or to move to another country. Nowhere else would IBM, for example, be able to find 65,000 IT specialists to replace its Indian workforce.

Nevertheless, one can also question the fundamental assumption that the shortage of IT engineers in India will continue widening every year. The financial crisis in 2008 has also had an impact on the Indian IT industry; all Indian IT firms have reduced their outlooks starting from Q4/2008 onwards and have become very careful with their 2009 forecasts. The main impact of the global economic crisis will not be seen before 2009. The former trend of 20–30% annual growth for the sector in India may also be a thing of the past – and the supply may start outstripping the demand very soon. For the time being the trend on the talent availability has been stopped.

Assuming that the economy will recover in 2010, however, one finds that those who are currently on the payroll of any IT company in India, be it local or international ones, know their value and rightfully and rationally take what opportunities they can find. In the long run, the salary increases of the past will not be sustainable, but this does not seem to bother today's employees too much. The attrition rates, which dropped in 2009 significantly, could rise again. There will be always at least one competitor on the market that will pay a little more – at the end of the day loyalty is always a matter of salary and opportunities. Of course, this puts specific challenges to employers in terms of keeping their employees at it.

Skill Discrimination: "Vastly Different Skill Levels (Employability) of Graduates"

Whereas one problem of the talent market is that the quantity of the graduates is insufficient to meet the industry demand, the greater challenge is actually to find the 'right' people. The quality of education varies from institute to institute, and one requires a deep understanding of these establishments to access the most suitable talent pools.

On the one hand, there are 200,000 IT engineers leaving the Indian education sector every year, but only 2% (approximately 4,000) are graduates from the top-notch IITs (Indian Institutes of Technology). Those 4,000 can already take great pride in having attended an IIT, where 250,000 young people try to get entry every year. It is a ratio of 1:500, at best, that gets one of these highly demanded seats. When leaving, not all of them would even look for a job in India; still, many of them go for jobs in the U.S. However, this percentage has declined since 2002, from 50% to 16% today (the number of Indian IT engineers in the U.S. has come down from 80,000 in its peak year 1986 to around 70,000 today).

Consequently, even though the skills and qualifications of IIT graduates are usually outstanding, it would be naïve to believe one could hire only from there. Most companies look well beyond the IITs into second or even third league universities when hiring directly from a campus. But there is also an end to it somewhere. Software product companies like SAP only consider approximately 20% of all engineering graduates to be employable for them, as either the engineering skills or the communication skills of the other candidates are insufficient. Of course, this causes difficulties in the selection. Although the number of CVs in the market is enormously high, the selection is an art by itself. At the end of 2008, one SAP manager recalls: "This year I had to fill just two positions in my team here. It took me 50 interviews to do that, just because the quality of applicants has dropped so dramatically, compared to the years before." Recruiting agencies usually go only by the CVs, so the pre-screening is more often than not based on the paper form. But once in an interview, candidates are getting tested a bit deeper on their knowledge and their thinking capabilities, and it turns out that the vast majority do actually fail in the interview process.

Strong Preference for the IT Sector: "Run into Engineering Jobs"

In any country, certain sectors have a high preference at specific times. This is the same in India, but for two things: on the one hand, it may be the only market in which IT engineering is currently the most-chosen study major overall; on the other hand, it is culturally also a place where the parents and the obligation toward the parents determine the subject of studies and the job of their dependent children. Education is a very costly affair in India. Most parents (regardless of status and wealth) spend one third of their income on the education of their children; the higher the income, the better the school that is chosen for the daughter or son. In some families, the most promising student is even financed by credit for his/her higher studies or friends and relatives might contribute money to help a young student of the family to become really successful. In India, more than anywhere else, success is defined by social status and salary. Therefore, career choice is certainly defined by the perspective of the money one can earn – and consequentially in today's economy, IT engineering is chosen quite often, if one is smart enough to get an entry into this sector. This is a very commonplace option in India, where many people still struggle to make ends meet and where the parent-son/-daughter relationship is very strong. Everyone in India feels this strong bond, which is certainly not only a matter of respect and love, but also of obligation and commitment. In the early years, the obligation is on the parents' side to make every possible effort for the child to be successful in school and studies – later it is the other way round when it comes to supporting the parents and taking care of them.

As a consequence, today one can say that many people who are not passionate about working in IT are still studying engineering or being employed by IT companies. As the choice was made for rational reasons, they do not really breathe and live the discipline. Thomas Vetter, one of SAP's vice presidents, says: "In an interview with candidates, I often see sparkles in the eyes of candidates, as long as we talk about literature or art. But when the subject changes to engineering, these sparkles are sometimes gone all of a sudden." A recent article in Germany's biggest online news channel 'Spiegel Online', entitled 'Engineers against their own will', referred exactly to this theme.

One can certainly be a good, solid engineer, if one has studied the subject just out of a rational decision and career ambition – but one may not be able to really excel in the subject or to achieve absolutely outstanding results. Managers who hire engineers must be aware of this and understand what kind of employees they are looking for, with respect to the specific job they have to offer.

6.2   Guiding Principles of People Management at SAP

From the very beginning, SAP has taken the approach that its global values towards its employees should hold good at SAP Labs India. At a local sales office in contrast, the localization and the closeness to the culture of the local customers have a slightly higher priority. Within the SAP labs network it was always felt that, due to the close global collaboration, one needs to believe in the same principles, otherwise one would fail in this set-up.

In the 1990s, Klaus Besier – the former head of U.S. Sales – clearly said to the executive board: "If you are in Rome, you have to live as the Romans do." He said this with reference to the U.S. field organizations, defending the fact that SAP Americas would always feel like a U.S. company rather than like being a branch of SAP Walldorf. This approach surely worked for the field organizations. When one sales manager in Singapore was asked about SAP's global values, he said: "Look, I have to bring in the numbers. As long as I sell, make my numbers and everyone in my team overachieves the target – we are successful. The team is happy and nobody will ask me about how I did it, with 'self-drive', 'teamwork' or 'responsibility'. We do not care about anything else. Nobody will ask."

Certainly SAP will always ensure that its global employees follow the same standard of behavior, the 'code of business conduct', which has to be observed everywhere in the same strict manner. The same applies to the guiding principles in book keeping (SOX standards) or the way how SAP is controlled internally. But there is no doubt that the local culture and people management have a much more local flavor in the field organization than they would have in any of the SAP labs around the globe. The reason for this is easy to understand: If you are a sales executive in a country, you usually spend your time with customers, local colleagues and preparing for demos. There is neither time nor need for traveling around the globe and meeting colleagues. This is different in the labs. Here an extensive communication is of paramount importance for good cooperation. How can one communicate, if there is no common base on how to do things, in what quality levels to believe, and if we don't speak the same language? Many of the sales people in China, Korea, and Japan may not speak a word of English, but this not may be required for them if they only talk to their local customers. However, if one works at SAP Labs in Shanghai, one cannot do any job in the global development network, if one is not able to talk, write e-mails, or phone other colleagues at a different location. Be it to clarify a question, address a problem, or just listen to some global roll-out information, language skills are important.

People management is therefore an art in the global context, because on the one hand, one needs to be able to meet the local expectations on how a company should work, in what it should believe, and what should be, at the end of the day, the perks and benefits it offers. On the other hand, there are certain ways how a global cooperation just 'does things' and manages its projects. Aligning those two worlds is the art of 'global management', and it does not only rest on the shoulders of the local Managing Directors (MDs) or depend on the work of the Human Resources (HR) department, but even more on all middle managers, who have to bridge the gap between the global projects and their local execution.

6.3 Culture and People Management

Like most companies, SAP has, strong and very well formulated values, which include, among other things, the belief in diversity and the belief that even two different cultures are able to work together efficiently, so that the best of 'both' comes out of it. However, as described above, a cultural 'misfit' is very often the reason for failure, may it be a failure of people, projects, and even complete products. In an R&D lab like SAP Labs India, different cultures come together for meetings on a daily basis, via different means of communication. Those cultures do actually influence how productive a meeting can be or whether the outcome is negligible.

By 1995, the world was simple, and for becoming a good manager in product development at SAP, it was sufficient to understand how Germans think, develop software and can be motivated. This has changed when India arrived on the map of the global SAP Labs and became an influential player. Intercultural competence became mandatory – not only on the side of the Germans, but also on the side of the colleagues working in India. Before some kind of understanding and agreement of the same standards was developed, a typical meeting between Indian and German colleagues could have happened as follows:

> *Its 10:00 CET (Central European Time) in the morning. The meeting is supposed to start at 10:00. The three German participants have gathered in the video room in Walldorf at 09:59, wondering why the camera in Bangalore is still showing an empty room. At 10:02, they start the meeting. No earlier than 10:10, the first of the Indian colleagues arrives, being surprised quite a bit that the meeting has obviously already commenced. With their thoughts still dwelling on the cricket match last night and on what they had discussed over lunch, they try to concentrate on what is happening over there in Germany. Meanwhile, those colleagues in Germany have reached the third topic of the agenda, after the first two (most important ones) had been finalized. At this point, they realize that the colleagues in Bangalore have joined (it is 10:20 and all three Indian colleagues are in the room now) and that it would make sense to switch from German to English. Nevertheless, among themselves they would continue to talk in German, not bothering too much about what the colleagues in India would think. Finally it is 10:45, the Indian colleagues have 'warmed-up'. They are now fully alert and ready to contribute. The first questions are asked towards the room in Walldorf. However, in Walldorf the conversation has changed towards less important topics. One colleague has already left for another meeting, another gets up to get some*

coffee. The remaining person would answer the questions in a more 'dry' manner without much emotion, but always repeating the same fundamental logic: "We have always been doing it like this. This is how it works here." For the Germans, the meeting is basically over, whereas in India it could just get started. Both sides leave the meeting being pretty much frustrated. The Indian colleagues are upset that they were not allowed to contribute and that the German colleagues would not listen to them. The German colleagues are upset that the Indian colleagues did not contribute anything valuable to the most important points and that they talked so much and so fast that actually, one did hardly understand a word.

This sample story is not exaggerated and the idea here is to show as to how even a simple issue can derail a project. Incidents like this happened again and again – until people on both ends understood how different they might think and behave and that there was no ultimate 'optimal' way of doing things. There are many ways – and as in conversations among Europeans, usually the most important things are discussed first, whereas in conversations among Indians, there is a longer warm-up time with casual conversation, before the core business topics are put on the table. Hence, it is important to be explicit at times in communication and also be flexible to adopt different working styles. Another true story of intercultural misunderstanding happened to Alain Lesaffre, one of SAP's first managers who was sent to India.

On New Year's Eve 2000, Alain had invited his team to his house for a big party. The house and the garden was decorated, many additional lamps and candles had been installed, the music system and band was in place, the buffet food was ready – everything was just prepared perfectly for a great party. His team members arrived at some time between 8 p.m. and 10 p.m. (the invitation had been for 7:30 p.m.) in good tradition, not to upset the host by an early arrival. Alain's wife Michelle started serving dinner immediately so that the real New Year's Eve party could begin as soon as possible. Specifically she wanted to ensure that the dinner part was definitely over before midnight. She had catered for Indian dishes and a nice conversation kept going while everyone was enjoying food and drinks. But to her and Alain's surprise, all their guests started leaving as soon as they had finished the last course of their meal, though Alain and Michelle tried to convince them to stay and though they told them that the party was now supposed to start with live music, drinks and dance. Within minutes, they were sitting in their house alone, although the clock just showed 11:30 p.m. – wondering whether they had done something wrong. And surely they had: they had served dinner, which in India is the signal for the last act of an evening, so their guests just wanted to be polite by leaving directly after dinner. The surprise may have been on both sides in the same way: "Why did they serve dinner so early and wanted us to leave?" on the one side versus "Hey, why did they all run away after dinner?" on the other side.

Today, such stories could still happen, but meanwhile cultural awareness has become much stronger on both sides. Most of SAP's Indian employees have been in Germany at least once, and many German employees have also been in India for a long period of time or at least long enough to understand some basic principles of the Indian culture. From a management point of view, SAP has invested a lot in intercultural training, both in India and Germany, in order to increase awareness of those differences, which one needs to understand for being able to communicate efficiently.

The Indian Perspective

Ten years ago, anyone traveling to India from Germany or vice versa, would not have believed that a distributed product development was possible from India on a large scale. At SAP, the language used for coding was German, the documentation of the software was in German, and Indian visitors who traveled to Germany came back to India with horror stories about their visits. Just to name a few examples, Indians normally do not carry a map with them since they are always hopeful to find someone – in their densely populated country – who would help them find any place. When they arrived in Germany, they could not even read anything or talk to anybody, since everything was written in German. And of course, Germany is not exactly the country where you can meet people everywhere at any time; the cities look deserted after the shops have closed (they already closed at 6 p.m. back then), and even if one would find a person to talk to, this person would be likely to react with fear or rejection, as he or she was not able to understand the Indian visitors.

Driving a car in Germany also seemed to be very difficult, given the super high speed Autobahns and all the rules to be obeyed, and in winter time, on the other hand, walking around was neither an option, due to the extremely cold conditions and the fact that most Indians would not have appropriate clothing for it. Sometimes, people in Germany appeared to be hostile towards foreigners, and it seemed to be risky to walk around alone in German cities. Given the fact that many Indians are vegetarians finding a suitable place for dinner was another challenge; it was hardly possible to find any restaurant that would not serve meat as part of its dishes. Most of the times, those Indian visitors did not know what they ordered in the restaurant, neither what they would get, since they did not know how the ordered dishes would look like or taste. The German concept of one dish per person, with a multi-component course served on one plate, was strange as well, because Indians in contrast are used to order many individual items and share them on the table.

In those early days, cultural issues on both sides resulted in many serious challenges for SAP Labs India and its staff. At that time, Franziska Ahl was part of HR Global Mobility Department in Germany. She took care of all the assignments of SAP employees inbound and outbound of Asia-Pacific, and 90% of those assignments were between India and Germany. Looking back to the times when Indian colleagues started to come to Germany and SAP business was growing she recalls: "I think the initial challenge at that time was that people were not used to work together. Both cultures are far away from each other, we were not used to traveling that much at that time and the Indian and Asian colleagues were generally not used to traveling to countries like Germany. As I see it, the main challenge for our Indian employees was that Germany wasn't an English speaking country, and people had problems in getting around and understanding what was going on."

Franziska Ahl remembers that all of a sudden, in 1999, SAP had some 100 Indian colleagues staying in Walldorf at the same time. Therefore it became difficult to offer an elaborate helpdesk to all these visitors. She says: "Our aim was to provide as much support as we could on our job level and to find out whether there was an employee who had big problems, for being able to offer immediate assistance and help solving them."

In fact, there were lots of different challenges and problems Indian visitors had to deal with. For example, according to Franziska Ahl, the greatest challenge for both her and her colleagues in HR and for all Indian engineers staying in Germany, was that the dependant visa process took such a long time. She states: "For all Indians, family is really important, much more than for Germans, and it was not that easy to get dependent visas for family members. We were always struggling to get them to Germany. I remember a lot of situations when I had told those colleagues that the immigration process was still ongoing, and they still kept coming to my office to explain how important it was to get their family here. I completely understood them, but the problem was that the company had no influence on the authorities and on how quickly they would proceed with the permits and the visas. Different from India, the German authorities would not give any priority even to a large employer like SAP to speed things up. It was quite a challenge to get all of them used to those long processes. The visiting employees might have to stay in Germany for a long time, which they were not used to, and being deprived of their family was a big burden for them. Most of the time, we were able to get the visas for the spouses and the children, but we had to learn that due to the close relationship to the parents, 'family' in India also included the employee's mother and father, sometimes even the mother and father in law, and that it was also important for them to make a visit to keep the family's life going."

It was also new to all German employees that their Indians colleagues had the tendency to appear in somebody's office only in groups, when they wanted to clarify certain matters. Franziska Ahl admits: "At this time, realizing that people would not come on their own, was quite odd for us. Now things have changed completely, but in those early days, I would always have visitors and I would always have a full office. My colleagues, who were responsible for other regions, found it funny that my office was always crowded and that so many people dropped by. The Indian employees always tried to clarify problems in a community. They tended to bring their fellows or friends with them and I learned that it was their way of supporting that something was a very serious concern to them."

The cultural differences and barriers for visiting Indians did even include ordinary things like the different climate, the food or just traveling with the German national railway, the 'Deutsche Bahn', proved a challenge to them. On the other hand, most of the Indians did not know to drive a car and if they did, they found it extremely difficult to drive on the right side of the street". Franziska Ahl states: "It took us a while to understand that driving in India is so completely different from driving in Germany, considering that the speed of cars is much higher here and that we drive on the right side of the road. So we had to set up certain processes and special rules for enabling the Indian colleagues to get some driving lessons, just for getting them into the German way of driving and for preventing accidents and damages to the rental cars."

Initially, the damage quota of rental cars used by the Indian colleagues in Germany reached 25 %, so the car rental agency complained and demanded a higher insurance premium from SAP. After the mandatory driving lessons and a change in the policy had been introduced (damages were no more fully covered by the insurance, but 50 % had to be paid by the driver), the accident quota came down to even less than 1 %.

Another cultural diversity that caused, when looking back, some amusing problems, was the fact that Indian employees always liked to stay in groups, specifically in their accommodation. Several times Franziska Ahl visited the landlords of the apartments and went to the hotels to make sure that the Indian visitors would feel comfortable and that their specific requirements were met. But on the other hand, she also had to becalm the landlords. It often happened that the kitchen equipment of many different apartments was moved to one apartment, because people would share everything and meet up for cooking and dinner; afterwards, the landlords had to search for those utilities and rearrange them again. Or *rotis*, traditional Indian breads, were grilled directly on the glass-ceramic cooking field, instead of using a pan – boosting the blood pressure of the landlords tremendously.

Some of the male employees lived for the first time in their life in an environment where not anybody, may it be a maid or a sister, would tidy up around them day and night. Being left alone in Germany in an apartment without such support, they had no clue, not even about a minimum of housekeeping. This resulted in absurd situations, when, for example, one colleague poured buckets of water through his apartment and only stopped when neighbors from the floor below complained about wet walls. Another one never opened a window for six months due to the hostile weather conditions outside, not realizing that minimum of ventilation was needed for the flat. Only after the fungus on the wall had reached the ceiling, he informed the landlord. SAP usually covered up for such damages, as long as one could assume that they arose from innocent lack of knowledge and not from gross negligence.

"I think the Indian visitors were on their own when they had to adjust to the culture and to integrate themselves, but I know they managed it by forming a strong Indian community in Germany. There are certain things you really enjoy, but there are also things that are not so easy to overcome like the food, the cold climate or people who are just different. But I still think those people enjoyed that they could travel around and see places they had never seen before.", Franziska Ahl remembers. On the other side, when German employees traveled to India, Franziska Ahl's experience was that the vast majority of those who visited India in those early days, shared her passion and admiration of the Indian culture, and they enjoyed staying in India, working with Indian colleagues and getting to know a different culture: "I did not receive any major complaints from employees who went to India."

But also the Germans faced some adaptation problems when they visited India, for instance regarding the different traffic rules or the food. While their Indian colleagues had problems with driving a car in Germany, they tried hard to understand the priority rules of the Bangalore traffic. Only after a while, they concluded that the biggest vehicles had the highest priority. Since in Germany cars would stop for people to cross the street, they were surprised to see the never ending traffic in Bangalore, which left them wondering whether they had to wait till the end of the day for crossing a street. Finally, they learnt the art of bravely dashing to the median of the road and then making it to the other side of the street. However, some of them gave up and decided to take an auto-rickshaw to reach the other side of the street.

While much of this sounds amusing today, it was really hard during the initial years of SAP Labs India to overcome all these hurdles and to get into a working mode. It would not have been possible without patience and perseverance. Not only has SAP changed during the past years, but also Germany and India as countries have become more open, more international and easier to adjust to for foreigners. Certainly, Germany is still not ranked very high regarding the prevalence of the English language (e.g. compared to Scandinavia or the Netherlands), but it has achieved a much more open view on immigration and on people from different nations who live and work there. This change was quite evident during the 'Football World Cup' in 2006. Germany could prove its hospitality as well as its attractiveness as a tourist destination. And many smart businessmen (many of them Indian) have also started offering specific services for the Indian community in Germany. Today, Walldorf has got Indian fast food facilities as well as international supermarkets, and even many of the Italian restaurants close to the SAP headquarters realized the potential of their new customers when they started offering 'Indian spiced vegetarian noodle dishes'. On the other hand, Bangalore has become much more cosmopolitan as well, offering foreigners nice gated communities to live in, where they would find clubs, pools and shops on an international level. Whereas 10 years ago, not even one international airline would fly to Bangalore, meanwhile there are ten of the top global carriers connecting the city with Europe, the Middle East, and Asia-Pacific.

Lessons Learned

A global company needs to act pro-actively in bringing cultures together. This is not about creating only one combined culture, but establishing mutual awareness and understanding of different cultures. Only if that can be achieved, a company can make positive use of diversity.

6.4   Management of People – the Role of Leadership

Today, SAP sees itself as a global company, and management of intercultural teams is considered one of the key elements of leadership at SAP. Aiming at diversity in leadership, SAP also strives for a manager team of diverse age, gender and ethnicity. Real talent does not know any barrier of age, and therefore career opportunities and moves may be based not on tenure, but on capability. This is often easier said than done since all human beings enjoy the comfort of being surrounded by people who understand their way of thinking and who communicate in their mother tongue, so that even nuances can easily be expressed and understood.

There is no doubt, management in India is more about managing people because, for example, mostly young colleagues need more detailed guidance and support to carry out their tasks. And as with many things, there is no simple way to understand nor is there only one precise formula on how to do things. However, it is very clear that the responsibility of a manager for her or his team members reaches much further than in a Western corporate culture. Managers in India are seen more as a 'father figure' by young employees, and those expect their managers to coach, guide and advise during the course of a project in a very intensive and comprehensive way.

Fig. 21. Educational meeting between colleagues at SAP Labs

SAP managers working from Germany had to learn that many people issues in India have a higher priority than they would have ever imagined from their German background. Whereas project management skills can be seen as universal, and project execution runs pretty similar across all countries at least in theory, the 'softer' part of management in India comprises a lot more aspects, for which many colleagues from outside of India were not prepared. One has to experience it: to understand that in rare cases, a marriage can completely derail an employee, and to realize that the employee's parents have a very large influence on his major decisions, may it be the next career step, the choice of employer or of the life partner. Any family crisis would have effect on the office life – although this principle may be valid universally, in India there is always a certain amount of drama involved, which really disturbs the individual's performance. Therefore it also becomes the manager's issue.

The managers in Germany initially felt very insecure in this environment. Unable to decide on how serious an issue really was (due to the lack of any reference point or any personal experience), they found it extremely difficult to appropriately classify certain cases: Is it justified that a developer asks for a transfer from India to Germany, due to his marriage with a woman whom his parents did not find suitable for him? Is a three-week vacation justifiable for a marriage? How should a parental request to leave Germany immediately, be handled, in order to take care of the sick mother for an unforeseeable amount of time? And what is this 'Native Place' concept all about? As a consequence of these many uncertainties some German managers would just approve whatever was demanded or would start consulting other colleagues in a quest for advice. Many of these questions do still appear in the daily life of a manager in India (or a manager of teams including Indians), but sometimes the situation is so complex that it requires substantial experience which no training courses can substitute in short time. Though things indeed work differently in India, there is still always a suitable response to any of those problematic situations, as strange as it might appear to the foreign observer. SAP realized this fundamental fact from the beginning and was lucky to have a talented HR manager, who was always able to advise the German managers in a language they would understand. Even if the situation looked really weird, the HR manager would listen, analyze and then give advice – and in most cases, an appropriate solution was found. At the same time, the labs management initiated cultural trainings in India and Germany to train employees on both sides how to deal with each other on cultural aspects. This certainly helped with the mutual understanding and created an attitude not to take things right away 'personally', but also to first think about whether something irritating was just meant from a different cultural perspective and whether it could also be considered just as a friendly remark.

One should not believe that leadership in India, and more specifically at SAP Labs India, has developed as something completely different from what is lived in Palo Alto, Walldorf or Shanghai. There are certain core beliefs that are part of every leader's job in a global organization, or they should at least be part of it: set *smart* objectives, give timely feedback, have meaningful career discussions, focus on delivery in spite of promising study opportunities, career advances, international internships and the like; and help the team members by means of coaching, mentoring or guiding them to build their networks, to learn, to get customer exposure and to communicate appropriately in an international environment, inside and outside the company. However, there might be a difference in India: a little bit of real attention and one-to-one discussion can mean so much more than following an HR procedure from the beginning to its end religiously.

The Talent Management Process

Since its foundation in 1998, SAP Labs India has grown within 10 years from 100 people to a large company employing more than 4,000 people. Many IT companies in India experienced similar or even stronger growth, but the Bangalore market has also been rife with cases of failed Indian operations of multinational companies. Of course, these flops often resulted in a bad press, and many times, companies decided to rollback all of their India strategy.

SAP Labs India has learned to manage the dynamics of a constantly changing job market and the specific behavior of the workforce in India. For achieving this goal, the Labs has invested early into a strong and capable HR team as well as into extensive market studies to prepare for the next movement. These measures enabled the company to systematically synchronize with the changing organizational priorities and thus, they ensured satisfaction of all stakeholders.

Though one would always expect a drop in quality when it comes to the selection and retention of people in a rapid growth scenario, the reality has been different at SAP Labs. It was possible to maintain a high standard due to the professional management combined with efficiently designed people processes. During the first years of SAP Labs India, these processes were simple, but the complexity slowly increased with the growth of the Labs.

Fig. 22. Attracting, retaining, and managing the talent within SAP Labs

For example, the business units' processes had to be continuously fine-tuned, as with the growth came different demands and expectations from the unit managers. The standard developer profile ceased to exist; now SAP Labs would look at the same time for highly specialized technical software architects, consultants with customer focus, lawyers for IT law, software testers and so on. Thus, the internal training curriculum had to offer flavors of all these different demands, which were usually worked out together with the relevant business units, whereas the very specific content had to be delivered always by the unit managers themselves.

Today, the talent management process at SAP Labs India contains six steps which are described in the following.

Talent Planning

At SAP, high-level budget planning normally starts two quarters before the beginning of the next financial year. During this period, business cases are reviewed and approved. The different Lines of Business (LoBs) make assumptions on the respective revenues to be expected for the next years, and they estimate the operating expenses they will incur, in order to realize those revenues. An important part of those expenses are of course the product development costs, and in software business is it predominantly the salaries of the software developers. Therefore, the amount of people in the budget for the coming financial years, the so called 'headcount figure', is one of the key planning variables in the overall budgeting process. It defines the growth or consolidation of business units – and as a consequence, it also defines the growth or consolidation of particular R&D locations like SAP Labs India.

The template for new business cases specifically requires planning managers to specify headcount split in high cost and low cost locations. Because of this, planning guidelines clearly contributed to the steep growth of Labs India, as now, for a given amount of budget, more developers could be put on a project in India, in Germany, or in the U.S. Although the high level budget planning starts pretty early, there are numerous rounds of refinement and detailed planning, before the executive board of SAP would approve the overall plans and budgets. These are then also part of market analysis and guidance. The real talent planning can start in a specific location only in the first quarter of a financial year.

Typically, a certain Line of Business would have completed and approved its global planning, and then it would approach SAP Labs India to help build new teams, extending the existing ones or in rare cases consolidating groups or programs. Normally it would ask for hiring support, consultancy for growth strategy execution, additional workspace, or advice on how to get the right managers aboard to build an organizational unit. After that, requests are consolidated, and Labs management identifies one local manager for each Line of Business as the head of the India operation, to develop and take ownership of the whole team. Hiring the Indian head is mostly done internally as the management wants to provide opportunities to existing employees before scouting for talent outside the company. The Indian manager works closely together with a German or U.S. counterpart to execute the plan. Foreign counterparts act as the bridgehead in the LoB, as this person is the channel and gateway to all the other groups within the headquarters. The composition of the team is then finalized and specific skill requirements are identified. Several issues like the long-term goal of the Line of Business, the period of management, the time line for hiring, job descriptions, the workplace, and hardware and software are finalized before starting the next steps. This prevents teams from rushing into hiring without understanding the long-term objectives, and thus getting the wrong profiles aboard. In the early days, most of this was done informally, just based on e-mail communication, but in the last years, these things have changed to formal processes and detailed procedures.

From the outset, Labs management, as well as the local LoB managers, were of the opinion that the workforce should not be hired based on today's pressing needs for a specific skill or technology, but that it should be hired with a long-term perspective. Team members were mainly hired for their attitude and character, and it was felt that they could be trained in the

Table 7. Employee profile of SAP Labs India

Most common qualification	Bachelor of Engineering
Average age	28 years
Average experience	4.5 years
Average SAP experience	2.1 years

required roles, products, and technologies. When he was asked about the qualities he would look for in new hires, Jack Welch of GE once mentioned that for him, 'integrity, intelligence, positive energy, decisiveness and the ability to execute' are skills an employee should have. This is exactly what the Labs management is aiming for, too.

Talent Sourcing

The actual hiring happens during the talent sourcing step. During the the planning stage, the focus is more on the size of teams or number of people to be hired, while the sourcing process focuses on the composition of such groups.

Usually, a small hiring team is formed, which consists of experienced colleagues from HR and managers from the hiring unit. This hiring team has to decide on the mix of the team members, in terms of hierarchy, competencies and experience levels. If a new team is formed at SAP Labs India, a standard ratio of one development manager per 15 team members is sought. This manager usually has 7 – 12 years of experience in the industry and is supported by three or four experts with a minimum job experience of 3 – 5 years. The remaining team members are younger, either fresh graduates or graduates with one or two years of experience. In case of a team extension, it is usually easy for the local manager to define the requirements for the new candidate, and then proceed according to the standard process. Forming a new team to develop a new product from scratch, is more complex, though. In this case an even more elaborate hiring process is needed.

Today, it is often not possible to get highly experienced engineers, as the competition for skilled people, depending on the cycle of the job market, is quite intense, and they are fewer in number. Therefore, the structure of teams at SAP Labs has also changed. According to the fast growth of the Lab, the teams also became larger, the range of experience for all team members became higher, and the teams became more diverse.

In general, SAP Labs recruits its employees through different channels, before they are grouped into teams and are assigned to the different development or organizational tasks. In India, the following channels are available to get talented people aboard:

Table 8. Recruiting channels of SAP Labs India

	Channel	Contribution of hires in %
1.	Employee referral	>50%
2.	Self initiated application and headhunting	~30 %
3.	Campus Hiring	<10 %
4.	Newspaper Advertising	<10 %

1. The most effective channel for hiring new people is the employee referral program. Initially, employees were offered incentives as high as 25,000 Indian rupees, (which at times was 50 % of a monthly salary), if they referred SAP Labs to friends, and those friends were eventually hired by SAP. Given the high reward of those early days, some employees even started referring people they did not really know and provided guidance to them on how to clear the interviews. However, in stray cases when the quality of referral dropped and when it was discovered by the management, this practice got stopped. It was made clear to the employees that they can refer candidates only when they know the candidate personally and can vouch for that person. In spite of the above experience the referral program is very successful and even today referrals account for a significant percentage of hiring. Since the applicant already has a friend at SAP, he or she knows quite well what to expect. This leads to a much lower rate of early resignations, and hence is a plus for both the employer and the employee.

2. A large number of employees join the company through self-initiated application or are directly contacted by recruiting firms that work for SAP Labs. Although this process works even on a large scale, it is at times very tiring for the recruiting team, as thousands of CVs have to be screened for hiring just a few dozen suitable colleagues. Usually this channel works for all levels, but it has a long lead time, due to the tedious selection process.

3. SAP also hires from institutes and universities – the so-called 'campus hiring' –, but this channel is least used by SAP. Less than 10 % of the new employees are hired as fresh graduates. The reasons for this are mainly the campus hiring demands and the long time it takes until the hired people are ready to start working. Campus hiring requires companies to provide written commitments / contracts already six month before the hired people would actually join. At the beginning of this decade, it was common for most of the Indian services companies like Infosys, Wipro, TCS, to give placements to candidates during their final term, even before their examination results were available. The offer letters were even given to the students one year in advance. Usually the so-called 'freshers' would join entry level positions and start working either on product maintenance or product development. At the time of signing up, they would not know the exact department or team they would join later. Though this was a lucrative sourcing option to get young, capable people on board, SAP did not take advantage of this due to the long lead time. Most LoBs would not take the risk of making an offer one year in advance, as their demands (once the planning is over and the approvals are there) are almost immediate. SAP only allows hires that are based on a specific, open job position. On the one hand, this makes it impossible to hire in SAP without knowing the target team or position beforehand. On the other hand, the expectations of candidates and managers can be met much more accurately if the exact team and role is known to both sides in advance.

4. Other channels like newspaper ads, bill boards, road shows and the like, are also used occasionally, but usually to increase public awareness of SAP Labs India as an employer, rather than to hire large numbers of people through such means.

However, awareness can be crucial as well, which was specifically true when SAP Labs was a new employer in India in the years 1999 – 2002. At that time, newspaper advertisements were released at periodic intervals to keep the buzz in the market. Usually Labs India would release combined job advertisements in the newspaper for 2 – 5 teams at the same time to reduce the hiring cost and to let the outside world know about the variety of jobs offered by SAP. Apart from information about the job location, the position, a brief description of the job, and the minimum qualification in terms of education and experience, the advertisement also contained a few statements about the culture of the company and the vision of the Labs. Every newspaper ad had a code to track the effectiveness of the medium. Most of the advertisements were published in Southern cities like Bangalore, Chennai, Hyderabad, and Trivandrum. Occasionally, hiring was also done in Pune, Mumbai, and Delhi, but success in those places was relatively lower, while the effort was higher compared to the Southern cities. Most of the early candidates were hired from Bangalore and Chennai, followed by Hyderabad, Trivandrum, Pune, Mumbai, and Delhi.

Fig. 23. SAP job advertisement in the year 1998

SAP also organized road shows during the early days to create awareness of the SAP brand in selected cities. Walk-in-interviews were conducted in the downtown hotels, and employees invited interested candidates. In this case, SAP had a hiring desk in the hotel that directed the candidates to the interview rooms. Several SAP experts evaluated every candidate for a full day. Candidates were called for two or three rounds of interviews on the same day, and offer letters were given immediately to the most promising prospects. At times, the crowd in the walk-in-interviews got out of control when hundreds of candidates showed up at the same time, and those who came too late had to be sent home. Recently, walk-in interviews have gone out of fashion, as the skill level of those who come for them has diminished dramatically; so today, most companies do 'walk-ins' only for very junior levels or low-level jobs.

Today, e-recruiting is becoming more and more important in the hiring process. It is part of SAP Human Capital Management and was developed in Bangalore by the ERP team. The tool is used by the Labs India HR team for sourcing talent. Prospective employees, head hunters, and employee referrals can be captured directly from the job postings at SAP's Internet

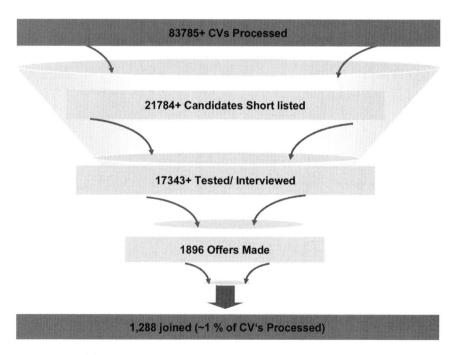

Fig. 24. Recruiting funnel SAP Labs India 2007

portal and transferred into the e-recruitment system. In the second step, the system makes recommendations for high caliber candidates through a CV and keyword queries.

These days, the job market is quite diverse, and it is also possible to advertise on job sites like Naukri and mine the thousands of candidate profiles stored there. At SAP Labs, there are different contractors from head hunting firms on the ground, to scan and load the selected profiles manually into the e-recruitment tool.

Talent Evaluation

Anyone who is not familiar with Indian conditions is usually very surprised and at times overwhelmed by the response to job ads. And indeed, the numbers are impressive: even way back in 1998, SAP received 4,000 applications for a single job advertisement in the newspaper. It was virtually impossible to search and scan all these CVs, as on the one hand, no decent desktop search tool was available at that time, and on the other hand, many hardcopy CVs were received. The number of applications for jobs at SAP Labs India has constantly increased, but one needs to keep in mind that only $1-2\%$ of the applications result in a hire.

For example in 2007, roughly 83,785 profiles were processed. Out of these, 21,784 were short listed, and with the support of a third party firm, 17,343 were tested and interviewed. 5,000 made it into the second round of interviews with SAP managers. Finally, 1,288 of those applicants were hired. Even universities in the Western countries do not administer tests to 17,000 candidates per year, which is a truly Herculean task. The profiles often include false or exaggerated assertions about projects and experience, and even though this can be found out easily in a short interview, a lot of time and commitment is required to do all those interviews with the same diligence. The biggest threat in this process is that the managers finally give up, and after 10, 15 or 20 disappointing interviews, they just fill the position. Thus, they may end up hiring the second-best person to fill the opening. For the company, this approach is dangerous in the long-run. Therefore, SAP Labs India has recently established a four eye principle to avoid hiring of mediocre engineers as a result of the project pressure and the low availability of suitable candidates. Overall, for the selection of people for management positions, there are usually three options:

- Promoting a colleague from SAP Labs India;

- Hiring a manager from the market (either from India or abroad);

- Getting an experienced manager from another SAP Lab or from another LoB.

Every company follows a certain approach for getting the best people into the top positions. All of the options have some pros and cons, but SAP believes to a very large extent in the development of its own talent.

Normally, at the entry level, candidates have to pass aptitude and technical tests that are used as a mechanism for short listing. At times, one can even find such aptitude tests used by big companies on the Internet, so candidates can use them in preparation. Whatever innovative ways companies may find to surprise the candidates with new questions, those candidates will find even more innovative ways to beat the system. Nevertheless, even then they prove their cleverness with various tactics to best selection mechanisms and in their preparation for the interview. Still, interviewer should be smart enough to surprise the candidate with new questions. Young graduates are also interviewed based on the results of the aptitude and technical tests, but normally the interview is kept lean.

For experienced candidates, the job interview typically starts with a brief introduction to the company, the location of the job, the position and the expected tasks. The candidates then explain their profile, starting with their family, schooling, college, career, and assignments. Usually a lot of emphasize is put on finding out the real motivation of the candidate to join SAP. After that, the interview moves to the functional and technical part, and finally it ends with the candidate's questions about the job, salary, and next steps. Job interviews at SAP Labs India are jointly handled by HR and the involved Line of Business, and if the candidate is suitable for the job opening, the offer letter may be given to them immediately.

Satish Venkatachaliah, Head of HR between 2002 and 2007 recalls: "The role played by the HR colleague in the interview process was very crucial. While the hiring manager focused on questions to check 'What the candidate knows?' the HR colleague focused on finding out if the candidate is the right fit for the company. HR was empowered by SAP to overrule any candidate found unsuitable due to the lack of behavioral competencies despite being technically competent. Hence HR team had to be possessing high functional competence to add value in the talent assessment process."

It is also a practice in India to request the candidate to sign a so-called 'surety bond' with the employer, to stay for a fixed period of time. One can say that this is done to discourage candidates who would leave the company immediately after training. If the employee still leaves within the stipulated time, the company will retain the bond amount. However, SAP has never requested new employees to sign a surety bond as it was felt unethical. One believed that if the right candidate was selected, this would immediately reduce the likelihood of that person leaving after a short period. Such 'misfits' or cases in which the new hire's expectations were not met, are rare at SAP Labs, and the attrition quota in the first year is much lower than in the following years. However, there have been cases where employees left a few months after joining, or even worse, they did not even show up on the first day of their contract.

Candidates who do not appear on their agreed first day of work, typically accept multiple offers in their job search, and they often make their choice just based on the salary. In 2006, NASSCOM, India's information technology trade body, introduced the National Skills Registry to stop such practices and to enable networking among HR managers to learn about ill-behaved candidates. This move was hailed by the industry, but the process is not consistently followed by the IT companies. In 2007 and 2008, in the mad rush for talent, many firms continued hiring ignoring the skills registry.

Many of the candidates collect several offers from different companies and negotiate hard to get the best possible deal. Besides the unprofessional behavior of accepting an offer and then not joining, there are of course many who get an offer letter, but never accept. Although there is nothing wrong with that, it created a certain hardship within the hiring teams: If an already chosen candidate still declines an offer letter, the whole hiring process has to start from scratch, and all efforts have to be made again. SAP managers lose additional 3 – 6 months in such cases. HR always maintains telephone or e-mail contact with the selected candidates to clarify any doubts and to learn about a potential disinterest well in advance – this is called in HR terms 'keeping the candidate warm'. Many companies risk offering more jobs than they actually have, expecting some no-shows in the process. Although there is only a small chance that all chosen candidates finally join, SAP never made additional offers, as it wanted to honor all its commitments in every possible scenario.

However, SAP Labs India also follows the practice of verifying information provided by the candidates through independent agencies. As a part of this verification, police records are checked and qualifications are cross-checked with education institutes. The company even had to terminate a few contracts after the employees had joined, when the investigations revealed false declaration of information.

In 2008, 1,900 candidates were given official offer letters, and out of this, about 80 % finally joined SAP Labs India. These numbers obviously display the great challenge that SAP has to cope with in India. This quota is a very important figure in the sourcing process; the so-called 'offer-to-join' ratio indicates the attractiveness of the offer and the employer. Whereas in the first five years of SAP Labs India, that quota had always been 95 % and above, in the overheating job market up to 2007, it dropped significantly. But from 2008 onwards, it got closer to the 90 % mark again, which the Labs management feels is a good figure to work with and to provide the LoBs with new talent. Satish Venkatachaliah adds: "One has to say with a sense of pride that we in SAP Labs **never** negotiated salary offered to a candidate despite the thousands of offers that we made. My philosophy on this was a very simple one – 'Be absolutely fair' – How could I have been fair to an employee, if I was not fair to him as a candidate. If a candidate could negotiate well – she or he would get a fantastic deal, if not, a very raw deal, and this isn't fair. I would ensure that we made the best possible offer that we could (based on our framework) and no negotiations. We did lose some candidates, but the ones who joined us were very happy."

Once hired, all new employees at SAP Labs India go through several weeks of induction training. Furthermore, they are usually assigned to mentors who accelerate their integration into teams and projects. During the first six months, new joiners are given a mix of classroom training, on-the-job sessions, and virtual electronic training. Everyone follows a certain learning map to get structured training. All these measures greatly help new employees become integrated into the company and to become productive 6 – 9 months after joining. Most fresh colleagues are also given the chance to travel to other development locations at least once in the first two years of their employment. This provides them with a good opportunity to develop their own network with experienced fellow employees. But later in their career, they are sent to other development locations to learn more about the different working styles, and to develop close working relationships with other senior colleagues.

The hiring process with internal candidates is a different one. Internal candidates are requested to inform their current managers before applying for other teams, and HR has published clear policies to avoid cross team conflicts caused by 'poaching'. They are also interviewed, but the process is a lot leaner when compared to external hiring. In addition to that, candidates are only eligible to move to another team after having spent at least three years in one unit. This rule helps both the management and the employees with their planning of workload, teams, and careers.

Hiring and Reassignment

Job rotation is encouraged to provide further career options and to give employees the possibility to widen their knowledge and experiences. The internal job portal helps them to find new job opportunities within the company. Finding a suitable position is no longer left to one's personal contacts and networks. As many IT companies, SAP offers its engineers a wide variety of career choices from Sales and Consulting to R&D around the globe. To support these assignments and transfers across countries, SAP has a globally valid and fine tuned 'Mobility Policy' that sets the guidelines and standards for such international job movements. From Labs India, every year about 3 % of the overall workforce make use of the transfer opportunities to Europe or the U.S., a figure that is much higher than the corresponding figures in Germany.

Performance Management

At SAP Labs, new employees are given a six-month probation period. During this period, both employee and the employer are entitled with special contractual provisions to separate within a short period. Employees are assessed during this period, and after those six months, HR provides formal letters to indicate the end of probation period and the beginning of a permanent employment.

Until 2000, SAP employees in development did not have formal performance appraisals. In Germany, the developers were generally considered to be competent in their tasks, without any need for the managers to tell them what to do. However, this situation has changed over the years, and today, performance appraisal is compulsory. Corporate goals cascade down to department goals, and individual goals that are communicated at the start of the year and reviewed at the end of the year. Progress is also reviewed for all goals, once mandatorily in the middle of the year and optionally several times during the year.

Basically, the performance appraisal, which is conducted at least twice a year, provides structured feedback to the employees about their own development, the way they have worked, the way they are perceived by others and what their share of the overall success is. At the same time, the company is able to develop a picture of its star performers, on those who exceed the expectations (the top 20% – 30%) or even consistently exceed expectations (the top 5%). The high performers and top talents of SAP are identified once a year as a part of the talent management exercise, a so-called 'calibration process', in which the senior management meets to discuss detailed proposals which were received from middle management. As a result, special opportunities are provided to further enhance the contribution of the top performers. These contain special training programs and internship opportunities, which offer participation in special projects. Meetings with senior executives are arranged as well for strong potentials to improve their visibility to the top management.

The majority of colleagues do a very good and solid job in a demanding environment and meet expectations by the end of the year, but on the other side of the spectrum, there are also some who do not meet their managers' expectations. If it is established that this is not a serious problem (e.g. due to some family crisis at home) or it is not a manager-employee relationship problem, then a special coaching and support program is provided for those poor-performing employees. This formal process is called "Performance Improvement Program (PIP)", and it is initiated together with HR to monitor the performance on a specific set of agreed and measurable short-term goals. After a period of three months, the employees have either improved and the PIP is stopped, or they have to leave SAP Labs.

To fill gaps in their skills and competencies, managers and developers alike are encouraged to attend at least five days of training per year. The respective managers are responsible that these trainings taking place effectively. Those can either be classroom trainings or sessions offered in the learning portal, which provides learning maps and several on-demand e-learning sessions. For special needs, SAP also provides mentors or personal coaches – specifically to those where the company feels that they are part of the high potential pool.

Retaining

In India, it is quite hard to find employees who have spent their entire career in one IT company. By contrast, most of the employees in state-owned corporations, banks and government offices spend their entire working life with only one employer. In the IT industry, employees tend to change jobs after 3 – 5 years, and this is seen as a healthy change. Professionals who stay with the same employer for more than five years are at times considered as low performers and less ambitious people. However, this is definitely not SAP Labs India's view: the company provides special loyalty incentives (like company cars) for those who stay with SAP longer than five years, and when filling management positions, it gives preference to those with a long SAP history. Most vice presidents at SAP Labs India have been with SAP more than 8 – 10 years. And the attrition quota in that segment is as well the lowest of all 'age of service groups'. A special focus has always been on those young performers who tend to leave the job after one or two years, as they are a big challenge particularly for product development companies. Special career steps and incentives have been created to retain those colleagues who may leave without having been really productive and without having been able to show their capabilities.

SAP Labs India also offers additional incentives like promotion hikes, company cars, annual vacation and stock options to retain its employees. The right mixture of performance-based pay and loyalty-based incentives has worked out to be quite successful for SAP Labs India. Besides the compensation and benefits, there are of course many more retention tools available and used by SAP Labs India, to remain an attractive employer: financial and administrative support for higher education is given, rotating programs with other subsidiaries are available, and special programs for the top talents of the company are provided.

In spite of the above mentioned efforts, roughly 10% of the entry level employees still leave their companies within their first year of service, which is typical in India. One has to learn to manage this. The software industry in India has increased its salaries on average by 10 – 15% p.a. over the last five years, because most companies saw attractive salaries as a precondition to maintain a competitive position in the 'hot' market for the best talents.

The SAP Labs India Career System

At the beginning of Labs India, the career model for young joiners always started with the classical profile as 'SW Developer' or 'Engineer'. After some years, when the colleagues understood the product and the technology much better, they got the opportunity to pursue either a technical career like a development architect, chief architect, or a managerial career growing from a development manager to vice president or even senior vice president. Both technical and managerial careers had equal status in terms of compensation.

In 1998, when SAP Labs grew to 100 employees, a career model was devised to bring together employees of K&V and SAP India. It included seven steps on the management or technical career ladder (called promotion

Changes of career levels in the last 10 years			
Global job description	Career Level		
	1998 – 2002	2003 – 2005	2007 – Today
	(500 Employees)	*(2000 Employees)*	*(4000 Employees)*
Developer	P1	L1	A
	P2		B
Senior Developer	P3	L2	C
	P4		D
Manager	P5	L3	E
	P6		
VP	P7	L4	F
SVP	n/a	L5	G

Career level and title are important motivation factors for employees in India.

1998 – 2002: Promotion Level (P)

2003 – 2005: Level (L)

2007 – Today: Job Bands (A-G)

Fig. 25. Career levels at SAP Labs India

levels P1 – P7). Employees could be promoted Developer, Senior Developer, Technical Leader, and Senior Technical Leader before becoming Development Architect or Development Manager (P6). The P7 level was reserved for Vice Presidents, which SAP Labs did not have at that time.

In 2003, when SAP Labs had grown to 700 employees, there was a strong move to harmonize the relatively flat global hierarchy. In alignment with the career model in Germany, three levels were removed from the system and from then onwards, there were only Specialists, Leads, Development Managers / Architects and Vice Presidents / Chief Architects. Those levels were then called L1 – L4, and those levels were consistent through all development locations of SAP. Satish Venkatachaliah explains: "One of the key challenges in making the transition to the new career model was to ensure that the benefits program associated with the 'P' level organizational model had to be redesigned. Every employee aspired to become a Manager at P5 (or P6) because they would get certain additional benefits while an Architect who would be at the same level wouldn't be eligible for the same benefit." He further adds: "When an organization reaches a size of 500 plus, it is necessary to introduce multiple career paths to facilitate the growth of employees in 'Individual contributor roles' rather than just aspiring for becoming people managers. The Career model in 2003 was based on the 'Triple Career Path' model and presented new avenues to employees to grow into Architecture, Project management and Experts without wanting to be just 'people managers' and the success of this was the massive change in the underlying benefits program. The model was robust enough to sustain itself till the organization grew to a few thousand employees. However by around 2007 SAP Labs had morphed itself from a 'Development Centric' organization to having over 17 distinct Lines of business and the Model had to be redesigned to suit the new organization and build it to provide different paths for LOBs to suit its business needs."

In 2007, when the organization reached a size of 3,500, the career model was revised again. Given the great size and strong growth, it was felt that additional levels were needed. Thus two intermediate levels were introduced, bringing the career model back to six levels (now called band A to band F). On the first four levels, the career path is now harmonized, independent of specialization. It starts with a title like Software Engineer (A), followed by Senior Software Engineer (B), Principal Software Engineer (C) and Associate Manager (D). Only then follows the career specialization to Development Manager, Project Manager, or Development Architect (E).

Overall, the career levels were adjusted to provide employees with 'regular' promotions. These shorter and regular steps on the career ladder motivate them to perform better. On average, an entry level employee gets a promotion every two years and therefore spends eight years in SAP Labs before getting into architect or managerial roles.

Lessons Learned

Attracting, building and retaining talent remains a key challenge for IT companies in India. It is less important how many career levels the model has, it is more crucial that the criteria for moving up the ladder are transparent and well communicated. A well worked out benefit basket will help to retain colleagues, but by the end of the day motivation to stay and to excel will only be sustained by excellent leadership, attractive work and continuous opportunities to learn new things and advance.

The Life Cycle of Employees

Whereas the above described talent management process shows more the HR view on the career talent. It is as well important to understand employee's point of view.

Developers

The most important skill for people joining SAP Labs India at an entry level, is to be a very fast learner. And indeed, we observe that most of the new colleagues are intelligent, energetic, and enthusiastic and technically competent team workers. They are flexible in terms of job assignments and very eager to learn new things every day. This becomes apparent during their first days and months after joining: they always carefully follow the instructions of the managers and try to get integrated with their team and organization by just working really hard. Therefore, most of the employees start contributing to the company goals even within their first six months, and enter a productive working mode very quickly.

Most of the knowledge required to develop good software at SAP cannot be taught through classroom training. Therefore, after the initial training courses, new employees at SAP are given a job to execute basic technical tasks. To do that, they have to gain knowledge mostly from different peers and to educate themselves on specific issues. In this way, most of them acquire basic and advanced skills during their first years working for the company. Though many colleagues have worked for at least one other IT company before joining SAP Labs, they often bring little or no business experience, and hence they find it difficult to acquire business process knowledge. Special industrial tours are organized to provide chances to meet end users and customers directly. We observed that it can take as long as two years to gain sufficient technical knowledge, five years to really master the business process knowledge, and even longer to acquire interpersonal-, communication- and presentation skills.

Though most of the employees have studied all their engineering subjects in English, the written and verbal communication skills are sometimes far below the standard that is necessary to work in a global environment. Initially, many young colleagues struggle with the task of writing a short, concise document or to give a presentation to a larger audience. Additionally, entry level employees sometimes are also quite casual in their attitude towards working life, and it takes them some time to understand the meaning of shouldering responsibility. In the past, many of them considered the working environment as an extension of the university campus, as several employee friendly policies were designed to retain them. Most of the employees did not even plan their vacations properly, and managers used to receive early morning phone calls informing them about their absence. Managers at SAP often had to explain the nuances of workplace etiquette to the young employees, specifically during their first 2 – 3 years.

Whereas appreciation for work is taken with pride, critical feedback is often not taken in the right spirit (as an important hint where to improve). Managers in India are always extremely careful when giving negative feedback, and they resort to indirect ways of communication. Strong negative feedback might even result in separation, and if it is given in public, one can be sure of adverse consequences. Promotion and salary hikes are shared openly with family and friends, and employees tend to publicly flaunt their successes.

Comparing the progress of Indian and German employees in their careers, one can say that employees in Germany normally make a slower visible progress at the beginning. It could take up to 10 years, until they are formally promoted for the first time, but during that time, they have reached a very advanced and expert level of competency with an enormous depth of knowledge in their core area of work. However, these days even in Germany, an employee would feel a bit lost if he had to work on the same career level for more than a decade without formal recognition of the expertise gained.

Indian employees reach new career levels quite fast – so they get 'officially' recognized in certain terms. But only in rare cases, they would reach the very deep expert level on a specific topic, because most of them would switch the area in which they work or change their job, before reaching such expert level. Much of the learning happens in the early stage by consulting colleagues and by working in a team thus, the initial learning happens fast. Sometimes employees would do a task without understanding the actual meaning behind it, but usually they are encouraged to ask questions and challenge common wisdom. But at the point where someone reaches a high level of expertise, he or she would often tend to fear that the investment could be lost in the event of that technology going out of demand; this also drives them to rather spread thin than dig deep.

When SAP started development in India, it was difficult to convince employees to work with ABAP (Advanced Business Application Programming) as most of them felt that the technology was proprietary to SAP. They suspected it to become a niche skill, which would not have the highest market value. Most of the developers preferred to work with technologies like Java or the Microsoft development platforms, as the demand for these was high in the Indian and in the world market. Though meanwhile everyone understands the tremendous advantage of having SAP skills, there is always discussion among developers on which technology is best and on which they should invest their time and develop expertise.

As long as the *learning and earning* is progressing at a fast pace, employees are highly engaged. Learning is seen as an opportunity to gain expertise on technologies with high demand in the market, thus creating a higher market value of oneself. The career level, a fancy title, and a salary raise always help motivating employees as these things give them a better position when negotiating with potential new employers. Apart from this, certain titles like 'manager' and 'director' also have social relevance in India and may therefore even help employees with their prospect on marriage.

Newspaper and magazine reports blame Indian IT professionals for behaving as if they were born with a silver spoon in their mouth, always asking what the employer can do for them, but never what they can do for their employer. Due to the high readiness to change jobs and employers in this industry, many people in India call the IT professionals irresponsible and unpredictable. At SAP Labs India, the experience with the majority of the staff has been quite different: most of the developers became productive very soon and demonstrated a high level of flexibility. As an example, employees even cancelled their vacations, worked over weekends and late in the evenings to complete their tasks. Managers always had the luxury of having the option to request team members for overtime and those sometimes considered this as a privilege and felt important. In most cases, the employees agreed to the requests and went the extra mile to satisfy the managers.

Manager and Directors

Developing into a Management Position at SAP Labs India

Becoming a manager at SAP Labs India is not a chance for everyone – especially the role as a people manager is only given to a selected few. It requires an excellent track record on previous projects, high integrity and leadership skills. Managers who are extroverted, with higher emotional intelligence and sense of humor, find it at times easier to motivate their teams than those who are introverted. One has to be careful not to simply promote the 'best developer' or the most excellent project lead to become a manager. One might find oneself in the situation of having one excellent developer less and one bad manager more. Therefore, apart from deep subject knowledge, the leadership and communication skills play a very important role in the selection process. During the first years after promotion, managers at SAP Labs learn from their peers, they learn on the job, and they are also sent to specially designed management trainings. In such courses, the art of setting objectives, motivating teams, rewarding them, giving commitments, and executing on commitments are taught on the job.

Managers need to be good communicators: they spend lot of time in meetings and in teleconferences with other management team members working in other locations around the globe, and they need to be able to get their points clarified or pushed through in such meetings. Maintaining good working relationships with seniors in other locations is as well critical for performing well on this job.

The Job of People Managers

Performance appraisal discussions used as an instrument for retaining and motivating employees is still a powerful tool if used in the right way. But managers have to be careful to deliver balanced feedback and to set realistic expectations. Some young managers may tend to make big promises they can never keep – which might make their life easier initially, but surely leads to problems in the team later.

Normally, managing a team during the first appraisal period is quite easy, as one can always refer to future prospects and projects. The second appraisal becomes a bit more challenging as many of the initial promises have to be fulfilled. If the manager happens to stay with the same team during the third appraisal, then it may become very hard to align the high expectations of the team members with the ground realities of the project execution. At times it may be impossible to satisfy demands, partly because they are unrealistic, partly because the team situation would not allow certain moves to happen.

Young team members often ask their managers about exact tasks and timelines to qualify for a promotion. "What do I need to do to reach the next level?", is a question a manager hears more often than not. It is difficult to explain to young employees that they have to acquire deep expertise to increase their value and contribution to the company, and that no automatic mechanism can be applied to reach a certain level. However, after having spent more time in the company and after having acquired some experience, for most of them, the procedures and realities become clearer, and they display a more mature behavior.

On the one hand, employees are highly demanding, on the other hand they often request for clear performance KPIs (Key Performance Indicators), and they want their goals to be stretched to more challenging levels. If the goals can be identified and if they can be measured objectively, the productivity can be quite high, as the employees go all out to achieve the targets. If encouraged to do so, team members also come up with ideas to improve processes and products, and they do not hesitate to communicate their suggestions to senior management during meetings.

Overall, managers either grow into senior positions or take lateral transfers to other teams when they want a change. The move to another location is also an option. Managers who stay with the same task for more than five years are quite rare. If they decided to stay on one position for a long period, they would have to release their potential successor, whom they had built up over the time, to move to another team. The attrition rate on the management level is very low at SAP Labs India, which provides high stability to the Labs.

One of the most challenging cases consists in the larger re-organizations at SAP that happen on a global scale. The reporting lines between the manager in India and his or her senior overseas manager are changed often due to re-organization in the company. This always results in a period of uncertainty and adjustment. Given the distance and the different time zones, it can take 3 – 6 months to get into a trusted working relationship and stable working mode again. Distributed development is based on close networks, which cannot be established by just painting a new organization chart. Thus, the creation of new network structures takes time, and it is very costly as it takes many overseas trips, initial on-site meetings and numerous conference calls before reaching a smooth state.

Managers at SAP Labs are also faced with meeting both the expectations of the business unit (LoB) and the expectations of the local labs management, specifically in terms of people related issues. The labs management requests them to participate in special assignments and events or to support neighboring business units with hiring assistance during times of rapid growth. Those demands need to be met as well, irrespective of the current pressure in their own business unit.

Lessons Learned

Visible recognition in terms of career movements is still very important for employees. After five to seven years of tenure most of them expect to reach a management level (DM, PM, Architect). Obviously, these kinds of movements are only possible during strong growth scenarios in the past decade. Only a higher focus on expert levels, job rotations and assignments will help companies to meet employee's expectations to progress.

Relationship and Expectation Management

Many managers from abroad felt overwhelmed with the importance of relationships in India and wondered how to handle the different expectations. SAP tried to tackle this issue by having, with Dr. Udo Urbanek, one very experienced manager posted in India from day one of the Labs India operations, who was known by all of the former K&V employees. He already had the necessary relationships with a large part of the organization. The other co-director of those early days, Werner Konik, had a history with the other part of the young Labs India staff. He had led a team within SAP before, which was responsible for the country versions of SAP R/3 for Asia-Pacific. SAP took care that existing relationships were not broken and that everyone at SAP Labs India, specifically all team leaders and managers, had at least one senior manager in India whom they could talk to, in terms of addressing problems, consulting for their or their groups' challenges or just to celebrate success together.

Relationship building is one of the key factors of any leader in a company in India. This does not mean that a manager has to be every team members' friend. It has more to do with the fact of understanding everyone's ambitions and feelings, and therefore, with the ability to translate the CEO's message into something that makes sense to the individual people. Just forwarding an e-mail from the top management does not help. The leader has to answer for each of the messages she or he delivers, the following questions:

- Why does this matter for my team members?
- How can they contribute to the goal and fulfill the vision?
- What is in it for them?

So managing does not only mean to deliver a share of what was requested by the board, but to break it down and to return feedback as well to the upper management. Leaders need to be able to understand new trends, think along new ways and understand how to take advantage of them. And they need to be able to take their teams with them. All this is easier said than done, because such leaders are people who love to work in a non-bureaucratic environment and demand personal freedom in their decisions, plus a boss who supports their risk-taking and constant intellectual challenges. The larger an organization gets, the more bureaucracy creeps in and prevents (with its rules and formal procedures) such an atmosphere to exist.

Nevertheless, in the start-up phase of SAP Labs India, this environment was certainly provided. The individual business units had a lot of freedom as their managers abroad (in Singapore and Walldorf) trusted in them fully. At the same time, the executive board, namely Peter Zencke, trusted his two co-directors a lot, so they were on their own setting up the Indian framework, ranging from the work environment to defining the first simple policies. Certainly one has to consider that it is easier to build and run an operation with 100 – 300 people, mainly based on strong relationships and a mutual understanding of goals and of what it takes to achieve them, than to do the same thing with an organization of 4,000 people or more.

The importance of relationships was one thing the organization realized; the other one was certainly the ability to deal with the employees' expectations. As mentioned above, the talent market in India was always, except for the years 2001 and 2002, recently and perceived as 'hot'. Most companies were growing in India with a speed similar to SAP, many even much faster – in a kind of accelerated turbocharged growth. This caused many younger employees to believe that it was a kind of natural law that accelerated personal growth would continue to happen. Accordingly, the expectations for career advancement, salary increase, opportunities, and work content have always been high – sometimes much too high for many managers to fulfill them.

Initially, this put the managers outside of India in a dilemma. As mentioned before, in the years 1998 and 1999, formal appraisal talks virtually did not happen in Walldorf, and managers were used to employees who did not actively push for their own career. A career in Germany normally just 'happened' if somebody appeared to be outstandingly qualified for a certain role, or it did not happen – which was mostly fine for many employees as well (or at least their managers believed so). A salary letter would be received at home; most managers would not bother to tell their employees in advance what the increase would be for a specific period. So they would not face the trouble of having to explain it. In India, the environment was quite the reverse. Managers were always confronted with clearly articulated demands in terms of the next career step or bonus. Initially, the need to explain all these things to everyone was experienced unpleasantly by many of the international managers. Most of them adjusted after one to two cycles at the latest, but some did not. This leads to the next section about the people who were sent to India from other countries.

Expatriates in India

From the beginning, there was one important SAP mandate –not to repeat the way in which SAP Labs Foster City had been established in the initial years, when German was the common language, because so many colleagues had taken that opportunity to settle down there. As a result, many of the opportunities in Foster City at the beginning were not really leveraged, as the lab itself was kind of 'expatriate' in California. This situation was corrected later, when the lab was moved to Palo Alto and was strengthened in the years under Shai Agassi with many new top level entries from other companies in the valley.

For Labs India, the expatriate quota was always limited to a maximum of 1 % – not more than 1 % of its employees should be assigned from other countries than India. Initially, these 'other countries' just comprised Germany, to be more precise: Walldorf. Still, SAP never faced a problem with an expatriate 'gold-rush' to Bangalore. Being considered as a 'hardship country', which imposed a lot of unusual difficulties (always from the viewpoint of someone who grew up in Germany or in the U.S.), the willingness to go to India and settle down there for some years has always been low. It required either a certain 'Abenteuerlust' (adventurousness) or some deep cultural interest to take this step. Initially, there were managers in the fields of Localization (Martin Prinz), HCM (Alain Lesaffre), Financial Industries (Ralf Besinger) and Apparel and Footwear Solution (Klaus Volkmer) besides the two lab directors (Dr. Udo Urbanek and Clas Neumann), who joined the company in 1999 and 2000. In 2001, SAP Labs India had exactly five expatriates while being a company of about 500 people.

The managers from abroad were brought in mainly for establishing a stronger link to the headquarters and to bring in knowledge that was not (easily) accessible in India. Actually, this principle became a successful concept for knowledge dissemination among the ramp-up of teams in India: bringing a manager with the required business knowledge from somewhere, hiring a team locally with the help of local HR, and then starting to make the team productive. After two to three years, a local successor would be built up in India who could take on the team, so the expatiate could move back to his or her home country. The concept is still followed today. SAP India has more than 4,000 employees, led by predominantly Indian senior and middle managers. But for certain topics where know-how is not yet available locally, expatriates are still coming to India. In

2008, the number of expatriates working at SAP Labs India was about 25, around 0.6 % of the overall workforce.

Of course, there were also assignment failures. Either the family did not fare well, or colleagues were just too overwhelmed by India – sometimes even the best planned assignment turns out badly for both sides. Luckily, such cases were rare, but whenever it happened, SAP could react fast and bring the expatriate back to his or her home country without a big loss of face for anyone.

Curiously, the highest 'failure quota' within the expatriate community, in terms of cultural misfits, came from Indians who returned to India after having spent 15–25 years in the U.S. These Non-Resident-Indians (NRIs) often had a completely different way of thinking, and found it much harder to adjust than many of the other expatriates with a non-Indian background. There were reasons for this on both sides: on the one hand, some of them displayed a certain sense of superiority towards local Indian colleagues – which as can be imagined, did not go over well with their hosts; on the other hand, local Indians' level of understanding and forgiveness regarding the mistakes made by foreigners, which certainly existed towards Europeans, was less compassionate concerning their own countrymen. They were expected to behave like 'Indians', which was not expected from Germans, to whom everyone in India would show some forgiveness regarding their cultural behavior or strange attitude.

Nevertheless, NRIs who return to India can provide a company with a lot of positive drive, bringing their extensive experience, different working style, and a new set of values. This is always much appreciated by a company. However, the fact remains that in the first 10 years of SAP Labs India, about 30 % of those assignments were canceled before the planned tenure, whereas the failure quota for all other assignees abroad is only 5 %. Certainly, in many instances, the individuals were not to blame for this, but the fact that the local culture was not able to deal with the situation.

Over all these years, more than 60 colleagues from different labs have spent two or more years of their professional career in India. Those colleagues then became 'ambassadors' who could also serve as knowledge hubs for others in Walldorf or Palo Alto, who would not know India that well. The lesson learnt by the company is that any assignment to or from India requires detailed planning, pre-assignment trips and a clear agreement on mutual expectations on such assignment. The family needs to be hundred percent behind it, and potential difficulties need to be addressed before the assignment starts. By these measures, the chances of success do increase a lot.

Virtual Teams

Most of SAP's senior managers do actually believe strongly in the value add and creativity of virtual teams – but still, there is always a difference between believing something and acting accordingly. How much easier it is to just call the people we have physically around us to a room, than to always dial in others? How much discomfort do we accept to hold meetings only at times that ensure everyone can attend? And how comfortable are we in staring at a phone without having a clue about the emotions of the participants at the other end of a teleconference. Virtual teams are groups of people who have a common goal, but who have to work across time zones, distance and cultures by means of modern communication.

Before SAP Labs India was created, nobody at SAP really thought about the necessity of virtual teams or even about best practices to make such teams work. Palo Alto always had a very thin overlap with work happening in Walldorf; U.S. teams only had a few chances to collaborate with Germany. So the honor was left to India to systematically think about how to make virtual teams work – something that has always been taken into account whenever creating organizational structures.

In terms of people management, the virtual team concept matters a lot, because it requires an open mindset from managers and individual contributors alike, as well as cultural awareness and high communication skills to get into a productive working mode. Not everyone is able to be part of a virtual team, and many people are never really happy with it, though they are forced to work in such environment. In India, employees get used to the virtual team environment from their first day of employment. Representing the 'off-shore' location from a German point of view, it is clear that those people out there need to make an extra effort to ensure their alignment with the headquarters. And it becomes everybody's daily routine to establish mechanisms supporting productive and transparent collaboration colleagues abroad, while at the same time ensuring that senior management expectations from outside of India are met.

On the other side, achieving this state of productive and transparent collaboration was not that easy since the majority of German employees were not used to working in such environment. Thus, an 'unlearning' process had to take place before they could master the new virtual team concept and appreciate its value. Until today, not all development departments have understood it completely, and sometimes important decisions are still first made in Germany, and are then announced in India, instead of being developed together with the colleagues from the Labs.

6.5 Conclusion

SAP Labs India has changed the way SAP handles people-related processes globally, due to its size and due to the fact that inculcating Indian employees in a real sense into the global workforce is a 'must succeed' issue for SAP on its path towards a truly global company. Many aspects of this learning process is still ongoing. Many people-related practices that were established at SAP Labs India early on, like a regular performance appraisals, talent management, management programs, outdoor team building exercises, and merger workshops, have meanwhile become global practices. This showcases Labs India's very strong people focus, where HR issues are always at the center of all top management activities. Slowly, the value of this people focus has become something that headquarters groups have also recognized. The people-based culture of India has also helped many managers overseas to focus more on people issues than they did before, and look upon their Indian colleagues as they do their non-Indian colleagues.

People management, as described in the chapter above, remains the most critical success factor of SAP Labs India in the years to come. SAP's ability to attract and retain the best talents will continue to make a difference to the company overall – but certainly to the lab in specific. No management team in India can claim success, if it fails on people-related issues. This requires a constantly alert mindset, a willingness to try new things, a comfort with ambiguity, the ability to dismiss preconceptions that restrict creative thinking, and the drive to continuously improve. What has worked up until now may be completely useless tomorrow – and even 10 years of experience may not help to solve the next big challenge just around the corner.

7 Infrastructure Challenges

The number one challenge in India is the huge infrastructure problem. This is not only a fact one can read from statistics or in newspapers and diverse internet blogs, it is also obvious to everyone who lives or travels to India.

For instance, if a visitor arrives in one of the metro cities, by the time he leaves the airport, this becomes apparent: depending on the time of the day, one can expect to spend up to three hours reaching the city center, and most of the time, the driver will be quite busy avoiding all the pot-holes in the street, the cows, other animals occasionally crossing, or trucks that have broken down on their journey left right on the road. Shortly after, at the check-in at the (five star) hotel, one has to be aware that it can get pitch dark at any time, as power cuts in many Indian cities are still a daily phenomenon, and the hotel-owned diesel generator may fail at that moment as well. The network connection for the laptop may or may not work, depending on the hotel management and the number of back-up arrangements they have. Even using the one's own cell phone, it is not that simple to get connected to the outside world. In Mumbai for example, one must be very lucky to have a 30 min. uninterrupted phone call, and in Bangalore the interruptions are even more frequent.

One may wonder what the reasons are for this situation. On the one hand, with its strongly growing economy and being a cash rich country, India is still a promising market. It belongs to the few countries in the world that have demonstrated their capabilities in developing nuclear weapons and fighter jets, and have sent satellites into the orbit. And on the other hand, you will not find a single kilometer stretch of pot-hole free driving in the biggest IT city of India, Bangalore. Putting this question to IT engineers in a company like SAP Labs India, would bring many different answers: "That's because the infrastructure does not keep pace with the strong economic growth", "That's because our politicians have neither the will nor the capability to do something about it.", "The weather is extreme in India, so with every monsoon, our roads get damaged." or even "Infrastructure problem? What's the problem?" Abdul Kalam, former president of India,

C. Neumann and J. Srinivasan, *Managing Innovation from the Land of Ideas and Talent: The 10-Year Story of SAP Labs India,*
DOI: 10.1007/978-3-540-89283-0_7, © Springer-Verlag Berlin Heidelberg 2009

was once quoted as saying: "Our roads are paved with corruption". But there may be as well a social component: "Why", asks V. Raghunathan in his book 'Games Indians Play', "don't I contribute in maintaining a beautiful park? Why is my concern for quality in whatever I do rather Lilliputian?" (Raghunathan, 2006).

So the questions and opinions around the whole infrastructure problem are quite diverse, and getting to its root cause is a very complex and complicated process. It may be even too difficult to get there, and it is certainly not the aim of this book to come to any conclusion on the causes for the infrastructure inefficiencies or even to a solution to fix them.

However, the fact is that central and state governments invest trillions of Rupees in fixing the symptom: new airports are planned or are already under construction in all major cities, and there is a huge interstate road project called 'Golden Quadrangle', which connects the big metro cities in the South and West of India. The telecom sector has been privatized to allow more investments and expertise to flow into the country in order to build a world class telecom and mobile network. Even the aviation sector is dominated by private players who run a safe and efficient network, but are helpless against the delays caused by the overcrowded airports and airspace. There cannot be any doubt that the politicians have understood the demand and are trying to act on this. Frequent travelers are often surprised to see new highways and bridges appearing, but this does still not satisfy the growing demand, and the planning and execution is not at the level where it should be. R. K. Mishra, winner of the 'Lead India campaign', in a recent talk he gave to SAP employees in Bangalore, asked: "Why does the government plan a multi billion dollar metro in Bangalore that connects four areas of the city nobody has ever heard about? Why don't they connect the most growing areas, like Electronic City and Whitefield, where all the thousands of IT companies are and where those people work who use cars and buses now and whom we want to get into public mass transport?" One can as well ask why so many politicians are engaged in a useless public debate on whether one should re-open the old Bangalore Airport, just after the brand new airport opened its gates.

In some way, the government and its execution arms always fall a bit short of the ever growing demand. And the demand is also created by companies like SAP, and other multinationals, that are hungry for energy, need a constant extension of bandwidth, and would like to see a smooth flow of employees to their offices every day.

Accordingly, the culture resulting from the success of the country and the foreign investments in the IT sector, has changed the economic status of the average middle class. With the increasing wealth of the middle class, there is also a strongly growing demand for proper roads and for a full and consistent flow of electricity over the whole working day, as there are millions who work in the IT market. For example, in a city like Bangalore, all IT professionals want to get to work every day using their own car without major interruptions by traffic jams. Ten years ago, a car was completely out of reach for 99 % of the employed workforce in India; today, it is only a quarterly salary away. By the time the so-called 'one lakh car', or in Europe known as the 1,500 Euro car, will hit the road in 2009, it will not only promote the people's mobility, it will also add to the congestion on the roads. In addition, if one imagines that every single one of India's IT professionals switches on his modern, big flat-screen TV, gigantic refrigerator (which would be sufficient for a soccer team), and of course the air conditioner at the same time, one might get another idea of the power problems that India's 'mega cities' have to face every day.

Multinational companies in India's high tech cities and foreign companies that plan to open a subsidiary there, have to be aware of these facts and the future trend. Without any doubt, the gap between supply and demand is still widening, and only a complete crash of the economy or a miracle, probably, will solve this problem.

7.1 How SAP Copes with the Infrastructure Issues in Bangalore

From the beginnings of SAP Labs India in 1998, SAP has tried to take a holistic view on the future infrastructure demand of its operations. At that time, the joint managing director Dr. Udo Urbanek was in charge of the first infrastructure setup.

K+V and the Early SAP India

In the beginning of 1998, SAP had acquired Kiefer & Veittinger, a small vendor for 'Sales Force Automation' software, headquartered in Mannheim, Germany. During the acquisition process, it turned out that it also had a larger development center in Bangalore. At that time, K&V certainly was a pioneer in leveraging the talent pool in India, and the whole setup of the development center in Bangalore, at that time was very much like a start-up. In Bangalore, they had rented a house in the middle of a normal residential area, since high class office space was just not available. At that time, office buildings actually did not exist, and the few that were there were mainly in the prime location in the city center and were occupied by large banks.

So the first setup of K&V was in a normal residence, a typical four bedroom villa in a quiet district, called Koramangala in the South of Bangalore. Obviously, the infrastructure problems there were even worse: nearly all the time, the electricity was coming from a huge generator in the attached garage, and the telephone connection was so weak that at any given point of time, no more than five employees could make a phone call. Data transfer was only possible at night, and with a transfer rate of 64 kB/s, it took the whole night to shift software packages back and forth. Space was a real constraint as well. As much as the first 20–25 software engineers found the villa spacious to work in, with the strong growth of K&V, it became more and more cramped and over-crowded. In the last summer in Koramangala in 1998, shortly before SAP Labs India was formally established in the brand new International Tech Park Limited (ITPL) office tower, there were 80 employees developing software under severe space constraints. To cope with the problem, PCs were set up virtually everywhere. Clas Neumann once found an employee who had even occupied a bathroom with his workstation! But it worked, the colleagues felt really 'connected' in its true sense and had fun at that place. On Friday evenings, everyone joined the beer and snack and TGIF ('Thank God it's Friday') party on the roof terrace. Everyone knew everyone; there was fun at work that made the infrastructure obstacles a secondary issue. Air conditioning was not expected, but something really appreciated if it happened to work for a few hours on a hot summer day.

Similarly, SAP set up its first office in Bangalore in the city center in 1996, in a small side road of the main Mahatma Gandhi Road (M.G. Road). Therefore, it was always just called the 'Brunton Road office'. Packed on a floor space of maybe 300 sqm, the number of colleagues, both from the field and the development organization, was growing fast as well, as SAP started early to develop a country version for India. At some point of time, the crowd became so large that there was no other way than renting another piece of floor space in one of the bank towers nearby, just to be able to continue working. This was quite a makeshift arrangement, as everyone expected to soon join the operations of SAP India and the K&V developers.

7.2   The Move to International Tech Park Limited (ITPL)

In spring 1998, it was already clear that SAP would not find enough floor space in the city center to join and develop its operations, which meanwhile were distributed to three different buildings. Therefore, the search went on for new and better office space. Coming from the Koramangala experience of K&V, it was clear for the managing director Dr. Udo Urbanek that the new office space had to fulfill some pre-conditions that would be more important than anything else:

- 100 % availability of power for 24 hours;
- excellent phone and data connectivity;
- well-working building infrastructure (elevators, water supply etc.).

What sounds as a no-brainer in most countries and even in many Indian technology parks today, was quite a challenge in Bangalore in 1998. Simple floor spaces opened here and there, but none of them would have fulfilled the expected quality standards or pre-conditions. Some facilities did not provide a data line, others had no reliable power backup and even others looked so shabby that nobody would have dared to ask people to move into such a place.

Finally, the decision was made to move into the first phase building of the International Tech Park Limited (ITPL), which was just being setup in the East of Bangalore, in an area called Whitefield. It had been a very quiet area till then, and it actually included a lot of farm land, a few villages and an area of villas and churches dating back to the British, who used to spend time there, on what they called the 'quiet country side'. Twenty kilometers from the city center, but connected by two roads to the city, this seemed to be the perfect spot for the government of Karnataka to establish its second IT hub in the city of Bangalore, after Electronic City, which is located in the South of Bangalore.

ITPL was the first Tech Park meeting international standards in India. Built by a consortium of the Tata Group, the government of Karnataka, and the Singapore Development Board, it also had quite a unique composition of shareholders. Together, the owners of the tech park brought not only the capital, but also the know-how to build and operate such technology park. As the arrangement was, the Singaporeans would provide the

Fig. 26. International Tech Park Limited (ITPL) at Bangalore in its early days.
Source: International Tech Park Bangalore 2009

park's management and managing directors, thus continuously bringing in
their know-how in tech park operations.

ITPL was a good choice for SAP Labs. On the official founding day of
SAP Labs India, all developers moved into the new premises on the 12th
floor of the brand new 'Discoverer Building' of ITPL. Though many colleagues missed the closeness to their home residences, as the company had
moved 20 kilometers outside the city, everyone felt more than compensated, seeing the new spacious office layout and the brand new infrastructure. There was no doubt, this space was of international standards: a nice
reception area welcomed all visitors and employees and smoothly working
elevators transported them to the 12th floor where a receptionist welcomed
them. The workplace had air condition 24 hours a day and a perfect view
across Whitefield. And the best part, of course, was the 100 % availability
of power and data connectivity.

Parks like ITPL have their own power plants to generate energy and their
own satellite links to transfer voice and data. Therefore, there cannot be
any doubt that such parks, which meanwhile exist in all bigger cities in India, are a perfect environment to start operations in a hassle-free way. Specifically when the setup is still smaller (up to 500 people), the construction

of a company owned building may not be the most efficient way of running an office. In parks like ITPL, one finds the perfect alternative that allows the company to concentrate on its core job and leave the rampant infrastructure issues outside the office.

ITPL provided SAP Labs India a reliable environment in which to grow. As the park expanded over time, SAP always found sufficient floor space to expand. Starting from one floor, the company soon rented another one, the 13th, then the 5th, 6th, and finally SAP Labs India was occupying five floors with a total of 10,000 sqm in the park. However, after three years, in 2001, it became clear that ITPL was only the starting point for SAP's continuous growth plans in India. A solution would have to be found, and this could only be the construction of a company owned campus.

7.3   The SAP Labs India Campus

Early in 2001, the principle decision to leave ITPL and to build a company owned campus was made by the two joint MDs, Dr. Udo Urbanek and Clas Neumann. They decided to discuss this proposal with the executive board, to express why a company owned campus made sense:

1. SAP Labs hoped for cost reductions and for a better planning of its cost base. Due to the relatively low personnel costs in India, infrastructure contributes a major portion of any company's costs. High-tech parks may be competitive in the base rent, but they usually charge quite substantial amounts as a 'maintenance fee' that includes air conditioning, electricity, and the general upkeep of the place. This maintenance fee can easily be another 50 % on top of the rent.

   In addition to that, the MDs had to take a long-term view: even though in 2001, the real estate market was rather flat, SAP Labs expected it to raise – a prediction that came true some years later and much stronger than expected. In 2008, the neighboring piece of land was sold at a price 20 times higher than the price SAP had paid in 2002. Just to repeat it: the prices had grown by 2,000 % in just six years!

2. A company owned campus is a matter of pride for the employees – it means a real mark in their hometowns, something they can show to friends and family members: "Look – this is where we work. This is

SAP Labs India!" Hence, an investment like this has a huge visibility in the market. The clear message is: "SAP is here to stay. We believe in India, in Bangalore and in its talent". This message was very important for recruiting talent as well as for selling software in India.

3. Finally, SAP wanted to develop the location in Bangalore, and therefore, it wanted its own piece of land, large enough for future expansion that gave it more flexibility to grow at a later point in time, independent of real estate and property markets.

In February 2001, with the help of the global finance head in charge, a proposal was presented to the executive board based on some initial estimates by builders and real estate companies. With total costs of EUR 15 million for about 1,000 workplaces, this proposal looked quite viable. Nevertheless, it was based on some rough estimates that the managing directors got from external consultants and vendors. The proposal was accepted by the board and after going through the details, is was soon realized that those initial estimates did not include all the 'nitty gritties' one had to consider: taxes, side costs, some of the furniture, landscaping and the like. By summer, it was clear that SAP could never buy land and build a campus on it for the estimated EUR 15 million. Thus, the MDs had to talk once again to the SAP executive board – in a meeting in September 2001.

This time, the proposal was perfect, based on ready-to-be-signed contract with multi-billion dollar real estate giant Bovis Land Leas. It was absolutely watertight, and the costs were in the 20 million EUR range, including the land. SAP Labs India was absolutely sure that it would make sense; the break would even be reached after eight years compared to rental, including all the financing costs. The preparation had been huge; Werner Brandt's and Peter Zencke's office had both gone through it a couple of times beforehand. Only the timing could not have been worse: two days after '09-11', the executive board had many things on the agenda, but the last thing was to approve an investment and cash outflow of EUR 20 million for the future growth project in India. The proposal was put on hold and not discussed any further. Companywide, SAP was trying to keep its cash together, as the financial markets became extremely nervous, and SAP had to expect the worst.

In India, nevertheless, the managers continued detailed planning and came back to the board with an updated proposal in February 2002. The basic figures were unchanged, and SAP Labs India suggested a timeline of 18 months (6 months for detailed layouts and design, and 12 months for construction) to build SAP's first company owned campus in the Asia Pacific. This time, the proposal was solid, and the time line was aggressive (SAP had already lost some months after the crucial '09-13 board meeting' the year before). The executive board approved the proposal after making some deep budgetary cuts, and so the new location had to be realized without fancy things like a multi-level car park or solar energy options.

From February 2002, the countdown was on, and SAP Labs' intent was an opening in September 2003. To build a large infrastructure on a 20 acre piece of land sounded like a pretty big project, but every country would have its own execution challenges. In India, it all started with the necessary government approvals. Some ministers would need to approve it, specifically as it was decided to buy the land from the Karnataka Investment and Development Board (KIADB), the investment wing of Karnataka's ministry of industry. KIADB was positive about the project, and despite cross fire from some ministries in the initial stage, the proposal was quickly accepted, and SAP Labs received the initial green light. Obviously, in every country, an entrepreneur has to deal with different governmental interventions. There are many terms and conditions a company has to fulfill, for example, the timeline until the proposed investment has to be completed, to the number of workplaces that have to be created, and the built-up space that has to be erected.

It might have been the timing that helped things go smoothly for SAP Labs India. In 2002, most companies were very careful with investments, so SAP experienced full support by the Indian government at that time. Even when at some point, certain previous land owners argued against the project and initiated an action against it – on the high court level, the IT ministry stepped in, compensated those people appropriately and thus resolved the matter in short period.

The detailed planning phase took the full six months SAP Labs had estimated. The company hired RSP, an Indian-Singaporean architecture firm, to do the exterior design of the building, the utilization concept, and the master design. And they did indeed set a new standard for building design in Bangalore. Even though the MDs did not have much experience in this area, they gave of course some guidelines to the designing team:

- *Modern, yet with a touch of Indian tradition*

  SAP wanted to build, of course, the most modern software campus in town, a kind of benchmark for all followers. At the same time, some traditional Indian elements and materials should be visible to the public, like courtyards, granite, or bodies of water. Today, the campus has achieved this integration: inside and out, there are courtyards and bodies of water, which are traditional elements of South Indian house architecture. But the building, with its huge transparent glass façade, looks quite elegant and adds a chic, modern high-tech look. At the end of the day, engineers want to work in a modern environment, not in a museum!

- *Campus layout*

  Designed in a ground-plus-two-floors layout, the SAP Labs campus buildings were conceived to set itself apart from the typical office blocks around it, which were usually attached blocks of seven to eight floors in rectangle form, clad with lots of aluminum. SAP especially wanted to have a lot of daylight in its buildings, which was achieved by three massive 400 sqm glass roofs across the courtyards. So everyone could work from 8:00 AM till 5:00 PM without having to switch on the light. And why was this important? Simply because we all know that the production of happy hormones starts from 2,500 Lux – creativity needs light!

- *Inspirative as an R&D center*

  From the beginning, the building was designed to function as an R&D hub. Thus, moving space, coffee corners and relaxation zones played a huge role. Space where people could meet, discuss ideas, or just have a coffee together, became a paramount design element, and SAP Labs created lots of such space: the best places with the best views were all reserved for the coffee corners. And outside, many inviting shady seats next to the bodies of water were provided.

- *Form follows function concept in all respects*

  Many rounds of discussion and sessions were invested into the actual setup of training rooms, meeting rooms, and work areas. It was decided to go for an open environment, with so-called 'cubicles', but not in a large boring floor layout, rather clustered around the courtyards. The management decided to choose an inside-out approach, first designing the work areas with their actual size and measures, and then the isles and meeting rooms around it, and finally the building design that had to bring it all together. This was maybe not the most intuitive way to design such a building, but it worked. No space was wasted, and all workplaces are kind of comparably located, with respect to light, reach and comfort. Another element were the water features inside the building. As SAP assumed that conversation noise would travel across courtyards and might disturb the engineers, fountains were installed internally so that the sound of nature and water would permeate building.

- *German building standards and norms*

  Even though building a campus in India, for SAP it was clear early on that it would like to see the good old German Industry Norm (DIN) to be followed for the construction and the specification of the campus. Luckily, the Indian building norms are not too much different, though not every building or builder seems to follow them. However, at least there was no need for a lot of knowledge transfer to the firms on the job. The structural design, the selection of façade or the heat absorbing windows, as well as the interiors (Lux levels of the lighting, safety measures, emergency exits, fire retardant carpets and materials etc.), were chosen according to the same standards SAP would use in any of its other buildings around the globe. Many of the materials were, of course, not available in India, so they had to be imported – but this was possible without causing any delays. Today, the building façade is from France, the revolving entry doors and IT room equipment are from Germany, the elevator is from Switzerland, the carpet from Italy, the air conditioning is from China, the generators are from the U.S. and the furniture is largely from Malaysia. From India, there are still many items, like the windows, the basic structure, the fixtures and all the granite that was used inside and outside of the building. So finally, it became a really global fusion product.

- *The 'experience'*

  The architects certainly insisted on a certain 'experience' for anybody who entered the campus – something different and very positive that encourages the employee or visitor to step in. This was achieved with a massive 'solarium' in the entry area, a transparent glass front and a hall stretching across all three floors with open balconies reaching into it representing the coffee corners. Initially, the MDs were not too convinced about it, but today, everybody enjoys this area as the communication center piece of the campus.

Fig. 27. Solarium and entrance in the main building, Phase 1 of SAP Labs India

The Construction Phase

In September 2002, SAP celebrated the groundbreaking of its new India campus – after a very thorough planning phase, and after all legal and commercial hurdles had been cleared. It was quite a journey for all people at SAP Labs India; at that time, there were not many multinational companies in Bangalore who had built a campus, though General Electric (GE) and Texas Instruments had gone that route much earlier.

One has to say to the credit of SAP's general contractor, Bovis Land Lease, that they really put their best people on the job, and under the leadership of their country head, Tom Mikus, this team really tried hard to keep to the budgets and timelines.

A key success factor was certainly the personal attention that everyone who was involved put into the project: from the Labs' MDs and the head of finance at that time (Kush Desai) to the Bovis team and the key architect – everyone felt very committed to the project and put a lot of energy into it. Every week, the team would meet three times, and Clas Neumann would also put on the boots two or three times per week and walk across the construction site to understand what was going on.

Fig. 28. Martin Prinz, Clas Neumann, Shri RV Deshpande, and Peter Zencke at the groundbreaking ceremony of the SAP Labs campus, Phase 1, in 2002

Fig. 29. Clas Neuman at the groundbreaking ceremony of the SAP Labs campus, Phase 1, in 2002

Of course, as in most projects of such scale, not everything went as expected. On one occasion, SAP had ordered all the glass windows from the only company in India that could do them as specified, which happened to be in Delhi. To ensure absolute top quality, Bovis had even sent an engineer to Delhi to monitor the final heat soaking process in that factory and the proper loading of the trucks. Then the engineer flew back to Bangalore, and the people at the campus were expecting the windows to arrive after a couple of days (the distance from Delhi to Bangalore is about 2,500 km by road). One week passed, but no truck arrived. Another week passed – still no truck. The MDs got very nervous, but even the glass factory had no clue about their whereabouts. Meanwhile, the monsoon season was about to start, and SAP's building still had no windows. However, the construction of the interior should have already started by then! After another couple of days, the owner of the trucks was able to track them down somewhere in Maharashtra, where one of the drivers had diverted his tour by a couple of hundred kilometers to attend the wedding of a relative. He just convinced the other drivers to follow suit. So these gentlemen spent a week celebrating a wedding, while the SAP Labs management was having nightmares, being scared their windows might have got robbed or destroyed

Fig. 30. Construction at the SAP Labs Campus, main building

on their journey down (which would have meant at least a two months delay!). But this is as well part of India and its culture: the family always comes first – and time is a very elastic term.

Two weeks before the official inauguration of the campus, SAP was already able to move the first 300 engineers into the building. A small 'pooja' (religious ceremony) was done in one of the courtyards, and work started one Monday morning, in Block C. Only 24 hours later the first catastrophe hit! The next morning at 5 AM, Clas Neumann got a wake-up call from one of

Fig. 31. Henning Kagermann visits the construction site

his administration managers with the words: "Sir, the campus is sinking!" Initially, Neumann quickly realized that it was something very serious: "I jumped into my trousers, pulled out any shirt I could grab and rushed to the site. Indeed, I saw kind of a 'horror scenario' – at least from the perspective of someone who wants to inaugurate a world class building in some weeks. The complete courtyard in one of the office blocks had gone down 3 – 6 feet, bursting all water and electrical pipes going across it. This had led to massive flooding of the ground floor and the basement, and one staircase that connected the floors was just ripped apart. We quickly checked the basement underneath this office block to assess the damage. It turned out that, though it was basically wet and partly flooded, the principle structure seemed to be okay. As the courtyard garden was built up on compacted sand, only that portion had given way, but the concrete structure was still okay. The structural engineers and architects gave it a 'safe to work' certificate, so work could resume as planned at 8 AM. But we got a bit alarmed on the overall workmanship of the building", Clas Neumann retells the story.

Detailed studies were requested by SAP and carried out by a senior team from Germany, which was flown in to assess the complete campus structure. It turned out to be okay, but some of the required safety margins (e.g. for earthquakes) were not factored in. Therefore, most of the columns and foundations had to be redone within 12 months – actually, the root cause were wrong drawings by some structural engineers, which nobody had checked properly. Again learning from this exercise – one better check everything twice – the four eye principle is somewhat of a 'must', specifically when dealing with manual labor and work.

The campus was finally built in exactly 12 months and got inaugurated together with Peter Zencke, the German ambassador, and the IT minister of Karnataka, in a big ceremony in September 2003. It became not only a matter of pride for all employees, it was also the expected new standard SAP could set, in terms of what a really high-quality workplace in IT would mean. Even though many colleagues who may have never experienced the times when IT engineers were sitting in a bathroom of a residential house in Koramangala, trying to develop software at 35° C, take this standard for granted – many still have this special feeling every day when passing through the revolving door into the campus.

Fig. 32. Main building on the campus of SAP Labs Bangalore, 2008

For SAP Labs India, the campus provides not only the space to grow, but also the best available infrastructure. There are not only diesel generators with a two Megawatt capacity, but the campus also has a UPS (Uninterruptible Power Supply) emergency device that is sufficient for one to two hours of backup. Actually, its full capacity was only needed once: somewhere outside, a caterpillar excavation machine had cut the main power line to the campus. On that very day, one of Labs' two generators was under maintenance and had basically been taken apart. The other one failed when it was initialized. So only the UPS backup saved all the work of the employees as it gave SAP sufficient time to inform everyone and shut down the PCs and servers in an organized manner. However, this was the only time in five years of operation at the campus, when SAP Labs was left without power at all. Besides this, the campus management was able to run the building 24 hours, seven days a week and 365 days of the year.

Data connectivity has improved very much over the last 10 years in Bangalore, at least with respect to the corporate sector: SAP Labs uses two 512 MB/s leased lines that lead from the campus to two mirrored data centers in

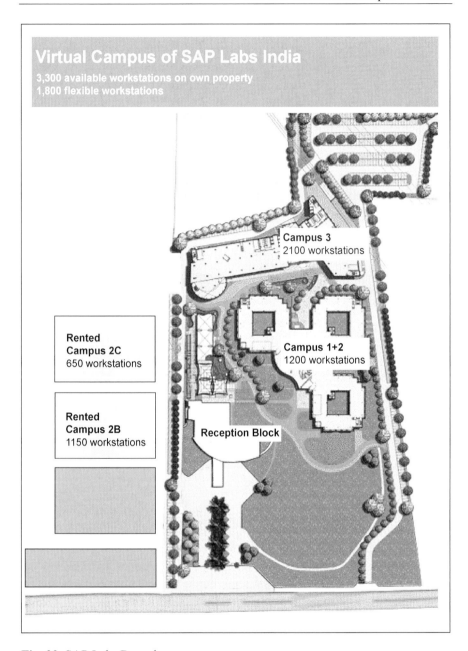

Fig. 33. SAP Labs Bangalore campus map

Germany on different routes. They have worked during the past five years with zero downtime. Both private service providers have always been able to provide SAP Labs with the bandwidth requested – and of course at competitive prices. Meanwhile, these lines are used for corporate internal phone calls as well as for video connectivity within SAP's global network. This is not only a very reliable, but also very cost effective solution.

Overall, the experience with SAP Labs campus has been very good. In the meantime, SAP Labs has also rented two buildings adjacent to its grounds. Since September 2008, SAP Labs has all 4,000 employees and 1,000 colleagues from partner companies working in one single campus in Whitefield, Bangalore. So today, the vision of 2002, of having the ability to grow to such number (which was really hard to imagine at that time) has became true.

In 2006, another location, besides the main campus in Bangalore, was opened in Gurgaon, in the North of India, to support the growth of the company. For the first two years, the location was remotely managed by Georg Kniese. He recalls: "The main idea behind opening a new location already started in 2004 when the board considered that it might be too risky to put everything into only one location in India. The basic reasons for opening the location in Gurgaon were political and local risks and the high attrition in Bangalore. In 2004, we also knew that the capacity of the campus we had built in Bangalore, would be too small in the future. Gurgaon was chosen because of the good international connection, the closeness to the government, to the public sector, to the different industries and to companies that are located there, apart from the IT sector."

By the time the location reached 300, it was decided that the location should no longer be managed remotely. V.R. Ferose was made the MD of Labs Gurgaon. He states: "Gurgaon, provides another option and offers a different talent pool besides Bangalore, to hire new talents. Today, Gurgaon is co-located with SAP India and SAP Labs India. In Gurgaon, 671 people are working on 90,000 square feet of rented workspace for various lines of business (with a presence of all the major board areas of Global Services and Support, Research & Development and Global Field Organization)."

The campus in Bangalore and the location in Gurgaon offer a perfect environment for innovative work, and at the same time, they provide a solid basis for the company's cost projections for the future and help to run SAP Labs India in an efficient and world class way.

**'Fun Facts' about the SAP Labs India Campus –
"We also develop software"**

To develop world class software from India, we also need to be an efficient power generating-, water procurement-, transportation-, security management-, hiring- and a catering services company!

- 25,000 – 30,000 liters of diesel are stored on the campus (the available storage capacity is 45,000 liters).

- On the campus, approximately 235,000 liters of water are needed per day (transported by water trucks).

- The campus has an installed capacity of 5,030 KVA (100 % backed up).

- SAP Labs India runs approximately 78 company busses on a day to day basis.

- SAP Labs India deploys 109 security personnel on its campus.

- SAP Labs deploys 88 people working in housekeeping.

- Approximately 5 million coffee cups are served on the campus free of cost per year.

- 4000 plates are served for lunch every day.

8 Mergers and Acquisitions

SAP followed different approaches to achieve its ambitious growth plans. The first approach was to enhance the product in an organic way by introducing breakthrough innovations and introducing continuous enhancements. Then SAP further complimented this successful organic growth strategy by expanding the partner ecosystem through co-innovation and strategic acquisitions. SAP followed the philosophy of mostly developing software in-house, instead of going through a cumbersome integration process. For several years, SAP proved that it could grow more than twice as fast as the rest of the market. SAP's CEO Henning Kagermann has often said that the acquisition strategy of SAP is aimed at filling gaps in the product rather than acquiring market share or customers.

Many of SAP Labs around the globe were started when SAP acquired other companies: SAP Labs Bulgaria came into existence when SAP acquired InQMy, a Java enterprise server company. Likewise SAP Labs Israel emerged from the acquisition of Ofek-Tech in 1998. SAP Labs India was also established together with SAP AG's acquisition of Kiefer and Veittinger GmbH in 1998. To start with, SAP retained these locations, enhanced them with additional development projects and finally converted them into a complete lab.

Over the last years, SAP has made several smart acquisitions to improve and add solutions. For instance, SAP acquired 'Triversity' and 'Khimetrics' to fill in gaps in retail solutions. Similarly, companies like 'Lighthammer' and 'Visiprise' were acquired in the area of manufacturing. While most of the acquisitions were small in nature, SAP surprised the market in October 2007 by taking over Business Objects for EUR 4.8 billion, which has been the largest acquisition in SAP's history so far.

India is very specific in a way, because most of the successful software companies have development facilities there, and whenever SAP acquired a company, SAP Labs India also got an addition from the acquisition's Indian subsidiary. In the last ten years, there have been three main acquisi-

C. Neumann and J. Srinivasan, *Managing Innovation from the Land of Ideas and Talent: The 10-Year Story of SAP Labs India,*
DOI: 10.1007/978-3-540-89283-0_8, © Springer-Verlag Berlin Heidelberg 2009

tions that impacted India: the acquisition of the enterprise compliance and risk management company 'Virsa' in 2006, the acquisition of 'Yasu Technology' in 2007, and the acquisition of 'Business Objects' in the same year. The acquisition of Yasu was initiated to add capability in the area of business rules management to the NetWeaver stack. All these acquisitions have provided Labs India with valuable opportunities to learn from new partners and from their organizational structures. Each of these companies commanded different business and background knowledge and had already tapped the Indian talent pool in different ways. New additions to Labs India further promoted innovations as synergies were identified and exploited after the integration.

Acquisitions also involve new challenges in terms of location strategies, and as a result of detailed planning, these challenges were treated instead as opportunities to initiate internal changes and improvements in the organizational structure.

8.1   The Acquisitions Process at SAP

Most of the acquisitions are handled with utmost secrecy during the initial stages of negotiation, and in most cases, the announcement comes as a surprise. The initial days after the press announcement are often chaotic. SAP has developed detailed processes to minimize disruption and to provide necessary guidance to manage the following transition. Most often, post merger integrations sometimes involve not only a dedicated integration team of the new enterprise, but also Indian operations. The project team reports to the executive board and prepares a detailed plan, orchestrating and supporting all the locations to complete the integration.

The acquisition process can be broken down into two main processes: the Investment Lifecycle (ILC) process and the Post Merger Integration process (PMI). The ILC starts with identifying and evaluating the opportunities, before moving on to negotiations and finally ending up with the closure and implementation of the deal. The corporate finance team is closely involved during all the stages, and the process typically ends with an audit of the investment. Once the announcement is made public, the project team follows the PMI process to integrate the newly acquired entities into SAP.

The PMI concentrates on the sixty days directly following the closure of the deal, but the integration planning typically begins much earlier during the due diligence stage. The PMI process consists of a preliminary planning, the creation of a blueprint that leads to realization, and finally ends with an audit. The post merger team consists of representatives from different departments like Sales, and Service and Support, as well as representatives from HR, IT, Controlling and Facilities.

The model focuses on a functional transition plan that emphasizes the goals to be delivered depending on the deal, enabling newly acquired employees, effectively addressing existing customer expectations, maximizing revenue opportunities, and finally ensuring a smooth transition into SAP. The idea is not to complete the integration within this sixty-day process, but to ensure that the acquired company can continue its business and at the same time begin to integrate its activities into SAP's organizational structures.

For every new deal, a business sponsor is assigned who reports to the executive board and is accountable for the operational success of the acquisition. In addition, key contributors from Product Development, Solution Marketing, and Product Management are identified.

During this process, SAP also takes time to share its core values with the newly joined employees, so that the acquired team can learn how and why SAP works the way it does. Post mergers require rapid decision making, and the idea behind this is to establish a combined organization as quickly as possible. The more time employees have to spend on thinking about the merger and about organizational issues, the less they will perform at high levels.

Key decisions employees have to invest effort on involving strategy and vision, organizational structure and alignment, product roadmaps, sales and marketing, and customers and services, will be critical to short and long-term business objectives. Central teams with experience from earlier mergers normally support the integration unit and support them in quickly coming to a decision.

The process also ensures a periodic review with the executive board to report the status of integration, to escalate challenges on-time and to get the necessary approvals ensuring smooth integration of the acquired entity. Even though these processes are to a large extent well-defined and provide the jumpstart for execution, every new acquisition brings its own set of challenges. Therefore, key information for every acquisition is documented and is used to enhance the process on an ongoing basis.

If opportunities in India are involved, SAP Labs India plays an important role during the early stages of the investment lifecycle: it commands a large ecosystem of developers, consultants, customers, and partners in India, and as a result, has access to rich market information. Labs India also gets queries from other subsidiaries and internal organizations on a constant basis about companies in India. There are plenty of opportunities, and when they match the strategy of SAP, experts from Labs India support conducting the due diligence phase. Experts from SAP AG conduct the initial analysis and work closely with corporate departments during the early stages of an acquisition.

8.2   Acquisitions at SAP Labs India

Acquisition of Virsa

Since its inception in 1998, Labs India has operated out of Bangalore. After careful deliberation during the last quarter of 2005, SAP started looking for another, alternate location. After having evaluated locations like Calcutta, Pune and Gurgaon, SAP decided to set up a Northern hub, which was closer to the capital New Delhi.

The Gurgaon office was opened in April 2006, and only one month later, Labs India was confronted with the acquisition of 'Virsa Systems, Inc.', which was based at Chandigarh in Northern India. Starting from that point, SAP Labs India not only had a second location to take care of, 2,000 km away from Bangalore, it also had a third location in Chandigarh, 250 km away from Gurgaon. Georg Kniese, former managing director of Labs India, states: "The acquisition had not been processed by the Labs management so we decided just to keep that third location in Chandigarh with another 100 people for the time being. The initial impression of the office was very good, although we did not know what the future would bring. However, over time, it turned out that it did not make sense to have a third location apart from Bangalore and Gurgaon. Firstly, the dream to grow to another 1,000 people did not come true; secondly, managing that remote outlet was difficult as it was not directly connected to SAP. Therefore, we decided to move people from Chandigarh to Gurgaon."

In 1996, Virsa Systems, Inc. was privately funded with venture investment from SAP Ventures, Kleiner Perkins Caufield & Byers, and Lightspeed Venture Partners and was promoted by Jasvir Gill and his wife Kaval. Virsa offices were located throughout the world, including the U.S., UK, Germany, France, India, Singapore, Australia, and Japan.

Jasvir Gill, a software specialist, was born in a Northern city of India, Punjab. Like many other Indian developers, he had moved to the U.S. in 1985 on a software assignment. Later, Jasvir got married to Kaval Kaur, a chartered accountant in India. When Jasvir's employer was acquired by IBM, he started his own consulting company with a focus on security issues, providing services on authorization and access rights to enterprise customers all around the U.S.

Virsa had more than 300 enterprise customers, many of them were 'Global 1,000 companies', across all major vertical market segments. In 2003, Virsa was worth about USD 3 million, growing at a rapid pace, and in 2006, it already reached over USD 100 million. At the time of the acquisition, Virsa Systems, Inc., was a global leader in cross-enterprise solutions for Governance, Risk and Compliance management. It provided the only solutions that dramatically simplified achieving compliance with regulations such as Sarbanes-Oxley in real-time, by enabling customers to embed automated control design, testing, and enforcement directly into their business processes. With more than 300 enterprise customers globally and more than 2.5 million end users, Virsa had the largest installed base in the sector.

In November 2004, Virsa had opened its development center in India. The subsidiary grew slowly, and it hired fresh graduates from universities. At the time of its acquisition by SAP, Virsa had over 65 employees in India, led by Rakesh Bhatia and they operated out of the development center at Chandigarh.

Before the acquisition took place, SAP and Virsa already had a highly successful relationship on three levels:

1. Technology: Virsa solutions were designed and delivered on the SAP NetWeaver platform, making Virsa one of the more than 1,000 independent software vendors (ISVs) who committed to build and market solutions on SAP's leading platform.

2. Go to market: SAP and Virsa were closely aligned in joint marketing, sales, and product development activities. Since March 2005,
   SAP had been exclusively reselling Virsa's flagship product, Compliance Calibrator™, as an add-on to mySAP ERP. In the one-year
   period since that agreement had been announced, SAP and Virsa
   had partnered on more than 150 customer wins. Additionally, SAP
   Ventures was an investor at Virsa.

3. Customer/vendor: SAP was also a customer of Virsa, running one
   of the largest global deployments of its Virsa's Compliance Cali-
   brator™, and Access Enforcer, with more than 40,000 users around
   the world.

The integration of Virsa products into the SAP portfolio was relatively
easy as the solution was already compatible with SAP and was built on an
SAP platform. SAP Ventures had already a stake in the company, and also
several large customers of SAP were already using their products and solutions. Today, the Virsa team in Gurgaon has grown to 70 people. Apart
from extending the solution, this team also provides support to the customers around the world.

Acquisition of Yasu

In October 2007, recognizing the increasing importance of the new breed
of professionals who help companies create and manage business processes, SAP announced the acquisition of Yasu Technologies, a privately
owned leader in business rules management systems. SAP decided to embed
Yasu Technologies' solutions into its NetWeaver technology platform to extend its footprint into the business process management (BPM) market.
With this, SAP believed that the customers would be able to comply easily
with regulatory policies and to better manage their business performance.

Unlike other acquisitions, Labs India was actively involved right away
from the early stages of the acquisition. Experts from the Labs, together
with colleagues from other locations, performed detailed due diligence
during the early stages of the investment lifecycle. The post merger integration lead was appointed from Labs India, and this greatly helped in the
overall integration.

At the time of the acquisition, Yasu had eight employees in the U.S. This
team mainly consisted of the CEO, few developers and solution architects

apart from the financial and administration staff. Yasu had its complete product design, engineering, sales, and marketing workforce in Hyderabad, India.

Satish Madhira, CEO of Yasu together with five other founders, had created a high performance organization that boasted of some of the best talents in India's IT industry, with several product development team members from premier institutes like the IITs. Yasu developed their business rule engine completely out of its headquarters in Hyderabad, and it had acquired around 100 customers. Many of these were some of the largest European and American companies in diverse industries such as insurance, telecommunication, manufacturing, banking, mortgage and financial services, airlines, automotive, and services. This customer base was built by a very small sales force of its own, primarily based in India, with a small outpost in the U.S., but no European presence. Yasu had one direct sales representative in the U.S., apart from 32 OEM partners and eight resellers, which included big names like IBM, Sun Microsystems, and BEA. Apart from the numerous partners, Yasu adopted innovative methods to acquire several new customers via Google AdWords. During this period, Yasu also had acquired vital experience in low-touch online sales channels.

Incorporated in 1999 with locations in Hyderabad and in the United States, and with 120 employees, Yasu was seen as a visionary in business rules management systems (BRMS). It brought market leading capabilities and expertise in this area to SAP. Solutions from Yasu Technologies enabled customers to centrally manage and monitor how business decision logic was formulated and maintained throughout their enterprise applications in a cost-effective manner. In early 2000, Yasu launched the first version of QuickRules BRMS, its flagship product. This business rule solution helped the company to accelerate its growth rapidly, and it offered a suite of products aiming at the enterprise rule management lifecycle.

Apart from adding valuable talent, Yasu added one topic that was entirely its own to the Labs India portfolio, the BRMS. It also came along with the challenge of another new location to be managed by SAP Labs, Hyderabad, which is about 500 km away from Bangalore.

Venkat Srinivas Seshasai, Vice President, BRMS (Business Rule Management System) development, explains: "One main difference to the Virsa acquisition was that the headquarters of Yasu was in India, so it was converted into a remote development location. While Yasu had all its development systems, servers and software in its own office it needed much more bandwidth to communicate closely with systems in other locations and Bangalore. Hence, SAP went ahead and upgraded the bandwidth to enable the colleagues to work the same way like other SAP development locations."

Today, the Yasu entity is completely integrated into SAP. NW BRM (NetWeaver Business Rules Management) which is shipped as a part of NW CE 7.11 (NetWeaver Composition Environment) is essentially a fully integrated version of Yasu QuickRules. This successful integration was achieved by the erstwhile employees of Yasu. While three of the cofounders left the company, the other three of them, along with many other employees, are still contributing to the overall success of SAP. By March 2009 all remaining Yasu employees moved into the SAP Labs India facility in Bangalore, which was the final step to complete the intergration.

Acquisition of Business Objects

In October 2007, around the same time when Yasu was acquired, SAP AG announced the acquisition of Business Objects, the biggest acquisition of its history. While many in the SAP community were surprised by the scale of the acquisition, SAP reiterated its strategy to grow organically and also explained that Business Objects would accelerate SAP's efforts to penetrate the strategic Business User segment.

Headquartered in Paris, France, Business Objects was widely recognized as the pioneer of business intelligence (BI) software. Business Objects was the world's leading BI software company with solutions spanning the information discovery and delivery, information management, analysis and performance management for more than 44,000 customers around the globe. Both companies announced that Business Objects would operate as a stand-alone business being part of the SAP group. SAP further said that the expertise and solutions from Business Objects would be complementary to offerings that SAP already provided to business users. CEO John Schwarz became part of SAP's executive board, and even after the takeover, he continued his responsibility as head of the Business Object teams inside SAP. Doug Merritt, who had earlier been responsible for the Business User development inside SAP, joined the Business Objects team and started reporting to John Schwarz. In addition, Herve Couturier, the R&D head of Business Objects, became executive vice president and head of SAP's technology platform, SAP NetWeaver. All these decisions helped to maintain a sense of continuity and security for Business Objects' employees and also facilitated accelerated integration.

In 2003, Business Objects started its operations in India with a local partner organization, and from its initial 150 team members, it grew to 300 by 2005. In 2006, Business Objects acquired the resources it needed from its partner to start its India development center.

Business Objects had a large development facility in India, which was located in Bangalore and was also close to the Labs India campus. This unit was among its four key global development facilities, and it actively participated in charting the strategic roadmap for the global R&D. Business Objects in India also had the vision to eventually develop several independent products over time, and the highly experienced R&D team was organized in a regional and global reporting matrix. Furthermore, the development center had a strong track record in the Indian market for hiring the best leadership and technical talents.

Srivibhavan Balaram, the former head of Business Objects in India says: "The communication of the acquisition to the employees was planned carefully, even the timing of the employee meeting in India was synchronized with the one in the U.S. However, it still provided some key lessons." He further adds: "It was surprising that the information reached Bangalore's unit of Business Objects faster, while, as in most cases, it took SAP Labs India much longer to receive information regarding the integration." This was a clear pointer on how size of the organization significantly slows down the flow of communication and it was one of the key learnings.

In 2007, Business Objects transferred major programs from its other development locations to Bangalore. During this time, it acquired complete accountability for the Business Objects 6.5 release apart from being responsible for key topics like lifecycle management and new initiatives in the mid-market area.

By October 2008, the Business Objects teams moved into the Bangalore Labs India campus, and senior members of the Business Objects team in Bangalore were integrated with the Labs India leadership. During the November 2008 SAP TechEd in Bangalore, the Business Objects team demonstrated its key capabilities to the large SAP community in India. The integration in India was formally completed when the Karnataka High Court approved the merge of Business Objects India into SAP Labs India in December 2008.

8.3 Summary

Over the years, SAP Labs India has gained immense knowledge and head-count through these acquisitions. Each time, they provided opportunities to review the current processes and also to learn from the experiences of the new colleagues. Labs India has performed successful integration of new teams with a human touch, and only very few employees left during these integration phases. Employees from Labs India and from newly acquired companies have found new careers in different teams, and this itself is a testimony to the lab's success and its acquisitions. Many employees from former Virsa, Yasu, and Business Objects are today working on innovations at SAP Labs India, and are contributing to its overall success. Different from many other countries where SAP Labs are situated today, Labs India always closed down the acquired facilities to maximize benefits, collaborate opportunities and gain efficiency. Engineers of the acquired companies were always transferred into one of the two SAP Labs facilities in Bangalore and Gurgaon.

9 Evolution and Way Forward

The world has certainly become a little flatter during the last 10 years. Thomas Friedman's book "The world is flat" starts with his tee-off at the KGA (Karnataka Golf Association) Golf course in Bangalore, where he was asked to aim the ball 'towards Microsoft and IBM', indicating to which large extent the city was and is shaped by the presence of the international IT companies (Friedman 2007). Ten years ago, the very same tee-off had already occurred, but if one had missed the green, the ball would not have landed in Microsoft's courtyard, but on a piece of barren land.

We still remember our first trip from Bangalore City to the Whitefield industrial area in 1997, where SAP Labs is located today. The route was dotted with several farm houses and nurseries, it was lush green, and one could occasionally see bullock carts on mud roads. It was a peaceful country-side scenery. The Discoverer Block of ITPL was coming up, and the only other landmark visible from there was the Container Corporation of India. We heavily debated the feasibility of working from a location like Whitefield as SAP was one of the very first companies considering to move there. It seemed so remote, a village outpost of Bangalore. Today, an estimated number of 50,000 IT engineers come to Whitefield alone, every day, while another 100,000 try to make it to Electronic City in the South of Bangalore. And many more live and work in different areas of the city.

India has seen a decade of 7% growth in GDP and was the second fastest growing economy in the world with 6,9% GDP growth in 2008–2009. This has definitely contributed to the prosperity, but it has not come without challenges. The gap between wealthy cities and poor villages has increased dramatically, and the growth in the urban regions has still not reached the 70% rural population in India. Still 60–65% of India's workforce depend on agriculture and the yearly monsoon. Droughts and floods trigger migration of population to the already crowded cities. Thousands of villages still do not have access to electricity and proper drinking water.

The amazing growth of the cities has not come without drawbacks, either: according to the State Road Transport Office, Bangalore adds close to 1,000

C. Neumann and J. Srinivasan, *Managing Innovation from the Land of Ideas and Talent: The 10-Year Story of SAP Labs India*,
DOI: 10.1007/978-3-540-89283-0_9, © Springer-Verlag Berlin Heidelberg 2009

vehicles every day to its streets – a number that is as amazing as frightening. The public infrastructure struggles under the burden of the demands of India's new middle class – young families who demand high grade apartments, cars and good roads, also have created an unforeseeable hunger for electricity. Most of the cities suffer from sever power outages and private enterprises rely heavily on expensive and highly polluting captive power generators to supplement the city's power. The Indo-U.S. civil nuclear cooperation, signed by former president George W. Bush, claimed to improve the situation. The nuclear deal between the U.S. and India, could enable India to generate additional 22,000 MW of nuclear power, and 15,800 MW of this would go to the villages. On the other hand, this deal could be seen as an Indian strategic measure to maintain a geopolitical balance with China and Pakistan.

Beyond the energy supply issues, India has another big problem to solve, which is the growing threat of terror attacks. India looks back on a 60 year history of hostility with Pakistan, and it is becoming increasingly difficult to cope with this highly unstable, nuclear armed neighbor. The death toll among Indians and foreigners that was caused by 10 terrorists at the end of November 2008 made this threat very visible to the rest of the world. The relationship between India and Pakistan has further deteriorated due to the high level of distrust and hostility.

Apart from those issues, there are also several internal challenges that India faces due to issues of governance, conflicts between federal and state bureaucracy, corruption, and tariffs that need attention. Capitalism and market driven policies are increasingly seen as the sole option for creating jobs, and for overcoming social challenges. Regional political parties have become increasingly stronger, and this has weakened the government's ability to accelerate the reforms. At the time this book was written, the outcome of the elections in India in May 2009 was still awaited. The results will have a large impact on the pace of reforms in India.

Finally, the global economic crisis was far away from being over at the beginning of 2009. The historic stock market crash in fall 2008 had triggered panic among international investors and financial markets. With the SENSEX trading on a 50 % low in March 2009, one wonders whether the Indian 'Wirtschaftwunder' (economical wonder) has come to an abrupt standstill. However, the impact of the international crisis on India is comparatively small because India is less dependent on exports than other Asian countries.

The current magnitude of the infrastructural, political and economic challenges has reached a level that makes us feel that the last 10 years may have been a time of relative stability and predictability. Now, with all these unforeseeable factors around, it seems to be impossible to look five years into the future, but we will try to describe a few trends we can foresee – which will in any case significantly shape the course of our business.

SAP's mission statement will remain unchanged as the most fundamental guiding principle:

"We will define and establish undisputed leadership in the emerging market for business process platform offerings, accelerate business innovation powered by IT for companies and industries worldwide, and thus contribute to economic development on a grand scale. In pursuing its open platform strategy, we will continue to deliver SAP applications that create unmatched value for our customers."

Apart from the fundamental challenge business is currently facing, SAP will continue serving its established business, while at the same time investing in new business that will help define the future for SAP and its customers.

For business solution software vendors like SAP, there are two mega trends that are driving them and customers alike: the emergence of a new software architecture (SOA – Service Oriented Architecture) and of a new deployment model (SaaS – Software as a Service). Both individually as well as in combination, have already started to transform this market significantly.

The transition to service-oriented architectures (SOAs) will create a new wave of IT enablement. SAP has carried on its SOA roadmap in the years 2007 and 2008, and with its Business Process Platform (BPP), it has been the first firm to have a completely re-designed platform on the market which is built entirely on SOA principles.

SaaS (Software as a Service) promises that ERP customers do not have to install and maintain large software packages in-house anymore, but instead get their application provided via the Internet. This reduces the upfront investment of enterprises a lot and releases cash flow that they are able to direct to other parts of their business. Thus, SaaS transfers the capital expenses companies previously had to pay for software into operating expenses. Companies that rely completely on SaaS have had tremendous market success in the last years, a fact that shows the acceptance of this new deployment model amongst businesses. With Business ByDesign (ByD), SAP has a new product on the market that offers this alternative to the customers.

Through 2010, SAP's strategy will center on four primary thrusts – advancing its core business, enabling its platform strategy, serving small and midsize companies, and winning over the information worker.

Large global enterprises are SAP's core business, and the current growth avenues all extend from the core. Continued growth will now depend on expanding SAP's presence in high-growth industries and economies, and on extending and improving the range of solutions it offers – in particular, extending its offerings by mission critical applications for its customers.

As mentioned above, SAP now has delivered on its platform strategy and is making its Business Process Platform (BPP) with all its advantages available to new and existing customers.

With the release of SAP Business ByDesign, the enterprise SOA solution for small and midsize companies, SAP has complemented its existing offerings and its leadership position with a solution for midsize companies, and has taken another major step forward in effectively addressing the needs of companies of all sizes. At the beginning of 2009, SAP had three distinct offers for the SME market: B1 (for small businesses), ByD (delivered using the SaaS deployment model) and A1 (which is a pre-packaged go-to-market variation of R/3). The fourth pillar of the strategy, addressing the 'information worker' in global and local businesses, will be served by new SAP products and to a large extent by the seamlessly integrated products of Business Objects, SAP's latest and largest acquisition.

Another theme of the next years will be sustainability. Not only can SAP reduce its own carbon footprint by optimizing facilities and reducing travels around the globe. It can also help its customers to intelligently monitor and steer their own sustainability efforts. With the announcement of a Chief Sustainability Officer in March 2009, SAP made its commitment clear that the company is determined to reduce pollution and wastage of resources.

9.1   Development Locations

Over the years, SAP has used its labs as a vehicle to translate global challenges into a true competitive advantage. Today, SAP labs are spread around the globe, and this R&D network enables SAP to leverage individual strengths of various locations and workforces.

The development workforce around the globe has grown in a fast and well-balanced way, and today, SAP is running large development hubs in Germany, India, China, North America (Canada and the U.S.) and Israel. There are also several focus labs in locations like Canada, Bulgaria, France and Hungary. While the development hubs participate in large scale R&D and contribute to every stage of the product lifecycle, smaller focus labs take up assignments in niche areas and accelerate the pace of innovation at SAP.

The labs network offers several competitive advantages, like faster reaction to the market and opportunities to engage with local innovation communities and ecosystems. By being close to the customers, SAP is able to understand and appreciate their needs, and the company is also in a better position to explain the capabilities of its products.

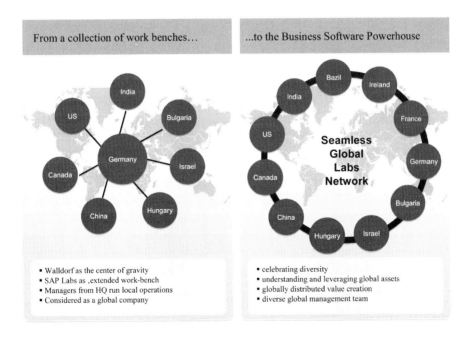

Fig. 34. Evolution of the Labs network

SAP's global governance model and a set of global practices and policies combined with unified tools, help employees around the world to collaborate and deliver support to customers worldwide, around the clock.

Even more importantly, SAP is transforming itself into a real global company, which has not only a very international executive board (in June 2009, the presumed six board members will have five different nationalities), but also develops its products across five continents. This diversity results in a high flexibility to continuously adjust to the ever changing business world – a fact that everyone in the company believes to be a corner stone for its future success.

In the future, the SAP Labs network will be able to further accelerate this competitive advantage. As the world becomes flatter, we will soon witness borderless labs with partners and customers contributing seamlessly. Further, with the SAP Labs network, SAP will be able to redefine co-innovation, collaborate and embrace new technologies and identify local synergies and take its innovation to a new level.

The challenge for the Labs network will be:

- consistently remain flexible enough to adjust to changing demands for resources and grow in the ability to up- and downscale quickly;

- develop an efficient operational model that makes the collaboration between global service lines and local execution a smooth experience without much friction;

- respond to the constant need for consolidation of R&D locations, which continuously emerge as part of acquisitions or as remainders of large-scale partner development projects; they need to be integrated efficiently into the Labs network;

- fine-tune the successful model of distributed development by including modern development philosophies and by implementing strict guidelines (like the maximum of three locations for any Line of Business).

Nevertheless, as the recent past has shown, most of SAP's Labs are based in countries where the legal framework is more flexible than in its headquarters in Germany. This allows a faster reactions on changes of the economical environment, may it be the reduction in positions or reorganization on a large scale. Going forward, SAP will continue to leverage its international locations and will gain in terms of growth perspectives.

9.2 Labs India

"At the beginning of our business in Bangalore, it was beyond a dream of mine, that 10 years later, there would be 4,000 people working as a lab for SAP. Things have developed dynamically, and everybody can be proud of being a part of a global SAP network, in which Bangalore plays and important role and is well prepared for the growth of the Asian market. It is a big achievement that today SAP is in the lead of the competition in this area", Peter Zencke, executive board member, stated in 2008.

SAP Labs India has grown from a humble beginning to a large development hub. The growth has helped it gain a wide variety of expertise. Every time the organization grew, the management was forced to move specialists and experts into management positions at the Labs to ensure quality and increase efficiency.

The job market in India is changing rapidly. Today, service companies like TCS, Infosys and Wipro have grown to approximately 100,000 employees each. Besides, these companies have started moving more and more to tier-two cities like Ahmedabad, Jaipur, Mysore and Nagpur, the IT capitals such as Bangalore, are getting too crowded and expensive. They have also realized that it will no longer be possible for them to maintain their annual 50% – 100% growth rates of the past. On the one hand, the job losses around the world in the current economical crisis will not allow for such growth rates, on the other hand, the global economy does not demand such volume of IT services for an unforeseeable period of time. The major IT vendors are under tremendous pressure to break the linearity between headcount and revenues. It is becoming increasingly difficult for the service companies to defend their profitability and to find a sustainable business model beyond today's successful services. The case of the Satyam fraud in January 2009, in which the CEO admitted to have inflated the balance-sheet by about one billion Euro in cash over the years, shows what the market and analyst pressure can do to some individuals.

Henning Kagermann, co-CEO SAP AG, states: "Today, India is SAP's third largest subsidiary in terms of employees, and it has been the fastest growing market in 2007 with a triple digit growth. In its 10 years of existence, Labs India has become an integral part of SAP's global research & development network and service & support network. I can proudly say that the Labs evolved into a true hub for innovation and research. It helped us understand the demands of our local customer and to adapt our products according to their special needs."

At SAP Labs India, the average age of developers and their average experience have increased over the years, and today, many of them have more than eight years of industry experience. Even though the industry will continue to grow in the coming years, its growth will be much slower, and it will become much more manageable. The stability of the workforce will increase, the salary levels, which have grown at an average of 10 – 15% in the last five years, will get tempered, and hence, the organizations will strengthen the quality of its workforce further. This will as well give the employees time to mature and will help them in the long run.

Today, Labs India has expertise in diverse areas, and it is in a good position to further increase the depth of its knowledge and to further accelerate the pace of innovation. As the Indian market continues to grow according to the increasing consumption of the middle class, the development teams will be able to work closely with growing companies in India. Experts predict that industry segments like healthcare, retail, automotive and the energy sector will witness strong growth once the current crisis is over. Indian companies are still acquiring overseas assets and are making India a headquarters for their global operations.

Increasingly global companies like General Motors, Suzuki, Boeing and Cisco are moving high-end design jobs to India to both take advantage of the skilled resources and to design products and solutions for the customers in the region. SAP Labs India is well positioned to co-innovate with these companies. According to a 2006 report by Booz Allen Hamilton and NASSCOM, India's share of advanced work is expected to grow and to become a USD 40 billion market by 2020.

The growing middle class has now tasted luxury, and it would be hard to reverse this trend. Events in 2008, like the cost-effective lunar mission 'Chandrayaan-1' and the announcement of the '1,500 EUR Tata Nano', are seen as examples of India's next generation of innovations. Apart from technological know-how, monitoring lifestyle changes and developing a deep understanding of the customer needs is seen as essential to foster innovation.

SAP Labs India will be participating in these trends. The challenge for the local management for the next 10 years will be to keep an innovative, high performing company together, which does not define its success by continuous (local) growth in terms of headcount, but in terms of contribution to SAP's global offerings. Along with that goes as well its share in the inventions and innovative products which SAP is going to release. This will require a shift mindset throughout the company, as managers and individual contributors alike have never experienced a scenario of a declining growth. But building on the flexibility and agility that the colleagues have displayed in the past, there is reason to believe that this shift in focus and mind can successfully be achieved.

On the other side, we can also imagine a scenario that builds on increasing confusion in the markets and insecurity of India's political landscape. In that scenario, India would not be able to get its act together and miss the opportunity for more inner stability and security. Such scenario would not only mean a stop of growth, but also involve reduced investment by multinational companies. Many potential investors are observing very carefully how the security issue after the Mumbai terror attacks is sorted out between India and Pakistan. And they will as well stay alert on how the regulators will act on the Satyam fraud and on what will be their measures to prevent such things from happening again.

9.3   Conclusion

Personally, we believe that even a scenario of uncertainty would offer some excellent chances, as the market for talent would become much better from the IT company point of view, and the cost advantage of India would sustain for a much longer period. As the gravity center of global economy shifts slowly to the East, India's democracy, diversity and determination will surely help it to realize its ambition of becoming a developed country.

In his speech on the occasion of the Labs 10 years celebrations on November 12th, 2008, Léo Apotheker, co-CEO of SAP AG, stated: "The fast growth of SAP Labs India is amazing, and the good news is that the IT sector in general, and software development in particular are just in their beginnings. There is a bright future for the software sector ahead. And all the increases in the digital world depend on enterprise software, so that gives us huge and strong possibilities in the market. It is in hard times that good companies make the difference! In future, we have to concentrate even more on our customer excellence, we shall deliver more comprehensive business solutions, not only software. That is what we have to focus on."

SAP always stated "We are here to stay" – and this will be the strategy going forward. If one believes in the people of the land of ideas, then the external environment will not change the equation to such an extent that innovation from India would one day not be possible anymore.

About the Authors

Clas Neumann

Senior Vice President and Global Head, Core SAP Labs Network

Clas Neumann is the Global Head of the core SAP Labs network which includes besides Labs India also North America, Brazil, Bulgaria, China, Hungary and Israel. Having been based in Bangalore for the last ten years, he was instrumental in establishing SAP's largest Research & Development hub outside of Germany. He grew it constantly to its current strength of 4,000 engineers, who are responsible for various products and solutions of SAP. In addition, Clas Neumann has held for four years the responsibility as Senior Vice President for SAP's latest product, 'SAP BusinessBy-Design', with teams in China, Germany and India, and he has held the role as the President of SAP Labs India.

In 1995, Clas Neumann joined SAP and worked in many roles across China, Germany and India. Prior to joining SAP he had served in one of Germany's major regional banks as well as in an ERP vendor start-up. Fluent in German, English, and conversational in Mandarin Chinese, he holds a diploma of the University of Applied Science in Ludwigshafen, Germany, and a MBA degree from INSEAD, Fontainbleau and Singapore (EMBA 2005).

As a member of SAP's Executive Leadership Team and of different German-Indian economic organizations, and because of his business achievements, he has been awarded with the 'Career 2005 award' by Germany's leading economic daily 'Handelsblatt'.

Clas Neumann is married to Bea and has three children, Celia, Beniyaz and Zarina.

Jayaram Srinivasan

Vice President, Supply Chain Management, Research & Breakthrough Innovation Unit

Jayaram Srinivasan is Vice President of the Supply Chain Management, Research & Breakthrough Innovation unit. He joined SAP in 1997 as a developer, when the company started its operations in India. During the early years, Jayaram developed the country version for India, and he worked closely with customers during the nascent stage of SAP in the Indian market. In 1999, he managed the extensive growth of the development team as a development manager of the oil & gas solution. In 2003, Jayaram Srinivasan became Vice President Manufacturing Industries, and he established a project based cross industry development team by leveraging expertise from different areas.

Jayaram Srinivasan has wide experience in different lifecycle stages of product development, ranging from research to customer support. Apart from developing standard software, he holds expertise in industry specific, country specific and customer specific developments. In the last 12 years, he has been managing several strategic global and local projects to improve effectiveness and efficiency of SAP Labs India. He has presented on the topic of distributed product development in several internal and external forums.

Prior to joining SAP, Jayaram Srinivasan had worked for Tube Investments of India for eight years and had had a brief stint for one year in Bahrain with the Jawad Group.

Jayaram Srinivasan holds a master degree in business administration and has also completed a one-year business leaders program at the Indian Institute of Management, Calcutta.

Jayaram is married to Sharmila and has two children Advaith and Sanmati.

References

External SAP Documents

SAP AG (2008): www.sap.com, November 2008.

SAP AG (2009): SAP Fact Sheet, http://www.sap.com/about/investor/pdf/ SAP_FactSheet.pdf, February 2009.

SAP AG (2008): SAP Annual Report, 'Innovation at the speed of your business', 2007.

Essays and Magazines

Hilmar Schepp (2002): Real Signs of the Times. In: SAP World, Employee Magazine, 2002, Number 3, p. 20 – 24.

John Hagel, John Seely Brown (2008): How SAP Seeds Innovation. In: Business Week, 2008, http://www.businessweek.com/innovate/content/ jul2008/id20080723_353753.htm, March 2008.

Michael Zipf, (2002): The Right Chemistry. In: SAP World, Employee Magazine, 2002, Number 3, p. 10 – 14.

Rafiq Dossani (2008): Orgins and growth of the software industry in India, http://iis-db.stanford.edu/pubs/20973/Dossani_India_IT_2005.pdf, November 2008.

Richard Lofthouse (2000): A statement of intent. In: Euro Business, 2000, November, Vol. 2 Issue 6, p. 68 – 75.

Thomas Ramge (2006): Healthy Paranoia, A success story in five episodes. In: brand eins, business magazine, 2006, Edition 10/01.

Books

Thomas L. Friedman (2007): The World Is Flat. A Brief History of the Twenty-First Century, New York

V. Raghunathan (2006): Games Indians Play: Why We Are the Way We Are, New Delhi / New York

Dr. Udo Urbanek, co-Managing Director and Joschka Fischer, German Foreign Minister, at SAP Labs India, 2000

Joschka Fischer, German Foreign Minister visits SAP Labs India at the ITPL Campus in Bangalore, 2000

Dr. Udo Urbanek, co-Managing Director SAP Labs India, Werner Mueller, Federal Minister of Economics and Technology, Dr. Peter Zencke former executive board member of SAP AG, Otto Schilly, Federal Minister of the Interior of Germany and Clas Neumann, co-Managing Director SAP Labs India at SAP Labs India, 2001

Dr. Udo Urbanek and Clas Neumann together with Goh Chok Tong, Prime Minister of Singapore, SM Krishna, Chief Minister of Karnataka and RV Deshpande, Industry Minister of Karnataka at SAP Labs office at ITPL, 2001

Martin Prinz and Georg Kniese, co-Managing Directors SAP Labs India and Roland Koch, Minister President of Hesse, at the SAP Labs Campus, 2005

Annette Schavan, German Federal Minister of Education and Research and Clas Neumann at the SAP Labs Campus, Bangalore, 2007

Dr. Peter Zencke, former executive board member of SAP AG and Léo Apotheker, co-CEO of SAP AG on the 10 year celebrations event at the SAP Labs Campus, November 2008

Kush Desai, Managing Director SAP Labs India, Dr. Peter Zencke, former executive board member of SAP AG, Clas Neumann, President of SAP Labs India, Léo Apotheker, co-CEO of SAP AG and Ferose V.R., Managing Director SAP Labs Gurgaon on the 10 year celebrations event, November 2008

Group picture of colleagues that have been working for SAP Labs India since 10 years together with Clas Neumann, Léo Apotheker, Dr. Peter Zencke, Ferose V.R. and Kush Desai

Group picture of SAP Labs India colleagues on the occasion of the 10 year celebrations of the Lab together with Kush Desai, Ferose V.R., Clas Neumann and Léo Apotheker

Clas Neumann visits the School of Hope in Bhuj, 2003. SAP Labs India organized an Earthquake relief fund with great contribution of SAP colleagues.

Ernie Gunst, COO SAP AG, visits the SAP Center of Hope in Bangalore, 2009

Henning Kagermann, at the groundbreaking ceremony of phase 3, 2004

Martin Prinz, Henning Kagermann, Peter Zencke and Clas Neumann at the groundbreaking ceremony of phase 3, 2004

Henning Kagermann at the Employee Address on the occasion of the board week in Bangalore, 2004

Georg Kniese, Henning Kagermann and Clas Neumann at the inauguration of phase 3 building, 2007

Gerhard Oswald at the inauguration ceremony of phase 3 building, 2007

Georg Kniese, Claus E. Heinrich, Werner Brandt, Léo Apotheker, Clas Neumann, Henning Kagermann, Gerhard Oswald and Peter Zencke at the inauguration ceremony of phase 3 building, 2007

Claus E. Heinrich, Henning Kagermann, Léo Apotheker, Peter Zencke and Clas Neumann at the board week in Bangalore, 2007

Printing: Krips bv, Meppel, The Netherlands
Binding: Stürtz, Würzburg, Germany